Computer Programming in C

A. Rajeswari,

Assistant Professor,

Department of Computer Science,

Velammal Engineering College, Chennai.

C.M. Nalayini,

Assistant Professor,

Department of Information Technology,

Velammal Engineering College, Chennai.

Published by

BONFRING®
Intellectual Integrity

Computer Programming in C

9 789386 638496 >

ISBN 978-93-86638-49-6

Authors

A. Rajeswari

C.M. Nalayini

Bonfring

309, 2nd Floor, 5th Street Extension, Gandhipuram,

Coimbatore-641 012.

Tamilnadu, India.

E-mail: info@bonfring.org

Website: www.bonfring.org

Phone: 0422 4213231

Dedication

Dedicated to my mother S. Mahalakshmi, to my husband U. Bhuvaneswaran and my sons B. Amit Vel and B. Vetri Vel

\- A. Rajeswari

Dedicated to my parents C. Mahalingam and M. Bhavani, to my husband A. Parimelazhagan and my lovable son P. Niswath

\- C.M. Nalayini

Preface

The advancements in technology have made Computer an essential tool in everyone's day-to-day life. The programming language also plays a vital role in developing software for various applications. Today, technology plays a major role in all areas where computers are used, including engineering, medicine, business, education and electronic commerce. The technological advancements and growing global competitions in the computer hardware and software systems have influenced many changes in the development of programming languages.

The most basic programming language that helps in understating other advanced programming language is C language. C is a general purpose, block structured, procedural, case-sensitive, free flow, portable and high-level imperative computer programming language developed by Dennis Ritchie at Bell Telephone Laboratories between 1969 and 1973. It was named C because it evolved from earlier language Basic Combined Programming Language (BCPL) and B.

By design, C provides constructs that map efficiently to typical machine instructions, and therefore it has found lasting use in applications that had formerly been coded in assembly language, including operating systems, as well as various application software for computers ranging from supercomputers to embedded systems. C language is used to re-implement the Unix operating system. It has become one of the most widely used programming languages of all time.

This text book is written for anyone who wants to learn the basic concepts, syntax, applications, and advances in C programming in a simple way. The focus of this book is to enable a novice to program in C by making them understand the concepts in a simple and easy way. Also this book specifically gives more examples and exercises for the reader to get more clarity.

Organisation of the Book

This book is organized into the following chapters.

Chapter 1 discusses the basic concepts of Computer which include the definition, components, limitations, applications, history and characteristics of database systems. This chapter explains the various generations and classification of the computer. Also this chapter describes the basic organization of computer and the basics of number system and its conversion with example. Finally this chapter presents the basics of algorithm, pseudo code and flowchart.

Chapter 2 deals with the basics of C programming. A clear understanding of the programming paradigm and problem solving is provided. This chapter explains the fundamental concepts of C such as constants, variables, keywords, data type and so on. There is a clear picture of the structure of C program. This chapter explains the operators and its types, storage classes, input/output statements to read a character, a string or any type of input and display any type of output on the screen.

Also this chapter provides the types of decision making and branching statements such as if, if-else, nested if, goto, switch, break, continue and return. Along with this, the chapter also describes the various looping statements such as for, while and do-while. All the concepts are discussed with the definition, syntax, example and work flow. Finally, explains the pre-processor directives, compiling and linking process. The most salient feature is the collection of programs for all the concepts discussed in the chapter.

Chapter 3 presents the concept of arrays and strings. The explanation includes the definition, declaration, initialization, general representation and the types of array. This chapter discusses the two important types of array which include one dimensional and two dimensional arrays with example programs for each. All the operations of matrix are programmed in this chapter.

The array is the collection of items of same data type. An array of characters forms a string. This chapter presents the basic operations of strings such as string length, string compare, string concatenate and string copy. The string operations are performed with and without the built-in functions. This chapter also gives an overview of sorting and searching techniques. The two basic types of sorting – internal and external sorting and two types of searching – linear and binary searching are explained in detail with worked out examples.

Chapter 4 explains the concept of functions and pointers. The basics of function include function prototype, function definition and function call. The built-in string and math functions are presented simply in a table with the role of the function, input/output, syntax and example. This chapter presents the most important concept in function called recursion. When the function has a call to itself, it is called as recursive function. Binary search is performed using this concept with few more examples.

Under pointers, the concepts discussed are-definition, void pointer, null pointer, initialization, dereferencing of pointer and so on. This chapter explains the pointer arithmetic and operations that can be and cannot be performed on pointers. Then comes the combination of pointers and arrays and array of pointers. The two important parameter passing techniques -pass by value and pass by reference are discussed with relevant examples for each. Finally, more example programs are given to make the reader understand the concept of functions and pointers and to enable them to program the same.

Chapter 5 discusses the concept of structures. Structure is a collection of data members of different data type. It is a user defined data type. The definition, need for structure, characteristics, syntax, declaration and initialization of structure are discussed in this chapter. The main advantage of going to structure is the ability to hold data members of different data type. This chapter deals with nested structure and self-referential structure. Nested structure is nothing but a structure within another structure and self-referential is the structure which has pointer member pointing to the same structure. Then comes the combination of topics such as structure and function, array of structures, structure and pointers. This chapter presents the dynamic memory allocation concept. The functions used for allocating, de allocating and re allocating the memory–malloc(), calloc(), realloc() and free() are discussed. Typedef is also discussed.

Also this chapter gives an introduction to data structure. The definition, need and classification of data structure are specified. This chapter focuses more only on singly linked list which is a linear non-primitive data structure. Abstract Data Type(ADT) is defined in precise with example. The basics of list include the definition, operations performed, implementation and types of list. The list can be implemented as array based implementation, linked list based implementation or cursor based implementation. The linked list can be classified as singly linked list, doubly linked list and circular (singly, doubly) linked list. In this chapter singly linked list is implemented using linked list based implementation. Finally this chapter presents the difference between array and linked list with few examples for linked list.

Chapter 6 deals with the concept of file processing. This chapter provides the basic knowledge on files, its types various functions to access the file. The file functions available in C are listed in the table and explained in specific with the syntax, purpose and example. The file functions include–fopen, fclose, fread, fwrite, rewind, fseek, ftell, remove, fgetc, fputc, fgets, fputs, fscanf, fprintf, ferror, feof, rename, putw and getw. This chapter describes the two types of file processing–sequential file processing and random file processing. The difference in sequential and random file accessing is made very clear and points are tabulated. This chapter also explains the concept of command line arguments with various examples based on it.

We sincerely hope that the content of this book will be useful to all learners of C Programming. Any constructive suggestion for further improvement of this book is most welcome.

A. Rajeswari

C.M. Nalayini

Acknowledgement

It is a great pleasure to acknowledge the support we received from various sources for writing this book.

First, we would like to thank the Almighty for his blessings to bring this book in a successful manner.

We would like to express our sincere thanks to our respected Chairman, dynamic Chief Executive Officer, beloved Advisor, supportive Principal, HoDs and colleagues of Velammal Engineering College for their encouragement and moral support for writing this book.

We express our special thanks to our ever encouraging guides and the family members for their support and encouragement for publishing this book.

We thank the publishers for their efforts to publish this book in a good and complete shape.

We also acknowledge the authors and researchers of Computer Programming whose work has helped us in enhancing our knowledge on the subject for developing this book.

A. Rajeswari

C.M. Nalayini

Unit	Contents	Page No
I	**Introduction to Computers**	**1**

	1.1. Characteristics of Computer	1
	1.2. Limitations	1
	1.3. Applications of Computer	1
	1.4. History of Computer	2
	1.5. Generation of Computer	6
	1.6. Classification of Computer	10
	1.7. Basic Organization of a Computer	12
	1.8. Number System	17
	1.9. Need for Logical Analysis and Thinking	22
	1.10. Algorithm	24
	1.11. Pseudocode	25
	1.12. Flowchart	27
	Exercise	31
II	**Basics of C Programming**	**32**
	2.1. Introduction to Programming Paradigm	32
	2.1.1. Problem Formulation	33
	2.1.2. Problem Solving	33
	2.2. Introduction to 'C' Programming	35
	2.3. Fundamentals	36
	2.3.1. C Character Set	36
	2.3.2. Identifiers	36
	2.3.3. Keywords	37
	2.3.4. Declaration and Definition	37
	2.4. Structure of 'C' Program	37
	2.5. Constants, Variables and Data types	40
	2.6. Enumeration Constraints	44
	2.7. Storage Class	45
	2.7.1. Automatic Storage Class	47

	2.7.2. Extern Storage Class	48
	2.7.3. Static Storage Class	49
	2.7.4. Register Storage Class	50
	2.8. Expression Using Operators in C	51
	2.8.1. Classification of Operators Based on Number of Operands	53
	2.8.2. Classification of Operators based on the Role of the Operator	53
	2.9. Managing Input and Output Operations	57
	2.10. Assignment Statements	60
	2.11. Decision Making and Branching Statements	61
	2.12. Looping Statements	68
	2.13. Pre-processor Directives	72
	2.13.1. File Inclusion Directives	72
	2.13.2. Macro Substitution Directives	73
	2.13.3. Conditional Inclusion	74
	2.14. Compilation and Linking Process	76
	2.15. Basic Example Programs	77
	Exercise	86
III	**Arrays and Strings**	**89**
	3.1. Introduction to Arrays	89
	3.2. Types of Array	90
	3.2.1. One Dimensional Array	90
	3.2.2. Two-dimensional Array	93
	3.3. Example Programs	95
	3.4. String	112
	3.5. String Operations	113
	3.6. Sorting	124
	3.6.1. Internal Sort Algorithms	125
	3.6.2. External Sort Algorithms	130
	3.7. Searching	131

	3.7.1. Linear Search	132
	3.7.2. Binary Search	133
	Exercise	136
IV	**Functions and Pointers**	**138**
	4.1. Introduction to Functions	138
	4.2. Function Prototype (or) Declaration	139
	4.3. Function Definition	139
	4.4. Classification of Functions	141
	4.5. Built-in Functions	147
	4.6. Recursion	150
	4.6.1. Linear Recursion	151
	4.6.2. Binary Recursion	152
	4.7. Example Program	155
	4.8. Introduction to Pointers	159
	4.9. Initialization of Pointer Variable	160
	4.10. Operations on Pointers	161
	4.11. Pointer Arithmetic	162
	4.12. Pointers and Arrays	165
	4.13. Array of Pointers	166
	4.14. Parameters	168
	4.15. Example Programs	172
	Exercise	178
V	**Structures**	**181**
	5.1. Introduction	181
	5.1.1. Structure Definition	181
	5.1.2. Need for Structure Data Type	181
	5.1.3. Characteristics of Structure	182
	5.2. Structure Declaration	182
	5.3. Structure Initialization	183
	5.4. Nested Structure	185
	5.5. Array of Structures	187

5.6. Structure and Functions 189

5.6.1. Passing Array of Structure to Function 190

5.7. Self Referential Structure 192

5.8. Union 193

5.9. Dynamic Memory Allocation 194

5.10. Typedef 200

5.11. Introduction to Data Structure 202

5.11.1. Classification of Data Structure 202

5.11.2. ADT 203

5.12. List 203

5.12.1. Implementation of List 204

5.12.2. Types of Linked List 204

5.13. Singly Linked List 204

VI File Processing 225

6.1. Why Files? 225

6.2. Definition 225

6.3. Types of Files 225

6.4. Files and Streams 226

6.4.1. File Declaration 228

6.4.2. File Pointer 228

6.5. File Operations (for Both Text and Binary Files) 228

6.5.1. fopen() 228

6.5.2. fclose() 230

6.5.3. fprintf() 230

6.5.4. fscanf() 231

6.5.5. fwrite() 233

6.5.6. fread() 233

6.5.7. fgets() 236

6.5.8. fputs() 237

6.5.9. fgetc() 239

6.5.10. fputc() 239

6.5.11. fseek() 243

6.5.12. rewind() 244

6.5.13. ftell() 244

6.5.14. feof() 249

6.5.15. perror() 250

6.5.16. Remove() 251

6.5.17. rename() 252

6.5.18. putw() and getw() 252

6.6. File Processing Types 254

6.6.1. Sequential Access File Processing 254

6.6.2. Random Access File Processing 258

6.7. Command Line Arguments 266

Exercise 279

Appendix

A Question Bank

B Solved University Question Paper

UNIT I

INTRODUCTION TO COMPUTERS

The term computer is derived from the word "COMPUTE". The word compute means *"to calculate"*. A computer is an electronic machine that accepts data from the user, processes the data by performing calculations and operations on it and generates the desired output results. Computer performs both simple and complex operations with speed and accuracy. In other words, a computer is a device that can be instructed to carry out an arbitrary set of arithmetic or logical operations automatically. The ability of computers to follow generalized sequences of operations, called programs, enables them to perform a wide range of tasks.

1.1. Characteristics of Computer

The key characteristics are

- Speed: The compiler is very fast in processing data at the rate of millions of instructions per second. For example: generation of payslip for 1000 employees.
- Accuracy: The Computer has a high degree of accuracy. For example: the quotient of a division can be gained with as many as decimal numbers.
- Diligence: The computer does not get tired as the human do when worked for a longer time. This property is termed as Diligence.
- Storage capacity: The capacity of the computer is too high as large volumes of data and information can be stored to it and retrieved back whenever required.
- Versatility: Computer is versatile in nature. Versatility means performing different kinds of tasks with the same ease.

1.2. Limitations

- The Computer works only as per the program given to it.
- It cannot do any work other than what is specified without getting instructions from the user.
- The computer does not have the decision making capability.

1.3. Applications of Computer

Computer is a fast, more accurate, reliable, diligent and versatile calculating machine which is used in following areas:

- Business: In offices, computers are used for payroll calculating, budgeting, sales analysis, financial forecasting, managing employee database, stock maintenance etc.

- Banking: Banks provide online accounting facilities like balance enquiry, deposits, withdraws etc. Insurance facilities like starting a new policy, extending a policy, knowing the maturity period etc. can be provided by computers.
- Education: Computer plays a vital role in the field of education. The computer based education is implemented in schools for making students understand the concepts better. Students can do self-learning in computers through internet.
- Health care: The technological improvement leads to great developments in the field of medicine. Few examples are diagnostic system, patient monitoring system, pharma information system, surgical system etc.
- Military: The modern smart weapons are accessed through computers in the war field. Missile control, military operation planning can also be done with the help of computers.
- Communication: Computer supports communication by providing features like E-Mail, chatting, Usenet, FTP, Telnet, Video Conferencing etc.
- Government: The major fields are income tax department, sales tax department, weather forecasting, election commission, generation of voters list, PAN card, driving license, male/female ratio etc.

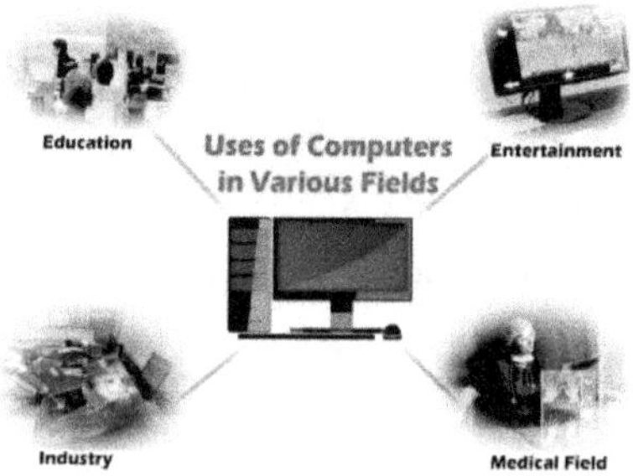

Figure 1.1: Applications of Computer

1.4. History of Computer

- Abacus: Abacus is the first counting machine used approximately 4000 years ago. This was invented by Chinese. It contains a wooden frame with metal rods and wooden beads. The beads in the first column values 1s, the beads in the second column values 10s, the beads in the third column values 100s and so on. Addition, Subtraction, Multiplication and Division are performed by moving the beads on the rods. The abacus machine is shown in the figure 1.2 below.

Figure 1.2: Abacus

- Napier's bone: John Napier invented the next better calculating machine called Napier's bone. Napier's made use of bones or carved ivory sticks with some numbers marked over it as shown in the figure 1.3 below. Napier's introduced the logarithmic values carved on the bone as an alternate to tables.

Figure 1.3: Napier's Bone

- Slide rule: Based on the invention of Napier, slide rule was built in England in 1632 and used worldwide. It is still in use by NASA engineers of the mercury, Gemini and Apollo programs which landed men on moon. The figure 1.4 below shows the slide that moves over the ruler.

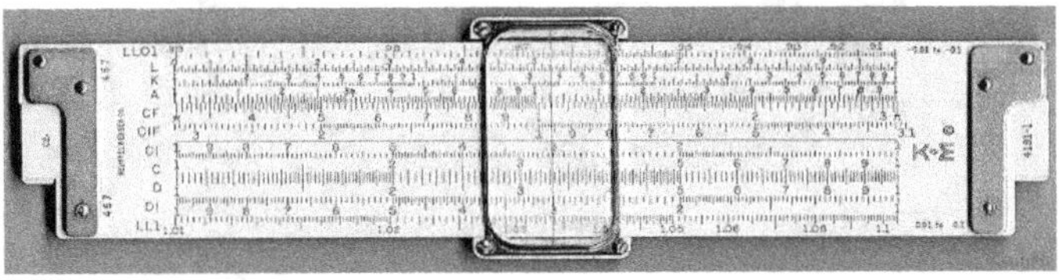

Figure 1.4: Slide Rule

- Pascal's adding and subtraction machine: Blaise Pascal, a French scientist invented the pascaline in the year 1642 to help his father who is a tax collector. Pascaline is an 8-digit digital calculating machine as shown in the figure 1.5 below. It contains eight wheels where the next wheel is incremented after the complete revolution of the current wheel.

Figure 1.5: Pascal's Calculating Machine

- Leibniz's multiplication and dividing machine: Gottfried Leibniz modified the pascal's calculating machine and invented a four function calculating machine called as Stepped Reckoner. He replaced the gear wheels with fluted drums ie., ten flutes arranged around the circumference of each drum as shown in the figure 1.6 below.

Figure 1.6: Stepped Reckoner

- Punch card system: In 1801, Joseph Marie Jacquard, a French scientist invented the Jacquard loom that appears like a weaving machine which is controlled by punched cards. The machine and the close appearance of the punched cards are shown in the figure 1.7 and figure 1.8 respectively.

Figure 1.7: Jacquard Loom

Figure 1.8: Punched Cards

- Babbage's analytical engine: In 1833, Charles Babbage invented a device called analytical engine that was running on today's programming language. For this invention, Charles babbage is known as the "Father of the Computer". This machine also used punched cards similar to Jacquard loom. The analytical engine is as large as the room size and powered by six steam engines.

Figure 1.9: Analytical Engine

- Hollerith's punched card tabulating machine: The next successful innovation is the Hollerith's tabulating machine invented by Herman Hollerith in the year 1890. The Hollerith's desk consists of a card reader that sensed the holes of the card, a gear driven mechanism for counting and a large wall of dial indicators to display the results. After this invention it took only 3 years to calculate 1890 census with the savings of 5 million dollars. The same calculation took 8 years prior.

Figure 1.10: Hollerith's Tabulating Machine

1.5. Generation of Computer

The evolution of computer from large sized calculating machine to a smaller powerful machine is defined in terms of generations of computer. There are five generations of computer which are discussed in terms of:

- The technology used by them(hardware and software)
- Computing characteristics
- Physical appearance and
- Their applications

1. First Generation(1940-1956): Using vacuum tubes
   - Hardware Technology:
     1 Vacuum tubes for circuitry
     2 Magnetic drums for memory
     3 Input was fed through punch cards and paper tapes
     4 Output obtained as printouts

- Software Technology: Instructions were written in machine language i.e., 0s and 1s for coding of instructions. It can solve only one problem at a time.
- Computing Characteristics: Computation time was in Milliseconds.
- Physical Appearance: Enormous in size and required a large room for installation.
- Application: It was used for scientific applications as they were the fastest computing device of their time.
- Examples: UNIVersal Automatic Computer(UNIVAC), Electronic Numerical Integrator And Calculator(ENIAC).
- Limitations:
    1. A large number of vacuum tubes were used which generated a lot of heat.
    2. They consumed lot of electricity and were expensive to operate.
    3. These devices were often subject to malfunctioning and required regular maintenance.
    4. Programming is difficult as machine languages were used.

2. Second Generation(1956-1963): Using Transistors

- Hardware Technology:
    1 Transistors replaced vacuum tubes of first generation which turned computer, smaller, faster, cheaper, energy efficient and reliable.
    2 Magnetic core technology was used for primary memory.
    3 Magnetic tapes and discs used for secondary memory.
    4 Inputs fed through punched cards
    5 Outputs obtained as printouts.
    6 It used the concept of stored programs in memory.
- Software Technology:
    1 Assembly language is used to write instructions i.e., mnemonics like ADD for addition and SUB for subtraction.
    2 Easier to code compared with machine language.
    3 High level programming languages such as early versions of COBOL and FORTRAN were developed during this period.
- Computing Characteristics: Computation time was in Microseconds.
- Physical Appearance: Transistors were smaller compared to vacuum tubes. Hence the size of computer was also reduced.

- Application: The cost of commercial products was high, though less than first generation. Transistors had to be assembled manually.
- Examples: PDP-8, IBM 1401.
- Limitations: They generated lot of heat but less than first generation systems
- Advantages: They require low maintenance compared to the early generation.

3. Third Generation(1964-1971): Using Integrated Circuits.

- Hardware Technology:
    1. Integrated circuits were used in which multiple transistors are placed on a silicon chip. Silicon is a type of semiconductor.
    2. IC chip increased speed and efficiency of computer.
    3. Inputs given through keyboard
    4. Outputs displayed through monitor.
- Software Technology:
    1. The keyboard and the monitor were interfaced through the operating system.
    2. Operating system allowed different applications to run at the same time.
    3. High level languages were used for programming.
- Computing Characteristics: Computation time was in Nanoseconds.
- Physical Appearance: The physical size was small compared to the second generation system.
- Application: Computers were produced commercially and were smaller and cheaper compared to predecessors.
- Examples: IBM 370, PDP 11
- Advantages:
    1. They consumed less power and generated less heat than second generation computers.
    2. The individual components were not assembled manually which reduces the cost to some extent.
    3. The maintenance cost was less compared to their predecessors.

4. Fourth Generation(1971-present): Using Microprocessors

- Hardware Technology:
    1. Large Scale Integration(LSI) and Very Large Scale Integration(VLSI) technology were used.

2. LSI-Thousands of transistors on a small silicon chip. VLSI-hundreds of thousands of components integrated in a small chip.
3. This era marked by the development of microprocessor which is a chip containing millions of transistors and components, designed using LSI and VLSI technology.
4. This generation gave rise to personal computer (PC) and linking of computers to networks.
5. Primary memory – Semiconductor memory (fast random access)
6. Secondary memory - Magnetic disks – small in physical size and larger in capacity
7. Mouse and Handheld devices were used in addition to the devices in third generation.

- Software Technology: MS-DOS and MS-Windows were developed which is a user friendly interface that allows user to interact with the computer via menus and icons. High level programming languages were used.
- Computing Characteristics: Computation time is in Picoseconds.
- Physical Appearance: Smaller that can even fit in the palm of the hand.
- Application: Used for Commercial purpose. PCs became available at home user.
- Examples:
  1. Intel 4004 chip - first microprocessor(CPU and Memory located on a single chip)
  2. IBM introduced first home use computers
  3. Apple introduced Macintosh
- Advantages:
  1. Smaller and cheaper than predecessors
  2. Portal and more reliable
  3. Much lesser heat and less maintenance
  4. GUI and pointing devices provides easy use and learning of computers.
  5. Networking helps in resource sharing and communication among different computers.

5. Fifth Generation(Present and Next): Using Artificial Intelligence
   - Hardware Technology:
     1. The goal of the fifth generation computers is to develop computers capable of self-learning and self-organization.

2. Super Large Scale Integrated (SLSI) chips are used which are able to store millions of components on a single chip.

- Software Technology: Parallel processing is done that allows instructions to be executed in parallel. This results in faster processing speed.
- Application: Fifth generation is based on Artificial Intelligence (AI) which simulates human way of thinking and reasoning. This includes areas like Expert System (ES), Natural Language Processing (NLP), Speech Recognition, Voice Recognition, Robotics etc.
- Examples: Intel dual core microprocessor.

1.6. Classification of Computer

The computers are broadly classified into 4 categories based on their size and type. They are:

1. Microcomputers
2. Minicomputers
3. Mainframe computers
4. Super computers

The detailed explanation is given below.

1. Microcomputers

Microcomputers are small, low cost and single user digital computer consisting of CPU, input unit, output unit, storage unit and the software. Microcomputers include:

- Desktop computer (or) PC
- Notepad computer (or) laptop
- Netbook
- Tablet computer
- Handheld computer (or) Personal Digital Assistant (PDA)
- Smartphones

Microcomputers can be connected through a network and made available for more than one user.

Desktop (or) PC: They are stand-alone machine. As the name suggest, they can be placed on the desk. It consists of three units- keyboard, monitor and a system unit containing the CPU, memory, hard disk drive etc. They are not very expensive. Hence, they are used at home, small business units and organizations. Example manufacturers are Apple, HP and Dell.

Notebook computers (or) Laptop: It resembles a notebook, small in size, can be carried anywhere (portable), has battery backup and has all functionality of the desktop. They are costlier than the desktop.

Netbook (InterNET + NoteBOOK): They are smaller notebooks optimized for low weight and low cost. They perform steaming of videos or music, emailing, web surfing or instant messaging.

Tablet computer: Portable computer has features of notebook computer but it can accept input from a stylus or a pen instead of the keyboard or mouse.

Handheld computer (or) PDA: Small computer held on the top of the palm. They are small in size, uses pen or a stylus for input. PDAs do not have a disk drive. They have limited memory and are less powerful. They are connected through wireless connections.

Smartphones: Smartphones function both as a phone and as a small PC. A Smart phone can have a stylus (or) pen (or) may have a small keyboard. They can be connected to the internet to access the electronic mail, download music, play games etc. The connectivity here is wireless.

2. *Minicomputers*

Minicomputers are digital computers. They are used in multi-user systems with high processing speed and high storage capacity than the microcomputers. The Minicomputers can support nearly 4-200 users simultaneously. They are used for real-time applications in industries, research centres etc. Example: PDP 11, IBM.

3. *Mainframe Computers*

Mainframe computers are also Multi-user systems. They are Multi-programming and high performance computers that work at very high speed and have large storage capacity. The mainframe computer can be accessed via a terminal that may be a dumb terminal, an intelligent terminal or a PC.

The term dumb terminal is given to the terminal that cannot store data or do processing on its own. It has input and output device only. An intelligent terminal is the one which has input, output and can do processing of its own but there is no storage of data.

They are used in banks or companies where many people require frequent access to the same data. Example: CDC 6600 and IBM ES000 series.

4. Super Computers

Supercomputers are constructed by interconnecting thousands of processors that can work in parallel. As many works are done in parallel, supercomputers are considered to be the fastest and the most expensive machines with high processing speed compared to other computers. The speed is measured in FLOPS (Floating Point Operations Per Second).

They are used for highly calculation-intensive tasks such as weather forecasting, climate research, molecular research, biological research, nuclear research and aircraft design. Example: IBM Roadrunner, IAM Blue gene and Intel ASCI red.

1.7. Basic Organization of a Computer

Computer is an electronic device that accepts data as input, processes the input data by performing mathematical and logical operations on it and gives the desired output. The computer consists of four parts:

1. Hardware
2. Software
3. Data
4. Users

1. Hardware

The physical devices of the computer those are required for input, output, storage and processing of the data. Example: keyboard, mouse, printer, hard disk, processor

2. Software

Software contains the set of instructions that tells the computer what tasks and how these tasks are to be performed. The hardware is instructed by the software to perform different kind of tasks.

Program is a set of instructions, written in a language understood by the computer, to perform a specific task. A set of programs and documents are collectively called software.

3. Data

The isolated values (or) raw facts on its own have no much significance but can be processed to generate some meaningful information.

4. Users

People those who write computer programs or interact with the computer. They are also known as skin ware, live ware, human ware or people ware.

1.7.1. The Input-Process-Output Concept

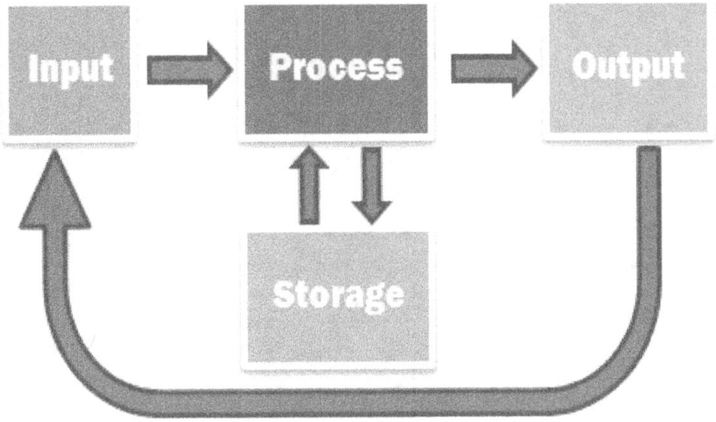

Figure 1.11: The Input-Process-Output Concept

The concept of generating output information from the input data is referred as input-process-output concept. The diagrammatic representation is shown above in figure 1.11.

- Input: The computer accepts input data from the user via an input device like keyboard. The input data can be text, characters, word, sound, image, documents etc.
- Process: The computer processes the input data by performing some actions by using the instructions or program. Some actions can be arithmetic or logical, editing, modifying documents etc. During the process, the data are temporarily stored in computer's main memory.
- Output: The output generated after processing the data is in the form of text, sound, image etc. they are displayed on monitor (or) printed using printers etc.
- Storage: The data are stored permanently in the secondary storage like disk or tape. The stored data can be retrieved whenever required.

1.7.2. Components of Computer Hardware

The three main components of hardware are:

1. Input/Output(I/O) unit
2. Central Processing Unit(CPU) and
3. Memory Unit

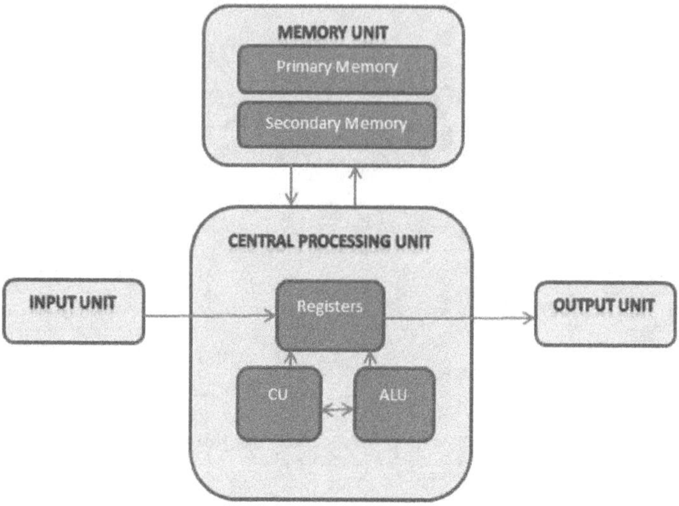

Figure 1.12: Basic Organization of Computer

1. *Input/Output Unit*

The user interacts with the computer via input/output unit. The input unit accepts the data from the user and converts it into the form understood by the computer. The input devices are keyboard, mouse, scanner, stylus, Microphone, Barcode reader. The output unit converts and provides the processed output in a form understandable by the user. The output devices used are monitor, printer, speaker.

2. *Central Processing Unit*

Central Processing Unit is the brain of the computer that controls, coordinates and supervises the operations of the computer. It consists of Arithmetic Logic Unit (ALU) and Control Unit (CU). In addition, it also contains registers for temporary storage of data, instructions, addresses etc. The components of the CPU are explained below in detail.

Arithmetic Logic Unit (ALU)

The arithmetic unit performs arithmetic operations such as addition, subtraction, multiplication and division on the data. The logic unit performs logical operations. For Example, comparison of numbers, letters. The logic operations are represented as greater than, less than or equal to conditions.

Control Unit (CU)

The Control Unit can control the overall operations of the computer. It checks the order of execution of instructions and controls and co-ordinates the overall functionality of the units of computer.

Registers (or) CPU's Working Memory

Registers are high speed storage area within the CPU, with least storage capacity. Different registers are shown in the figure 1.13 below that are used to serve specific purposes.

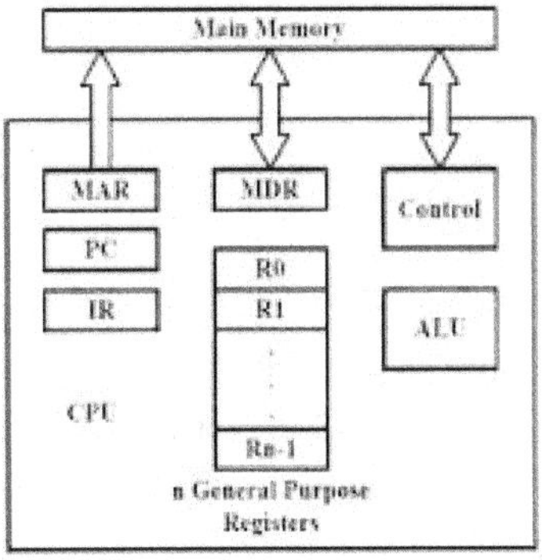

Figure 1.13: Registers in CPU

The important registers are

- ACC – Accumulator to store results of arithmetic and logic units.
- IR – Instruction Register contains current instruction most recently fetched.
- PC – Program Counter contains address of next instruction to be processed.
- MAR – Memory Address Register contains address of next location in the memory to be accessed.
- MDR – Memory Buffer Register temporarily stores data from memory and to memory.
- DR – Data Register stores operands involved and any other data involved in the processing is also stored.

3. *Memory Unit*

The data, instruction, results and programs processed in the CPU are stored in the memory. There are two classes of memory namely primary memory and secondary memory. The hierarchy of memory is shown in the figure 1.14 below.

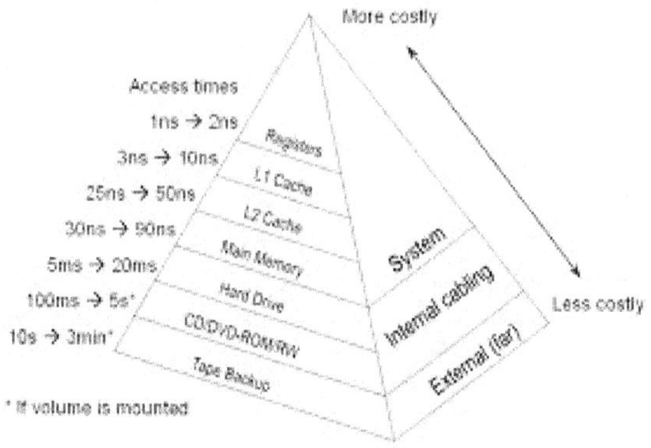

Figure 1.14: Memory Hierarchy

Internal (or) Primary Memory

The main memory contains one or more levels of cache and Random Access Memory (RAM). The data, instruction, intermediate results are temporarily stored in the primary memory. Hence it is also called as volatile memory. Random Access Memory (RAM) is a random selection of memory location where the data stored is lost on power failure. Static RAM (SRAM) and Dynamic RAM (DRAM) are also the examples of Volatile memory.

The cache is a small amount of fast memory that sits between normal main memory and CPU. When processor attempts to read a data from memory it first checks the cache. The most recently and frequently used data is stored in cache. When the cache is full, the data will automatically be pushed to the main memory.

External (or) Secondary Memory

Secondary memory is external and permanent memory and so it is also called as Non-Volatile Memory. They can store bulk or mass amount of data. Read Only Memory (ROM) is an example of non-volatile memory that allows only read operation.

Programmable Read Only Memory (PROM) allows write once and read many operation but does not supports erase operation. Erasable Programmable Read Only Memory (EPROM) overcomes the problem with ROM and PROM by erasing the data by passing ultraviolet light and the chip becomes reprogrammable.

Electrically Erasable Programmable Read Only Memory (EEPROM) is similar to EPROM but the data is erased using electrical beam. The external storage media used are floppy disk, magnetic disks, magnetic tapes, optical discs etc.

1.7.3. Fetch-Execute Cycle

With the architecture described above, the computer can execute the program by following the fetch-execute cycle which involves four steps.

1. Fetch the next instruction
2. Decode the instruction
3. Get data if needed
4. Execute the instruction

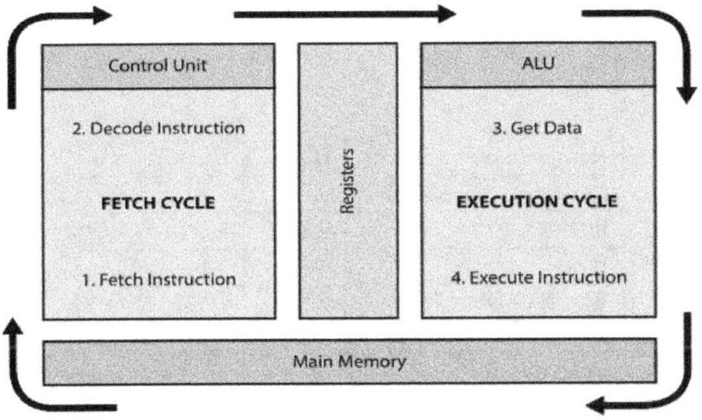

Figure 1.15: Fetch-Execute Cycle

To start the cycle, the data is first loaded into the main memory and the address of the first instruction is assigned to the Program Counter (PC). In order to fetch the next instruction, the PC is incremented by one to point to the next address in the memory. The instruction is fetch from that place and the control unit decides what kind of instruction is that and then decodes the instruction into control signals. In the third step, the data necessary to process the decoded instruction is fetch from main memory. Finally now the control unit is ready to execute the instruction. At the time of execution, the communication happens between the ALU, CU and registers. The cycle continues after executing each instruction till the end of the program.

1.8. Number System

A Number System in base r (or) radix r uses unique symbols for r digits. One or more digits combined to get a number. The *base* of a number decides the valid digits that are used to make a number. The *position* of digit starts from the right hand side of a number. The digits of a number have two kinds of value:

- Face Value: The digit located at that position.
- Position Value: the position value is given by $base^{position}$

For Example, Consider the number 52,

The face value at position 0 is 2 and at position 1 is 5.

The position value of digit 2 is 10^0 and digit 5 is 10^1.

The number is sum of *face value * base*^{position}.

i.e., $(5*10^1)+(2*10^0)=(5*10)+(2*1)=50+2=52$.

There are four kinds of Number System. They are

1. Decimal Number System – Base 10.
2. Binary Number System – Base 2.
3. Octal Number System – Base 8.
4. Hexadecimal Number System – Base 16.

Number System	Base	Digits	Largest Digit
Decimal	10	0-9	9
Binary	2	0,1	1
Octal	8	0-7	7
Hexadecimal	16	0-9,A-F	F(15)

Table 1.1: Number System

Decimal	Binary	Octal	Hexadecimal
0	0000	000	0
1	0001	001	1
2	0010	002	2
3	0011	003	3
4	0100	004	4
5	0101	005	5
6	0110	006	6
7	0111	007	7
8	1000	010	8
9	1001	011	9
10	1010	012	A
11	1011	013	B
12	1100	014	C
13	1101	015	D
14	1110	016	E
15	1111	017	F
16	10000	020	10

Table 1.2: Sample Values of All Four Number System

Conversions

Converting Decimal to Binary, Octal and Hexadecimal

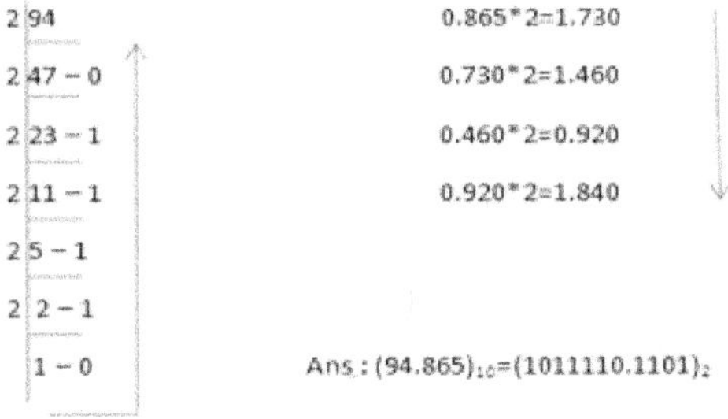

A number has two parts: Integer part and Fraction part.

Example: $(25.2345)_{10}$ where 25 is the integer part and 0.2345 is the fraction part.

The steps to convert vary for both the parts as explained below.

Integer part:

1. The operation performed is division.
2. To convert decimal to
    2.1. Binary - divide the integer by 2
    2.2. Octal - divide the integer by 8
    2.3. Hexadecimal - divide the integer by 16
3. The converted answer is obtained by writing the reminder of the division method from bottom to top.

Fraction part:

1. The operation performed is multiplication.
2. To convert decimal to
    2.1. Binary - multiply the fraction by 2
    2.2. Octal - multiply the fraction by 8
    2.3. Hexadecimal - multiply the fraction by 16
3. The converted answer is obtained by writing the integer part of the multiplied answer from top to bottom.
4. Only the fraction part of the multiplied answer is considered for the next iteration.

Convert $(94.865)_{10}$ to Binary, Octal and Hexadecimal.

Decimal to Binary

2 | 94	0.865*2=1.730
2 | 47 – 0	0.730*2=1.460
2 | 23 – 1	0.460*2=0.920
2 | 11 – 1	0.920*2=1.840
2 | 5 – 1	
2 | 2 – 1	
1 – 0	Ans : $(94.865)_{10}=(1011110.1101)_2$

Decimal to Octal

8 | 94
8 | 11 – 6
| 1 – 3

0.865*8=6.92

0.730*8=7.36

0.460*8=2.88

0.88*8=7.04

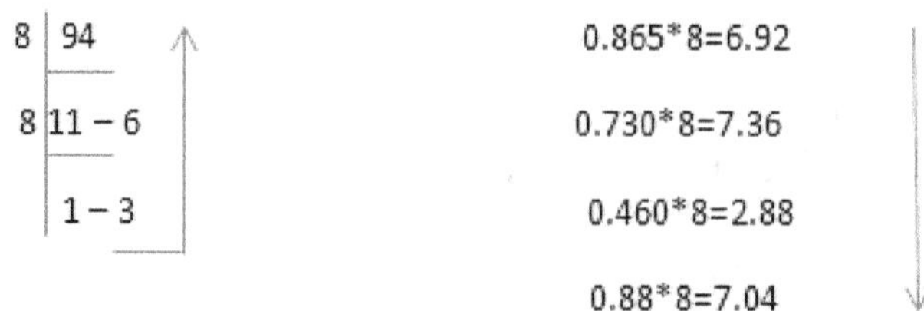

Ans: $(94.865)_{10}=(136.6727)_8$

Decimal to Hexadecimal

16 | 94
16 | 5 – 14
| 0 – 5

0.865*16=13.84

0.84*16=13.44

0.44*16=7.04

0.04*16=0.64

14 → E and 13 → D

Ans: $(94.865)_{10}=(5E.DD7)_{16}$

Converting Binary, Octal, Hexadecimal to Decimal

1. Find the sum of the *facevalue*(from base)*^{position} for each digit in the number.
2. Before the decimal, the position is assigned from right hand side and starts from 0.
3. After the decimal, the position is assigned from left hand side as -1,-2 and goes on.

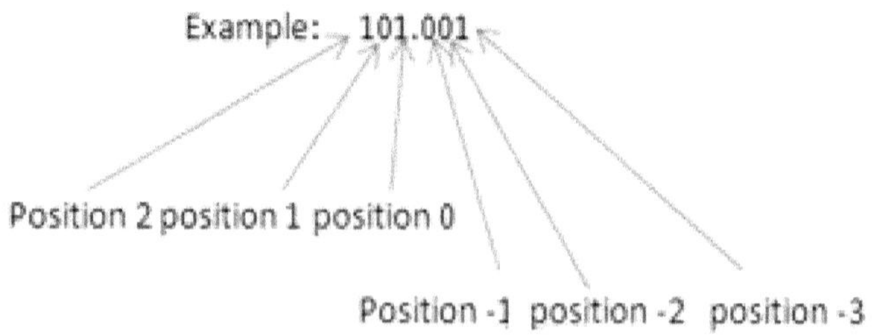

Convert $(1011.1001)_2$ to Decimal

$\Rightarrow$ $1*2^3 + 0*2^2 + 1*2^1 + 1*2^0 . 1*2-1 + 0*2-2 + 0*2-3 + 1*2-4$

$= 8+0+2+1 . (0.5)+0+0+(0.0625) = 11.5625$

Ans: $(1011.1001)_2=(11.5625)_{10}$

Convert $(24.36)_8$ to Decimal

$\Rightarrow$ $2*8^1 + 4*8^0 . 3*8^{-1} + 6*8^{-2}$

$= 16+4 . (0.375)+(0.09375) = 20.46875$

Ans: $(24.36)_8=(20.46875)_{10}$

Convert $(4D.21)_{16}$ to Decimal

$\Rightarrow$ $4*16^1 + 13*16^0 . 2*16^{-1} + 1*16^{-2}$

$= 64+13 . (0.125)+(0.00390625) = 77.12890625$

Ans: $(4D.21)_{16}=(77.1289)_{10}$

Converting Binary to Octal and Hexadecimal

The steps to convert from binary to octal is

1. Group the binary number in part of 3 digits from the right side of the integer and from left side of the fraction.
2. For each group of 3 digits, write their equivalent octal digit.

The steps to convert from binary to hexadecimal is

1. Partition the binary number and group in part of 4 digits from the right side of the integer and from left side of the fraction.
2. For each group of 4 digits, write their equivalent hexadecimal digit.

Example: Convert $(1110101100110.11)_2$ to Octal and hexadecimal.

1 | 110 | 101 | 100 | 110. 11 = 001 | 110 | 101 | 100 | 110. | 110

1 6 5 4 6 6

Ans: $(1110101100110.11)_2=(16546.6)_8$

1 | 1101 | 0110 | 0110. 11 = 0001 | 1101 | 0110 | 0110. | 1100

1 D 6 6 C

Converting Octal, Hexadecimal to Binary

This conversion is very simple as each digit is merely replaced by its equivalent binary number. (3 digit – octal and 4 digit – hexadecimal)

Example:

Convert $(473)_8$ to binary

$(473)_8 = (100\ 111\ 011)_2$

Convert $(2BA3)_{16}$ to hexadecimal

$(2BA3)_{16}=(0010\ 1011\ 1010\ 0011)_2$

1.9. Need for Logical Analysis and Thinking

Planning the Computer Program–The Programming Process

Programming is not a straight forward task. The process of programming follows the program development lifecycle. The program development lifecycle is given in the figure 1.16 below.

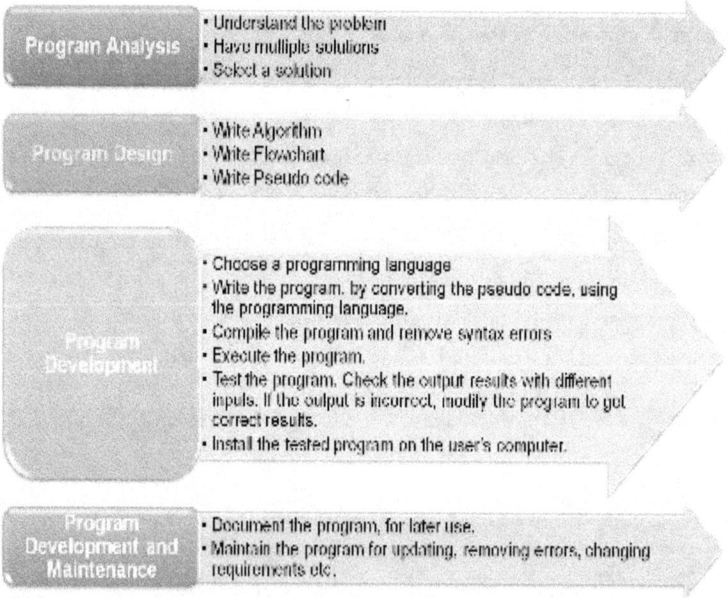

Figure 1.16: Program Development Lifecycle

The programming process involves the following steps

1. Understand the Problem
    - Read the problem statement
    - Question the users about their requirements
    - Collect the Inputs required
    - Decide on the required Outputs
    - Special formulae if any
    - Talk to users to get clarity
2. Plan the logic

    The following tools can be used for planning the logic better, understandable and simpler.
    - Visual Design tools
        1. Input record chart
        2. Printer spacing chart
        3. Hierarchy chart
        4. Flowchart
    - Verbal Design tools
        1. Narrative description
        2. Pseudocode
3. Code the program
    - Before coding the programming, the basic step is to select an appropriate language on which the programming can be done.
    - To follow the order of instruction and easy coding without logical errors, convert flowchart and/or pseudocode instructions into programming language statements.
4. Test the program

    The program coded should be tested for errors. Only on resolving the errors the expected output can be achieved successfully. The various kinds of errors are given below.
    - Syntax errors
    - Runtime errors
    - Logic errors
    - Test data set-It is the sample set of input given to check the functioning of the code.

5. Implement the program

   The implementation part requires the following:

   - hardware
   - software
   - Train the users
   - Implementation styles- can be
     1. Crash (or)
     2. Pilot (or)
     3. Phased (or)
     4. Dual

6. Maintain the program

   - Maintenance is done by programmers trained for it.
   - Legacy systems
   - Up to 85% of IT department budget lies in the maintenance phase

Problem solving with computers involves the following steps

- Clearly define the problem
- Analyse the problem and formulate a method to solve it
- Describe the solution in the form of an algorithm
- Draw a flowchart of the algorithm
- Write the computer program
- Compile and Run the program
- Test the program
- Interpretation of results

1.10. Algorithm

Algorithm is an ordered sequence of finite, well defined, unambiguous instructions for completing a task. It is a step-by-step English like representation of logic. Different algorithms differ in their requirements of space and time. The characteristics of a good algorithm are:

- Precision – The number of steps in the algorithm is defined (or) precisely stated.
- Uniqueness – The results of each step are uniquely defined and only depend on the input and the intermediate results of the preceding steps.
- Finiteness – The algorithm should stop at the end of finite number of executions.
- Unambiguous – each step should be clear and should project only one meaning.

- Input and Output - The algorithm should read the inputs required and display the outputs expected.
- Ordered – The steps in the algorithm should be sequential i.e., in order with start and stop at the beginning and end of the algorithm.

  Advantages:

  - Its step-by-step representation helps for easy understanding.
  - It is independent of programming languages. So any person without programming knowledge can understand the process.
  - It is easy to debug.

  Disadvantages:

  - It is time consuming and cumbersome.

Example: Algorithm to find the greatest of three numbers.

Step 1: Start.

Step 2: Read the three numbers a,b and c.

Step 3: Compare a and b. if a is greater, goto step 4 else goto step 5.

Step 4: Compare a and c. if a is greater, output "A is greatest" else output "c is greatest".

Step 5: Compare b and c. if b is greater, output "b is greatest" else output "c is greatest".

Step 6: Stop.

1.11. Pseudocode

Pseudocode consists of short, readable and formally-styled English language for explaining an algorithm. It is not based on any programming language and does not include variable declaration, subroutines etc.

It cannot be compiled or executed. There is no SYNTAX. Some terms are commonly used to represent the various actions. For example:

To input data – INPUT, GET, READ

To output results – OUTPUT, PRINT, DISPLAY

To calculate – COMPUTE, CALCULATE

For incrementing – INCREMENT

For initialization of variables – INITIALIZE

For arithmetic calculations – ADD, SUBTRACT, MULTIPLY, DIVIDE

For assignment of values - ASSIGN

The control structures are represented as follows

- Sequence structure: sequence of steps executed in linear order.
- Selection constructs: two kinds of selection statement namely if-statement and case statement
- Iterative statements: WHILE, DO-WHILE

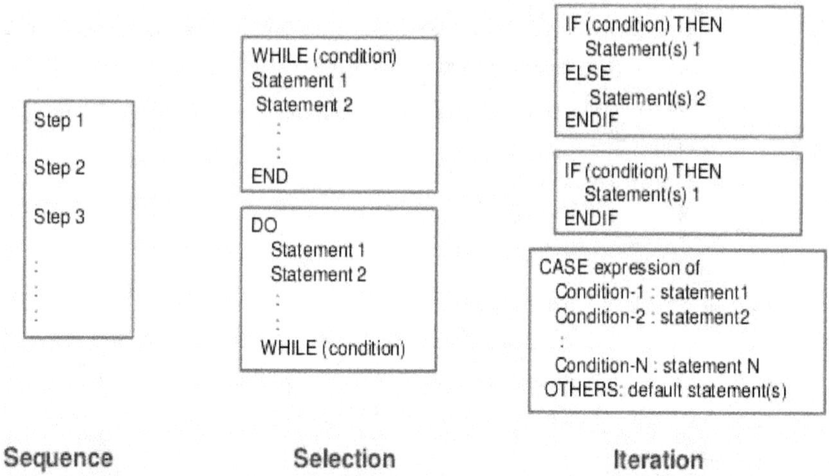

Step 1
Step 2
Step 3
WHILE (condition)
Statement 1
Statement 2
END
DO
Statement 1
Statement 2
WHILE (condition)
IF (condition) THEN
Statement(s) 1
ELSE
Statement(s) 2
ENDIF
IF (condition) THEN
Statement(s) 1
ENDIF
CASE expression of
Condition-1 : statement1
Condition-2 : statement2
Condition-N : statement N
OTHERS: default statement(s)
Sequence
Selection
Iteration

Advantages:

- Easier to write and modify in a word processor.
- Converting a pseudocode to a program code is easy compared to converting a flowchart into a program code.

Disadvantages:

- There are no standard rules. So it can vary from programmer to programmer.
- It's not visual.
- Creates an additional level of documentation making it difficult to maintain.

Example: Write a pseudocode to find the greatest of three numbers.

READ values A,B and C

IF A is greater than B THEN

ASSIGN A to MAX

ELSE

ASSIGN B to MAX

ENDIF

IF MAX is greater than C THEN

PRINT MAX is greatest

ELSE

PRINT C is greatest

ENDIF

END

1.12. Flowchart

A flowchart is a diagrammatic representation of the logic for solving a task. The purpose of drawing a flowchart is to make the logic more clear in a visual form.

"Pictures speak louder than words"

A flowchart is drawn using boxes of different shapes with lines connecting them to show the flow of control.

Flowchart Symbols

A symbol used in a flowchart is for a specific purpose. They use variety of symbols out of which few important symbols and their purposes are represented in the table below.

S.no	Symbol Name	Symbol	Description
1	Process		Operation (or) Action step
2	Alternate process		Alternate to normal process
3	Decision		Decision (or) a branch
4	Data		Input/Output to (or) from a process
5	Predefined process		Process previously specified
6	Internal storage	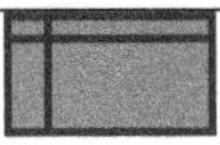	Stored in memory

7	Document	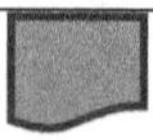	A Document
8	Multi document		More than one document
9	Terminator		Start or stop point
10	Preparation		Set-up process
11	Manual Input		Data entry from a form
12	Manual Operation		Operation to be done manually
13	Connectors		Join flow lines
14	Off-page Connector		Continue on another page
15	Card	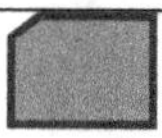	I/O from a punched card
16	Punched tape	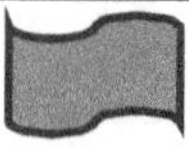	I/O from punched tape
17	Summing Junction		Logical AND
18	OR	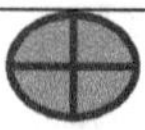	Logical OR
19	Collate		Organize in a format
20	Sort		Sort in some order

21	Extract		Split Process
22	Merge		Merge in a predefined order
23	Stored data		General data storage
24	Delay	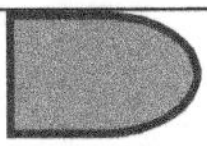	Wait
25	Sequential Access Storage		Stored on magnetic tape
26	Magnetic disk		I/O from Magnetic disk
27	Direct Access Storage	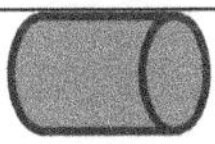	Stored on hard disk
28	Display		Display output
29	Flow lines		Indicates the direct of flow

Table 1.3: Flowchart Symbols

The control structures are represented as shown below.

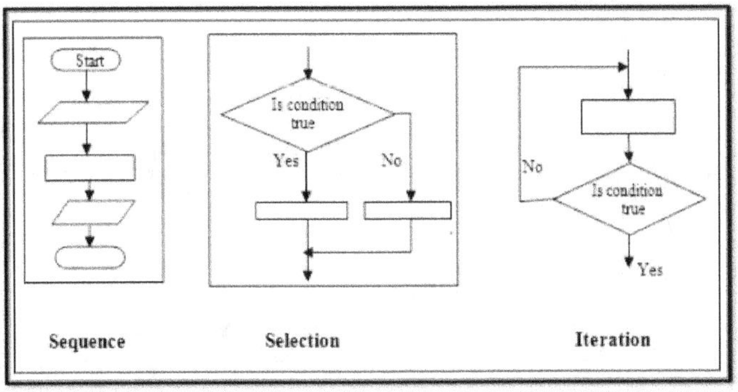

Rules to draw the flowchart

1. A flowchart should have a start and end symbol.
2. The direction of flow in a flowchart must be from top to bottom and left to right.
3. The relevant symbols must be used while drawing a flowchart. Sequence, selection or iterative structures to be used (as shown above) wherever necessary.

Advantages:

- The pictorial representation makes it easy to understand.
- Easier to identify any errors while drawing the flowchart
- Relevant symbols used reflect the proper meaning.

Disadvantages:

- Drawing a flowchart is time-consuming.
- It will be complex if the program contains complex branches and loops.
- Flowchart will be difficult to understand if it is drawn for too many pages.

Example: Draw a Flowchart to find the largest of three numbers

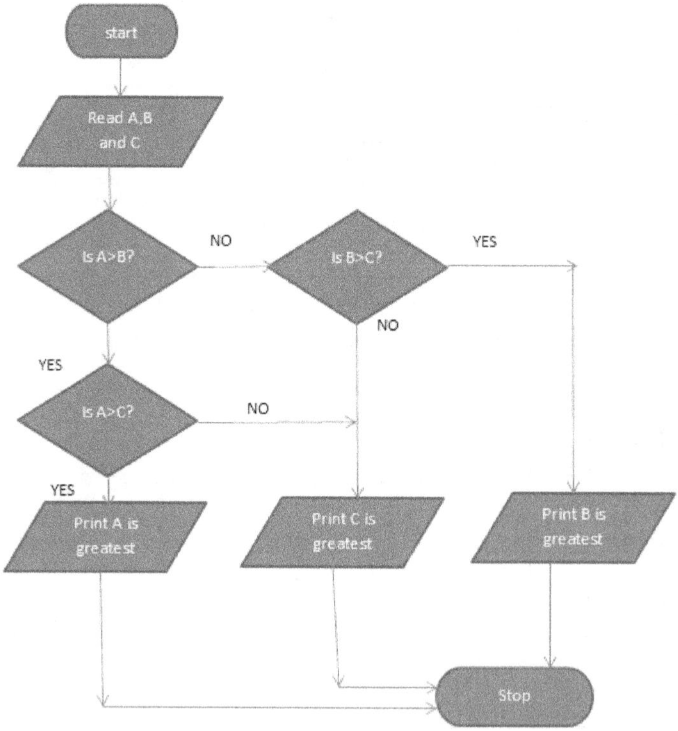

Exercise

1. Convert $(3598.714)_{10}$ to Binary and Octal
2. List the bases of Decimal, Binary, Octal and Hexa-Decimal and justify.
3. Differentiate Algorithm and Pseudo code
4. Write an algorithm and Pseudo code to find GCD().
5. Draw a flow chart to perform binary search.

UNIT II

BASICS OF C PROGRAMMING

2.1. Introduction to Programming Paradigm

Paradigm refers to an example that serves as a pattern or a model. Programming paradigm arise as a result of developer's idea on how to solve a problem. To define, Programming Paradigm is a set of coherent abstractions used to effectively model a problem. Few problem solving procedures are discussed below in this chapter. The programming language can be classified under multiple paradigms based on their feature. Some common programming paradigms are

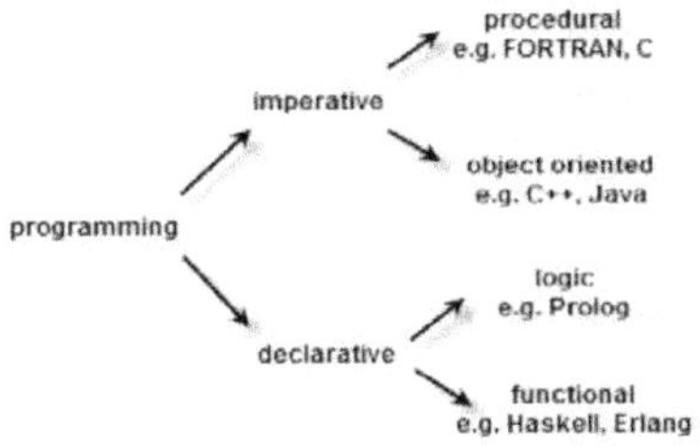

Imperative Paradigm

Imperative paradigm uses statements in natural language that changes the state of the program. It focuses on how a program operates. It is further classified into two-procedural and object oriented paradigm.

- Procedural: It is a structured paradigm that consists of algorithms and data. It is based on the concept of procedure call that is implemented through a stack register. It is good for decomposition.
- Object-oriented: It is based on the concept of objects that contains data in terms of attributes and methods. This object based paradigm is good for encapsulation.

Declarative Paradigm

Declarative paradigm focuses on what the program should accomplish without specifying how the program should achieve the results i.e., it deals with the computation without any information on the control flow. It is further classified into two–logic and functional paradigm.

- Logic: Logic paradigm is based on the formal logic that includes facts and rules about the problem. This type of paradigm is good for searching.

- Functional: Functional paradigm builds a program that performs computation as an evaluation of mathematical functions. This avoids state change and mutable data. This type of paradigm eliminates side effect as function inputs (arguments) produce the same output irrespective of the state change. Functional paradigm is good for reasoning.

2.1.1. Problem Formulation

Before attempting to solve the given problem, it is important to first define (or) formulate the problem. This formulation or definition gives clarity to the problem and helps in arriving at a solution. In order to make a good problem definition:

- The definition should be as precise as possible.
- The definition should address the following
    - The objective of the problem (what is required?)
    - The input to be given (Initial Condition)
    - The output to be obtained (desired results)
    - The relation between the input and the output

2.1.2. Problem Solving

Problem solving is the sequential process of analyzing information related to a given situation and generating appropriate response options. The diagrammatic representation of the steps involved in shown in figure 2.1 below.

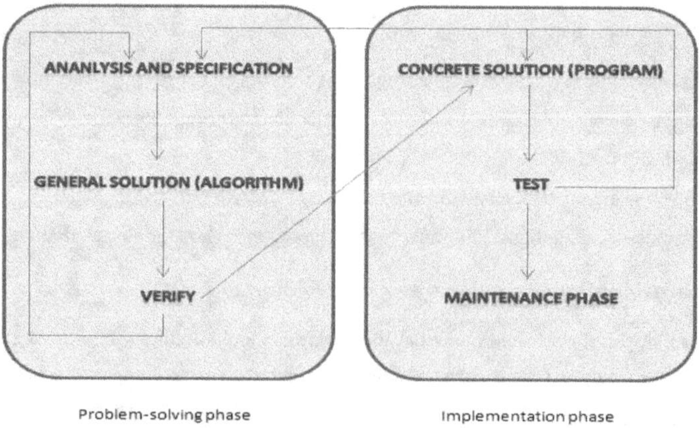

Figure 2.1: Programming Process

The programming process involves the following steps

1. Understand the Problem
    - Read the problem statement
    - Question the users about their requirements
    - Collect the Inputs required
    - Decide on the required Outputs
    - Special formulae if any
    - Talk to users to get clarity
2. Plan the logic

    The following tools can be used for planning the logic better, understandable and simpler.

    Visual Design tools:

    - Input record chart
    - Printer spacing chart
    - Hierarchy chart
    - Flowchart

    Verbal Design tools:

    - Narrative description
    - Pseudocode
3. Code the program
    - Before coding the programming, the basic step is to select an appropriate language on which the programming can be done.
    - To follow the order of instruction and easy coding without logical errors, convert flowchart and/or pseudocode instructions into programming language statements.
4. Test the program

    The program coded should be tested for errors. Only on resolving the errors the expected output can be achieved successfully. The various kinds of errors are given below.

    - Syntax errors
    - Runtime errors
    - Logic errors
    - Test data set-It is the sample set of input given to check the functioning of the code.

5. Implement the program

   The implementation part requires the following

   - hardware
   - software
   - Train the users
   - Implementation styles-can be:
     - Crash (or)
     - Pilot (or)
     - Phased (or)
     - Dual

6. Maintain the program

   - Maintenance is done by programmers trained for it.
   - Legacy systems
   - Up to 85% of IT department budget lies in the maintenance phase

Problem solving with computers involves the following steps:

1. Clearly define the problem
2. Analyse the problem and formulate a method to solve it
3. Describe the solution in the form of an algorithm
4. Draw a flowchart of the algorithm
5. Write the computer program
6. Compile and Run the program
7. Test the program
8. Interpretation of results

2.2. Introduction to 'C' Programming

C is a general purpose, block structured, procedural, case-sensitive, free flow, portable and high-level imperative computer programming language developed by Dennis Ritchie at Bell Telephone Laboratories between 1969 and 1973. It was named C because it evolved from earlier language Basic Combined Programming Language (BCPL) and B.

By design, C provides constructs that map efficiently to typical machine instructions, and therefore it has found lasting use in applications that had formerly been coded in assembly language, including operating systems, as well as various application software for computers ranging from supercomputers to embedded systems. C language is used to re-implement the Unix operating system. It has become one of the most widely used programming languages of all time.

2.3. Fundamentals

2.3.1. C Character Set

A character set defines the valid characters that can be used in a source program or interpreted when a program is running. The set of characters that can be used to write a source program is called a *source character set* and the set of characters available when the program is being executed is called an *Execution character set.*

The basic character set of C language include:

1. Letters
   1.1. Uppercase letters: A,B,C,...,Z
   1.2. Lowercase letters: a,b,c,...,z
2. Digits: 0,1,2,...,9
3. Special Characters: ,.:;!"%^#&(){}[]<>|\/_~ etc.
4. White space characters:
   4.1. Blank space character
   4.2. Horizontal tab space character
   4.3. Carriage return
   4.4. Newline character
   4.5. Form feed character

2.3.2. Identifiers

An identifier refers to the name of an object. It can be a variable name, label name, tag name, structure/union name etc.

The syntactic rules to write an identifier name in C are as follows:

1. Identifier name can have letters, digits (or) underscores.
2. It should start only with a letter (or) underscore and not with a digit.
3. Keywords and reserved words can't be used as identifier name.
4. No special characters, blank space and comma can be used.
5. The maximum number of characters depends on the compiler but the limit imposed provides enough flexibility to create a meaningful name.
   Example: studentname, student_name, student1

2.3.3. Keywords

Keyword is a predefined reserved word that has a particular meaning in the programming language. There are 32 keywords in C. They are

auto	break	case	char
const	int	float	double
continue	default	switch	while
do	if	goto	else
enum	struct	union	extern
for	long	register	return
short	signed	sizeof	static
typedef	unsigned	void	volatile

2.3.4. Declaration and Definition

Declaration only introduces the name of an identifier along with its type to the compiler before it is used. During declaration, no memory space is allocated to an identifier.

Definition of an identifier means declaration plus reservation of space for the identifier in the memory.

The general form of declaration statement:

Datatype identifier [=value[...]]; //the content inside the bracket is optional.

Example: introllno;

float mark1=87.5;

2.4. Structure of 'C' Program

The basic structure of 'C' program is shown in figure 2.2 below. The components in the structure are explained in detail:

Documentation

The documentation section consists of a set of comment lines that gives some information like name of the program, programmer details, date of modification etc. This kind of information can be given at the beginning of the program. Comment lines can also be written in between the program coding to give some information about the code (or) the purpose of that particular line of code. This increases readability. These lines are not processed by the compiler.

There are two types of comments:

1. Single line comment
2. Multi line comment

Single line comment: it starts with two forward slashes (i.e. //) and is automatically terminated with the end of the line.

Multi line comment: it starts with a forward slash followed by an asterisk (i.e. /*) and is terminated with an asterisk followed by a forward slash (i.e. */). It is used when more than one line of text are to be commented.

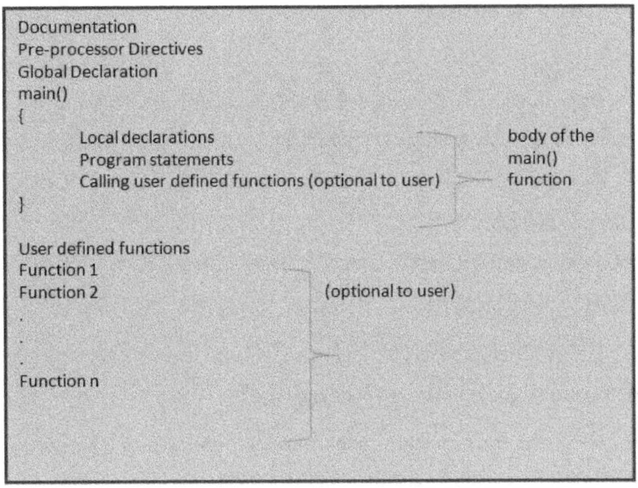

Documentation
Pre-processor Directives
Global Declaration
main()
{
Local declarations
Program statements
Calling user defined functions (optional to user)
body of the main() function
}
User defined functions
Function 1
Function 2
Function n
(optional to user)

Figure 2.2: Structure of 'C' program

C program is composed of three main sections:

Section 1: Pre-processor directives

Section 2: Global declarations

Section 3: Functions

Pre-processor Directives

The pre-processor directive always starts with a pound (or) a hash (#) symbol which is a non-white space character. The pre-processor is terminated with a new line character and not with a semicolon. They are executed before the compiler compiles the source code. It instructs the compiler to include C pre-processors such as header files and symbolic constants.

Example: #include<stdio.h>

#define pi 3.14

The first example includes a standard input/output header (.h) file. The second example defines the value of the variable pi as 3.14.

Global Declarations

The global declaration is an optional part where the variables are declared before the main() function as well as user defined functions. The global variables can be used inside all the functions (main() as well as user defined) without locally declaring the variables inside the function. These variables have global scope.

Functions

Every program should contain only one main() function. This indicates the start of the program written in lowercase letters and not terminated by a semicolon. Every function has two parts:

1. Header of a function
2. Body of a function

The general form of the header is

return_typefunction_name ([argument_list])

The term inside the [] are considered optional.

The body of the function contains a set of statements enclosed by a pair of curly brackets known as braces. { indicates start and } indicates end. There are two types of statements:

1. Non-executable statement. Ex: Declaration statements
2. Executable statement. Ex: function call statements

Local Declarations

The variables that are declared inside the function in the local declaration section are called as local variables. These variables are local to the function where it is declared and can't be used in other function without declaring it in that function. The scope of the variables is local.

User Defined Functions

The subprograms written by the user to perform a specific task is called as user defined function. It can be written before or after the main() function. The user can write any number of user defined function and the purpose of the function is also user dependent. The detailed description about the function can be studied in unit IV.

Example:

```
//program to display a global and a local variable
#include<stdio.h> //header files
#include<conio.h>
int age;            //global declaration
void main()
{
float weight=34.5; //local declaration
clrscr();
printf("Enter the age");
scanf("%d",&age);
printf("Age=%d\n Weight=%f\n",age,weight);
getch();
}
```

body of the function

2.5. Constants, Variables and Data types

Constants

A constant is an entity whose value remains the same throughout the execution of a program. It cannot be placed on the left side of the assignment operator because it does not have modifiable value. Constants are classified as:

1. Literal constants
2. Qualified constants
3. Symbolic constants

The detailed explanation of the constants is given below.

1. Literal Constants

Literal constant denotes a fixed value, which may be an integer, floating point, character or a string.

The types of literal constants are:

- Integer literal constant
- Floating literal constant
- Character literal constant
  (i). Printable character
  (ii). Non-Printable character

- *String literal constant*

Integer Literal Constant

The rules to write the integer values are:

1. It must have at least one digit.
2. It should not have any decimal point and no special characters and blank spaces are allowed.
3. It can be either positive or negative. If no sign, then it is assumed to be positive.
4. If the integer literal constant starts with

   O – it is octal number system

   Ox – Hexadecimal number system
5. The size of the constant can be modified using length modifier (l,L,u,U,f or F).

Floating literal constant

It can be written in a fractional form (or) in an exponential form. The rules for writing are

1. It must have at least one digit with a decimal point.
2. It can be positive or negative value. If no sign is mentioned then it is assumed to be positive.
3. Special characters and blank spaces are not allowed
4. Be default it is assumed to be of type *double*
5. The size of the floating literal constant can be modified using length modifier f or F
6. In an exponential form, it has two parts – the mantissa and the exponent part separated by e or E.

Character Literal Constant

The character literal can have at least one or at most two characters enclosed within a single quote ('). For example, 'a', '\n' .

The two types of character literals are as follows.

- Printable character literal constant: All characters except quotation, backslash and newline character when enclosed within a single quote form a printable character literal constant. Ex:'A','#'.
- Non-printable character literal constant: The non-printable characters are represented using the escape sequence. An escape sequence consists of a backward slash (i.e. \) followed by a character and both enclosed within a single quote.

The list of escape sequences available are:

Escape Sequence	Name	Description
\'	Single quotation mark	prints '
\"	Double quotation mark	prints "
\?	Question mark	prints ?
\\	Backslash character	prints \
\a	Alert	alerts by generating a beep
\b	Backspace	moves the cursor one position to left of its current location
\f	Form feed	moves the cursor to the beginning of next page
\n	Newline	moves the cursor to the beginning of the next line
\r	Carriage Return	moves the cursor to the beginning of the current line
\t	Horizontal tab	moves the cursor to the next horizontal tab stop
\v	Vertical tab	Vertical tab movement
\0	Null character	points nothing

Table 2.1: Escape Sequences

- String literal constant: It consists of a sequence of characters enclosed within double quotes and implicitly terminated by a null character. The null character occupies one byte in memory even though it is not counted while determining the length of the string.

  Example: The length of "John" is 4 bytes but in memory it occupies 5 bytes including the null character.

2. *Qualified Constants*

The qualified constants are represented using *const* qualifier. Qualified constants are non-modifiable values.

Example: const int a=10;

The keyword const represents the variable 'a' in read only mode i.e., the variable can only be read and not modified. If it is initialized as int a=10, then the value of 'a' can be modified.

3. *Symbolic Constants*

The symbolic constants are created using define pre-processor directive.

Example: #define PI 3.14

The symbol PI is assigned the value 3.14. The value 3.14 is placed wherever the symbol PI is used throughout the program.

Variables

A variable is an entity whose value can vary during the execution of a program. It should be given a unique name called identifier. Rules for writing a variable name:

1. Variable can be composed of letters (both upper and lowercase), digits and underscore (_) only.
2. The first letter can be a character or an underscore but preferably a character.

Example: sum, name, mark_eng.

Data Types

In C, the variables should be declared before it can be used in the program. Data types are keywords, which are used for assigning a type to a variable. They are classified as:

1. Basic data types (or) primitive data types
2. Derived data types
3. User defined data types

1. Basic Data Types

The basic data types used are

- Character (char)
- Integer (int)
- Single precision floating point (float)
- Double precision floating point (double)
- No value available (void)

The storage size and the value range for all the basic data types is given in the table 2.2 below. The precision for float is 6 decimal point, for double is 15 decimal point and that for long double is 19 decimal point.

Type	**Storage size**	**Value range**
char	1 byte	-128 to 127 or 0 to 255
unsigned char	1 byte	0 to 255
signed char	1 byte	-128 to 127
int	2 or 4 bytes	-32,768 to 32,767 or -2,147,483,648 to 2,147,483,647
unsigned int	2 or 4 bytes	0 to 65,535 or 0 to 4,294,967,295
short	2 bytes	-32,768 to 32,767
unsigned short	2 bytes	0 to 65,535
long	4 bytes	-2,147,483,648 to 2,147,483,647
unsigned long	4 bytes	0 to 4,294,967,295
float	4 byte	1.2E-38 to 3.4E+38
double	8 byte	2.3E-308 to 1.7E+308
long double	10 byte	3.4E-4932 to 1.1E+4932

Table 2.2: Data Types

2. *Derived Data Types*

The data types derived from the basic data types are called as derived data types. The various derived data types are

- Array type. Ex: char[], int[] etc.
- Pointer type. Ex: char*, int* etc.
- Function type. Ex: int(int,int), float(int) etc.

3. *User Defined Data Types*

The new data types defined by the user are called as user defined data types. They are

- Structure
- Union
- Enumeration

The derived and user defined data types are explained in detail in the fore coming units.

2.6. Enumeration Constraints

Enumeration is a user-defined data type with the keyword "enum". The only constraint of enum is that it fits in only with the integers i.e., it is a collection of integer values and it takes only one value out of the collection. The size of the enumeration will be the size of the integer as shown in the second example program. This makes enum the right choice for the use of flags.

Syntax:

```
enum identifier
{
Enumeration_list,
};
```

Example:

```
enum week { sunday, monday, tuesday, wednesday, thursday, friday, saturday };
```

In the above example, the default values are used where Sunday takes 0, Monday takes 1 and so on. The values can also be initialized as follows in the example below.

```
enum suit
{
  club = 0,
  diamonds = 10,
  hearts = 20,
  spades = 3,
};
```

Program:

```
#include <stdio.h>
enum week { sunday, monday, tuesday, wednesday, thursday, friday, saturday };
int main()
{
  enum week today;
  today = wednesday;
  printf("Day %d",today+1);
  return 0;
}
```

Sample output: Day 4

```
#include <stdio.h>
enum suit
{
  club = 0,
  diamonds = 10,
  hearts = 20,
  spades = 3
} card;
int main()
{
    card = club;
    printf("Size of enum variable = %d bytes", sizeof(card));
    return 0;
}
```

Sample output:

Size of enum variable = 4 bytes

2.7. Storage Class

Storage class determines the scope and lifetime of a variable. The storage class of a variable determines the following:

- the sections of code that can use the variable.
- how a variable can be used in a multiple source-file program.
- how long the variable persists in memory

Scope of Variable

1) File scope: variable visibility is from the definition to the end of file
2) Block scope: variable visibility is from the definition to the end of the block
3) Function prototype scope: The variable is visible till the end of the function prototype declaration (int funct1(int a, double b);)

Linkage of Variables

1) External linkage: The variable can be used anywhere in a multifile program.
2) Internal linkage: The variable can be used anywhere in a single file.
3) No linkage: The variable can be used only in the block in which it is defined.

Note: Variables with block scope or function prototype scope have no linkage.

Storage Duration of Variables

Static storage duration: The variable exists throughout the program execution.

Automatic storage duration: The variable can exist only while the program is executing the block in which the variable is defined:

Syntax:

storage_specifier datatype variable_name

Types of Variable

1. Local Variables are variables defined inside a function. They have function or block scope
2. Global Variable are variables defined outside the functions. They have file (or program) scope

Advantages of using global variables:

- simplest way of communication between functions
- efficiency

Disadvantages of using global variables:

- less readable program
- more difficult to debug and modify

Types of Storage Class

1. automatic
2. extern
3. static
4. register

2.7.1. *Automatic Storage Class*

1. An automatic variable has automatic storage
2. The life time of an automatic variable is only within the function or block it is defined in.
3. Consequently, it has no meaning outside the function or block. It is called the local variable of the corresponding function or block.
4. The automatic variables are deleted after execution of the corresponding function or block where they are defined.
5. It is because they are no longer needed and memory occupied by the variables can be reused.
6. Consequently, the value stored in an automatic variable is lost after exiting from a function or block.
7. An automatic variable has block scope
8. Only the function in which the variable is defined can access that variable by name.
9. An automatic variable has no linkage
10. The variable cannot be declared twice in the same block.
11. An automatic variable can be defined explicitly using the keyword auto

Example:

```
#include<stdio.h>
#include<conio.h>
void main()
{
auto int c=40;
clrscr();
printf("%d",c);
{
auto int c=78;
printf("%d", c);
}
printf("%d",c);
getch();
}
```

Output:

40

78

40

2.7.2. *Extern Storage Class*

1. A variable defined outside a function is external
2. An external variable can also be declared inside a function that uses it by using the extern keyword.
3. If the variable is defined in another file, or after the function definition, then declaring the variable with extern is mandatory
4. External variables have external linkage.
5. External variables have static storage duration.
6. For external variables, the compiler may not distinguish between upper- and lowercase, and it may recognize only the 1st 6 characters in a name

```
int n = 75 ;
void display();
void main()
{
extern int n ;
printf("value : %d",n);
display();
}
void display()
{
extern int n ;
printf("value : %d",n);
}
```

Output:

Value: 75

Value: 75

2.7.3. *Static Storage Class*

The duration of a static variable is fixed. Static variables are created at the start of the program and are destroyed only at the end of program execution.

If a static variable is present inside the local scope, the associated object is initialized only once. The object will not be reinitialized even if the program control re-enters the block in which the variable is declared. Thus the value of static variables persists between the function calls. Static variables can be defined inside or outside of a function.

```
#include <stdio.h>
void function();
void main()
{
int i;
for (i=0; i<3; i++)
function();
}
void function()
{
static int;
static_var=0; /* static variable */
int auto_var = 0; /* automatic variable */
++static_var;
++auto_var;
printf("The value of the static variable is: %d\n", static_var);
printf("The value of the auto variable is: %d\n", auto_var);
}
```

Program output

```
The value of the static variable is: 1
The value of the auto variable is: 1
The value of the static variable is: 2
The value of the auto variable is: 1
The value of the static variable is: 3
The value of the auto variable is: 1
```

2.7.4. *Register Storage Class*

1. An automatic variable can be defined using the keyword register
2. Inform the compiler that variables will be referenced on numerous occasions and, where possible, to use the CPU registers
3. Instructions using register variables executes faster than instructions that use no register variables.
4. There are limited number of registers available.
5. Applicable to automatic variables and function argument only
6. Restricted to certain data types (is machine dependent), often int, char and pointer
7. Not allowed to take address of register variables, i.e., & operator will not work with register variables.

```
#include<stdio.h>
#include<conio.h>
void main()
{
register int i=0;
clrscr();
for(i=0;i<=2;i++)
{
printf("value of i is:%d\n",i);
}
getch();
}
```

Output

```
value of i is: 0
value of i is: 1
value of i is: 2
```

Storage Classes for Different Variables

Variables	Keywords	Scope	Linkage	Storage Duration
Automatic	Auto	block	No	Automatic
External	Extern	File/program	External	Static
Static	static	File/block	Internal	Static
Register	register	block	No	Automatic
Local	None/auto/static/register	block	No	Automatic/static
Global	None/extern	File	Internal/external	Static

Table 2.3: Comparison of Storage Classes

2.8. Expression Using Operators in C

An *expression* is made up of one or more operands and operators. An *operand* specifies an entity on which an operation is to be performed. An *operator* specifies the operation to be applied to its operands.

Example: In the expression, a=a+2

a and 2 are the operands

+ and = are the operators

There are two kinds of expressions. They are:

- Simple expression: The expression has only one operator
- Complex expression: The expression has more than one operator

When there is more than one operator, the order in which the operators will operate depends on:

1. Precedence of operators
2. Associativity of operators

1. Precedence of Operators

Each operator in the expression has a precedence i.e., priority associated with it. In a compound expression, the operator with higher precedence operates first.

2. Associativity of Operators

When several operators of same precedence appear together, the operators are evaluated according to their associativity.

An operator can be left-to-right (or) right-to-left associative. The precedence and associativity associated with the operators are shown in the table 2.4 below.

OPERATOR	NAME	ASSOCIATIVITY	PRECEDENCE
()	Function call	Left to Right	highest 14
[]	Array subscript		
.	dot(member of structure)		
->	arrow(member of structure)		
!	Logical AND	Right to Left	13
~	One's Complement		
-	Unary minus		
++	Increment		
--	Decrement		
&	Addressof		
*	Indirect		
(type)	cast		
sizeof	sizeof		
*	Multiplication	Left to Right	12
/	Division		
%	Modulus(Reminder)		
+	Addition	Left to Right	11
-	Subtraction		
<<	Left Shift	Left to Right	10
>>	Right Shift		
<	Less than	Left to Right	9
<=	Less than or equal to		
>	Greater than		
>=	Greater than or equal to		
==	Equal to	Left to Right	8
!=	Not Equal to		
&	Bitwise AND	Left to Right	7
^	Bitwise XOR	Left to Right	6
|	Bitwise OR	Left to Right	5
&&	Logical AND	Left to Right	4
||	Logical OR	Left to Right	3
?:	Conditional Operator	Right to Left	2
=,+=,*=,etc	Assignment Operator	Right to Left	1
,	Comma	Left to Right	Lowest 0

Table 2.4: Operators

2.8.1. *Classification of Operators Based on Number of Operands*

There are three types of operators based on the number of operands used in the expression. They are:

1. Unary operator: Operates on only one operand. Ex: -3 and a++
2. Binary operator: Operates on two operands. Ex: 2*3 and a+b
3. Ternary operator: Operates on three operands. Ex: Conditional Operator - a>b?a-b:b-a

2.8.2. *Classification of Operators based on the Role of the Operator*

The types of operators based on their role are:

1. Arithmetic operators
2. Increment and Decrement operators
3. Assignment operators
4. Relational operators
5. Logical operators
6. Conditional operator
7. Bitwise operators
8. Miscellaneous operators

The various operators, purposes and examples are discussed below.

1. *Arithmetic Operators*

The basic arithmetic operators are given in the table below with the example. Assuming the value of a is 5 and that of b is 2. Then the answers are also given in the table 2.5.

Operator	Description	Example	Answer
+	Addition (or) unary plus	a+b	7
-	Subtraction (or) unary minus	a-b	3
*	Multiplication	a*b	10
/	Division	a/b	2
%	Modulus	a%b	1

Table 2.5: Arithmetic Operators

2. *Increment and Decrement Operators*

There are two kinds of increment and decrement based on when the operation is done. They are pre and post operations. The operator for increment is ++ and decrement is --. Assuming the value of a as 5. The example value of a used for evaluation is shown in the table 2.6 below.

Operator	Name	Description	Example
++a	pre-increment	first the value of the operand is incremented and then used for evaluation	the value of a used for evaluation is 6
a++	post increment	first the value of the operand is used for evaluation and then it is incremented by 1	the value of a used for evaluation is 5
--a	pre decrement	the value of the operand is first decremented by 1 and then used for evaluation	the value of a used for evaluation is 4
a--	post decrement	after the evaluation is done, the value of the operand is decremented by 1	the value of a used for evaluation is 5

Table 2.6: Increment and Decrement Operators

3. *Assignment Operators*

The basic assignment(=) operator is used for initialization of values. Before taking about assignment operator it is necessary to know the concept of L-VALUES and R-VALUES.

L-VALUES are used at the left side of the assignment expression but can also be placed at the right side but R-VALUES are used only at the right side of the expression. Consider the example, x=1 where '1' is the R-value and 'x' is the L-value. The R-value is put up at the memory referred by L-value. Now, the L-value can also be put at the right side as y=x. The assignment operators are given with the example in the table below. Assume the value of a=5 and b=2, then the value of a after applying assignment operator is shown in the table 2.7 below.

Operator	Example	same as	Description	Answer
=	a=b	a=b	assigns the value of b to a	2
+=	a+=b	a=a+b	assigns the sum of a&b to a	7
-=	a-=b	a=a-b	assigns the difference of a&b to a	3
*=	a*=b	a=a*b	assigns the product of a&b to a	10
/=	a/=b	a=a/b	assigns the quotient to a	2
%=	a%=b	a=a%b	assigns the reminder to a	1

Table 2.7: Assignment Operators

4. *Relational Operators*

The relational operator checks the relationship between two operands.

If the relation is true, it returns the value 1 and if the relation is false, it returns the value 0 (zero). Only these two outputs are possible when relational operator is used. The relational operators with example is shown in the table 2.8 below.

Operator	Description	Example
==	equal to (checks the equality condition)	a==b
>	greater than	a>b
<	less than	a<b
>=	greater than or equal to	a>=b
<=	less than or equal to	a<=b
!=	not equal to	a!=b

Table 2.8: Relational Operators

5. *Logical Operators*

Logical operators are used to logically relate the sub-expressions. The operators are shown in the table below. For a logical AND to be true, both the sub-expressions should hold true. For a logical OR to be true, any one (or) both of the sub-expression need to be true.

Operator	Description	Example
&&	Logical AND	(a==5)&&(b==4)
||	Logical OR	(a==0)||(b==0)
!	Logical NOT	x!=0

Table 2.9: Logical Operators

The truth table for AND, OR and NOT is shown below in order.

Operand 1	Operand 2	Result
F	F	F
F	T	F
T	F	F
T	T	T

Operand 1	Operand 2	Result
F	F	F
F	T	T
T	F	T
T	T	T

Operand	Result
T	F
F	T

6. *Conditional Operator*

Conditional operator is also called as ternary operator that takes three operands with two symbols ? (question mark) and : (semicolon). This operator can be used for decision making.

Example: (a>10)?(a-1):(a+1);

In the example above, the value of a is checked first. If it is greater than 10, then the first expression i.e., decrement the value of a by 1 is evaluated else i.e., the value of a is less than 10, then the value of a is incremented by 1 i.e., the second expression is evaluated.

7. *Bitwise Operators*

Bitwise operator operates on individual bits of the operand. The operators are shown in the table 2.10 below.

Operator	Description
&	Bitwise AND
|	Bitwise OR
^	Bitwise XOR
~	Bitwise Complement
<<	Shift left
>>	Shift right

Table 2.10: Bitwise Operators

The bit values for AND, OR and XOR operation is shown in the table below.

Bit 1	Bit 2	AND	OR	XOR
0	0	0	0	0
0	1	0	1	1
1	0	0	1	1
1	1	1	1	0

Example: a&b where a is 4 and b is 2.

Binary value of 3 is 0011 and 2 is 0010

Now, the answer is 0010.

8. *Miscellaneous Operators*

The other operators used apart from the operators described above are called as miscellaneous operators. The operators are tabulated below.

Operator	Description
()	Function call
[]	Array Subscript
.	dot(Direct member select)
->	Arrow(Indirect member select)
*	Indirection operator
,	Comma
sizeof	Sizeof
&	Address of

Table 2.11: Miscellaneous Operators

The first five operators will be discussed in detail in the fore coming units.

Comma is used to join multiple expressions together. sizeof operator is used to determine the size in bytes, which a value or a data object will take in memory.

General form:

sizeof(expression);

The address-of operator is used to find the address of an object.

General form: &operand.

2.9. Managing Input and Output Operations

One of the most important operations performed in a C language programs is to provide the input values to the program and output the data produced by the program to a standard output device. There are two ways of providing input to the program. They are:

1. Assigns the values using assignment operator. Ex:x=5.
2. To read the data from the user using scanf statement.

The function used to carry out input and output operations are available in the standard input/output library i.e., #include<stdio.h>

The various forms of providing input and receiving output are explained below.

Single Character Input/Output:

- getchar() is used to read a single character input. scanf() function can also be used.
- putchar() is used to write the single character.

Syntax:

Variable_name=getchar();

Putchar(variable_name);

Example:

a=getchar();

Putchar(a);

String Input and Output:

- A string is an array (or) set of characters.
- gets() is used to read a string and puts() is used to write a string.

Syntax:

gets(variable_name);

puts(variable_name);

Example:

gets(str);

puts(str);

Formatted Input for scanf():

The formatted input refers to input data that has been arranged in a particular format. Input values are taken by scanf() function.

Syntax:

scanf("control_strings",&arg1,&agr2,...,&argn);

The format field is specified by the control strings and the arguments arg1,arg2,...,argn specifies the address of location where data is stored. The various control strings (or) format specifiers are given below.

Datatype	Control String	Description
char	%c	single character
int	%d	signed integer in decimal number
int	%i	signed integer
unsigned int	%o	unsigned integer in octal number
	%u	unsigned integer in decimal number
	%x (or) %X	unsigned integer in hexadecimal number
long int	%ld	signed long
short int	%hd	signed short
unsigned long	%lu	unsigned long
unsigned short	%hu	unsigned short
float	%f	signed single precision float
	%e	signed single precision float in exponent
	%E	same as %e (E used instead of e)
	%g	signed value in either e (or) f
	%G	same as %g (E used instead of e)
double	%lf	signed double precision float
string	%s	array of characters
pointer	%p	address of the variable

Table 2.12: Control Strings

Example: scanf("%d",&age);

The above example reads the age of a person from the user which is of integer datatype.

The corresponding control string is used based on the type of the input to read. The field width can also be specified along with the format specifier i.e., %xd, %xs where x is an integer.

Example: %3s is used to read the first 3 characters of the string.

While reading a string using scanf(), it is not mandatory to use &(addressof) operator as it is a continuous set of characters. scanf() can also be used to read a selected set of characters using *search set*. A *search set* is the possible characters that can make up a string. The character in the search sets are written in [].

Example:

- [abcd] – This implies to read only a,b,c,d characters from the string. '
- [^abcd] – This is used to read all strings except the characters a,b,c,d. (^ caret symbol is used).
- [a-f] – This implies to read the characters between a range i.e., from a to f.

  Basically there are two types of input functions namely

  - Buffered input: Buffered input receives the data and internally buffers into the event buffer and read the data from the buffer at the time of processing.

    Example: scanf(), getchar(), gets()
  - Unbuffered input: The data here are not buffered, the events are just polled.

    Example: getch(), getche()

Printing Output on Screen

There are two ways to print the output to the screen using printf() function. They are

1. *without using format specifier*

   The content is given in double quotes.

   Example: printf("Hello");

2. *with format specifier*

   The specific format specifier is used based on the data type.

   Example: printf("The sum of two numbers is %d",sum);

   The output for the example is: The sum of two numbers is 5 (i.e., the value of sum is 5)

Example program:

```
#include<stdio.h>
void main()
{
    char ch, str[20];
    int age;
    printf("Enter your name");
```

```
        gets(str);
        printf("\nEnter your initial");
        ch=getchar();
        printf("\nEnter your age");
        scanf("%d",&age);
        printf(" \nYour Details.........\n");
        printf("Name=");
        putchar(ch);
        printf(".");
        puts(str);
        printf("\nAge=%d",age);
}
```

Output:

Enter your name Abi

Enter your initial S

Enter your age 25

Your Details............

Name=S.Abi

Age=25

2.10. Assignment Statements

The values in the left side of the operator is taken by or assigned to the variables in the right side. The assignment operator is "equal to"(=) symbol. In C language, "double equal-to"(==) is used for equality relations in order to avoid confusion between assignment and relational operation. Example of a Simple Assignment statement is a=5, where the value 5 is assigned to the variable a. The assignment operator can be used along with other operators too. For example:

- flag ? count 1 : count2 = 0; which says **if** (flag)
  count1 = 0;
  else
  count2 = 0;

- while ((ch = getchar())!=EOF)
  {...}

The assignment statement must be parenthesized because the precedence of the assignment operator is lower than that of the relational operators.

2.11. Decision Making and Branching Statements

Branching statements are used to transfer the program control from one point to another. They are classified as

1. *Conditional Branching (or) Selection Statements*

The program control is transferred from one point to another point based upon the outcome of a certain condition.

Example: if, if-else, nested-if, switch.

2. *Unconditional Branching (or) Jump Statements*

The program control is transferred from one point to another point without checking any condition.

Example: goto, break, continue and return.

If Statement

The simplest form of branching statement is if statement. It takes a condition in the parenthesis and a block of statement inside the curly braces. When the condition is true, the block of statement will be executed. If the condition is false the block of statement will be skipped. It is not mandatory to used curly braces when there is only one statement.

Syntax: if(expression)

```
{
 Statements;
}
```

Flowchart:

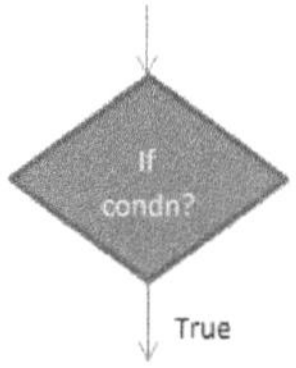

Example: if(a>0)

```
{
c=a-b;
}
```

If the value of a is greater than 0 then the statement inside the curly bracket will be executed. If a value is 0 or less then the statement will be skipped.

If-else Statement

There are two parts–if and else. When the condition is true, if part will be executed and when the condition is false, the else part will be executed.

```
Syntax: if(expression)
        {
                statements;
        }
        else
        {
                statements;
        }
Example: if(a>b)
        c=a-b;
        else
        c=b-a;
```

Flowchart:

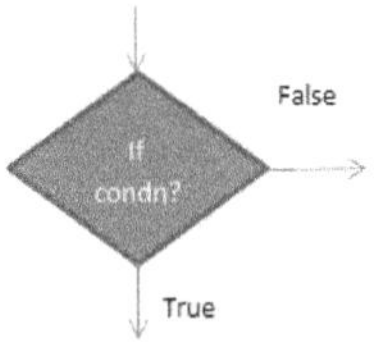

Nested if Statement

If the body of the if statement contains another if statement then it is called as nested- if statement.

```
Syntax:if(expression)
        {
         If(expression)
         {
                Statements;
         }
        Statements;
}
```

Example:

```
if (a>b)
{
        if(a>c)
        {
        printf("%d",a)
        }
printf("%d",b+c);
}
```

Nested if-else Statement

If the body of the if part or else part contains another if-else statement then it is called as nested if-else statement.

Syntax:

```
if(expression)
{
 if(expression)
        statement1;
 else
        statement2;
}
else
{
 if(expression)
        statement1;
 else
        statement2;
}
```

Example:

```
if(a>b)
 {
 if(a>c)
 printf("a is greatest");
 else
 printf("c is greatest");
 }
```

```
else
 {
 printf("b is greatest");
 }
```

Flowchart:

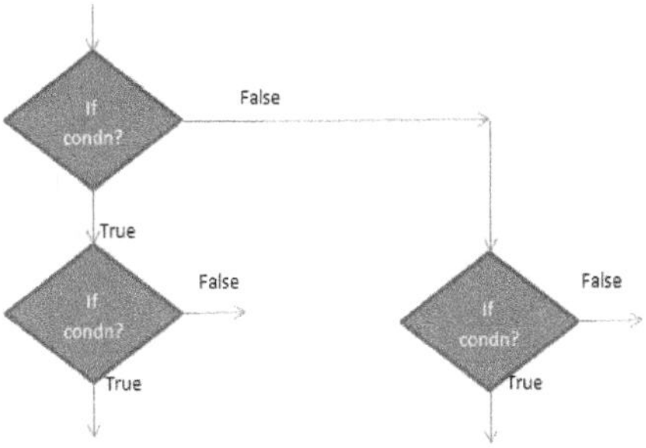

Else-if Ladder

When there are different test conditions with different statements, then we can go for else-if ladder.

```
Syntax:if(condition 1)
    {
            statement1;
    }
    else if(condition 2)
    {
            Statement2;
    }
    else if(condition 3)
    {
            Statement3;
    }
    else
    {
            statement4;
    }
```

```
Example: if (year%400==0)
         {
                 printf("It is a leap year");
         }
         else if(year%100==0)
         {
                 printf("It is not a leap year");
         }
         else if(year%4==0)
         {
                 printf("It is a leap year");
         }
         else
         {
                 printf("It is not a leap year");
         }
```

Switch Statement

Switch is used to control complex branching statements. When there are many conditions or options, it is difficult to use else-if ladder. So switch statement is used.

```
Syntax: switch(choice)
     {
             case 1:
                     statement1;break;
             case 2:
                     statement2;break;
                     .
                     .
                     .
             case n:
                     statementn;break;
             default:
                     statement;
     }
```

Example:

```
switch(ch)
{
        case 1:
                c=a+b;
                printf("Sum=%d",c);
        case 2:
                c=a-b;
                printf("Difference=%d",c);
        case 3:
                c=a*b;
                printf("Product=%d",c);
        case 4:
                c=a/b;
                printf("Quotient=%d",c);
        default:
                printf("Enter a valid choice");
}
```

Goto Statement

Goto statement can jump from one point to another by pointing to a label name without checking any condition. There are two types of jump: Forward jump and Backward jump.

Syntax: goto label;

Forward jump
goto label;
....
label:
statement;
Backward jump
label:
statement;
...
goto label;

Example:

```
goto add;
printf("Addition process is going to happen");
add:
printf("Sum=%d",a+b);
```

Break Statement

Break statement is used to terminate the nearest case (or) a loop. It occurs only inside the body of the switch statement (or) a loop and conditions inside the loop.

Syntax: break;

Example:

```
for(i=1;i<=10;i++)
{
 if(num<=0)
        break;
sum+=num;
}
```

Continue Statement

Continue statement is used to terminate the current iteration of the loop and moves the execution to the header (or) starting of the loop. It is only present inside the body of the loop and conditions inside the body of the loop.

Syntax: continue;

Example:

```
for(i=0;i<10;i++)
{
 if(i%2==0)
        continue;
printf("i=%d",i);
}
```

Return Statement

Return statement is used to terminate the function and return the control to the calling function.

Syntax: return;

(or)

return expression;

The first form is used when the function type is void i.e., no data is returned from the function. The second form is used when the function returns some specific type of data.

Example:
```
int add(int a, int b)
{
int c;
c=a+b;
return c;
}
```

2.12. Looping Statements

Looping (or) Iteration is a process of repeating the same set of statements again and again until the specified condition holds true. Loops are classified in two types as follows.

1. Counter Controlled Loops

The number of iterations is known in advance. A control variable, known as *loop counter* is used to keep track of the loop iterations. Since the number of iteration is fixed. It is also called as *Definite Repetition Loop.*

Example: for loop.

2. Sentinel Controlled Loops

The number of iterations to be performed is not known in advance. So it is called as *Indefinite Repetition Loop.* The execution (or) termination of the loop depends upon a special value called the *Sentinel Value.*

Example: while and do-while loop.

There are three iteration (or) looping statements. They are:

1. For statement
2. While statement
3. Do-while statement

The different looping statements are explained with example below.

1. *For loop*

The for loop contains three sections inside the parenthesis. They are-Initialization, Condition and Loop Counter(Increment/Decrement). The sections are separated using a semicolon(;).

Syntax

```
for(initialization;evaluation/condition;counter/increment(or)decrement)
{
Statements;
}
```

Example:

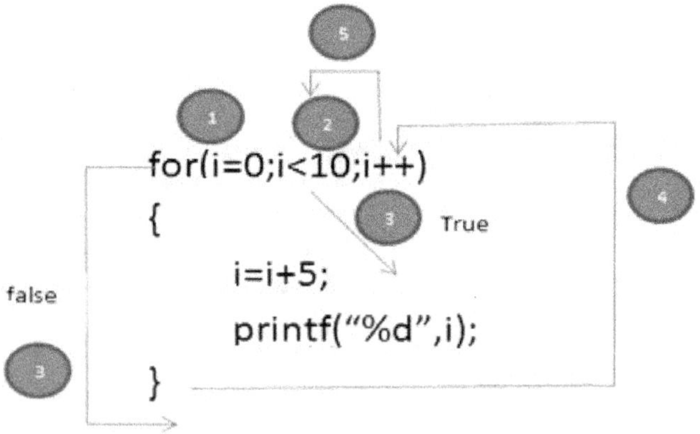

The working process is

1. Initializes the value of i. (i is 0 in the above example).
2. The condition part is checked. (in the ex. i should be less than 10 to execute the body of the loop).
3. If the condition is true, the body of the loop is executed. If the condition is false, the loop is terminated and the control comes out of the loop.
4. The counter is incremented to start the next iteration.
5. Again the condition is checked to decide whether the body of the loop to be executed or not. The process continues until the condition fails.

2. *While Loop*

Syntax: while(condition)

{

Statement;

Increment/decrement;

}

Flowchart:

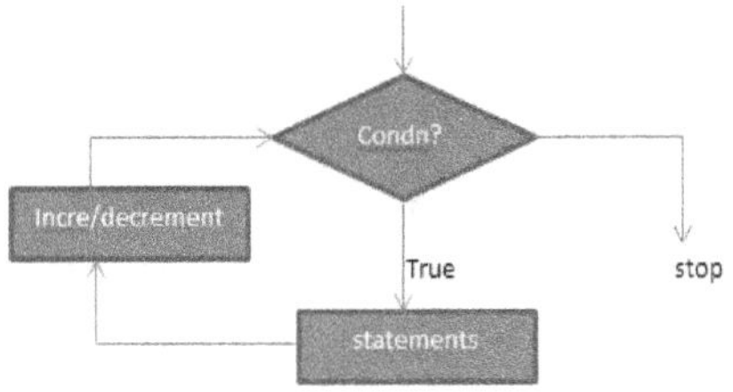

The working process is

1. When the condition is true, the body of the loop is executed and the loop variable is incremented.
2. The control flows back to the header of the loop for next iteration. This continues until the condition is true.

Example: while(num>0)

{

sum=sum+num;

num=num%10;

}

3. *Do-while Loop*

Syntax:

do

{

statements;

incre/decrement;

}while(condition);

Flowchart:

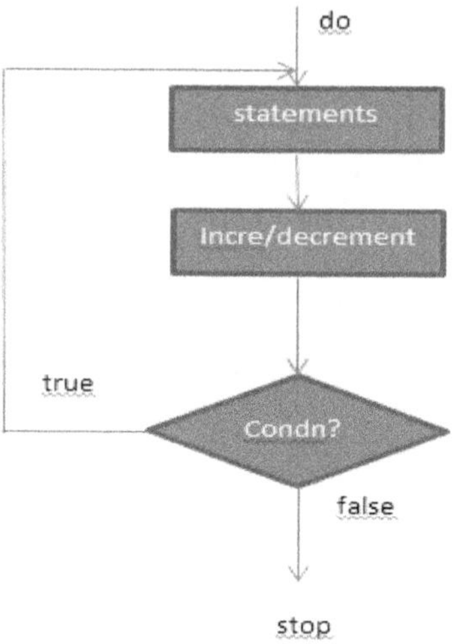

The working process is

1. The body of the loop is executed before checking the condition.
2. If the condition is true, the control moves to the start of the loop else the loop terminates.

Example: do

```
{
sum=sum+num;
num=num%10;
} while(num>0);
```

The difference between while and do-while statement is as follows.

WHILE	**DO-WHILE**
This is also called as *top tested loop*	This is also called as *bottom tested loop*
The condition is first tested, if it is true then the block is executed until the condition becomes false.	It executes the body once, after it checks the condition, if it is true, the body is executed until the condition becomes false.
Loop will not be executed if the condition is false.	Loop is executed at least once even if the condition is false.

Table 2.13: Difference between while and do-while

2.13. Pre-processor Directives

The preprocessor is a program that executes before the source program is compiled. The preprocessor is controlled by directives known as preprocessor directives. Any preprocessor directive starts with **#.** It can only have whitespace before it. Rule to write a preprocessor directive:

1. It should begin with # symbol
2. It is always placed before the main()
3. It cannot be terminated with semicolon
4. There is no assignment operator in #define statement
5. The conditional macro must be terminated ie., #ifdef should have #endif

Preprocessor Directives

#define : Defines a macro substitution

#undef : Undefines a macro

#include : Specifies a file to be included

#ifdef : Test for macro definition

#endif : Specifies the end of #if

#ifndef : Test whether macro is not defined

#if : Test a compile-time condition

#else : Specifies alternatives when #if test fails

The various preprocessor directives available in 'c' are as follows

1. File Inclusion
2. Macro Substitution
3. Conditional Inclusion

2.13.1. File Inclusion Directives

- It includes one or more files in the program
- A copy of the specified file to be included in place of the directive

Syntax:

1. #include <filename> : It includes standard library header files and searches in the special directories
2. #include "filename" : It searches in the current directory and used for programmer-defined files

Example:

1) #include<stdio.h>
2) #include<conio.h>
3) #include<string.h>
4) #include "pari.c"

2.13.2. Macro Substitution Directives

It uses #define directive and also defines symbolic constant

Macro or the identifier defined in the program is replaced by the macro substitution.

Syntax:

```
#define  macro value
```

Types of Macros

1. Simple macros : It allows simple functions, expressions, more symbols and operators
2. Argumented macros: It allows complex functions and expressions
3. Nested macros: one macro can be placed inside another macro

```
#define Null 0
#define sum(a,b)  (a+b)
#define n 3
#define cube(n)   n*n*n
```

Example program

```
#include<stdio.h>
#include<conio.h>
#define n 3
#define cube(n)   n*n*n
#define sum(a,b)  (a+b)
void main()
{
int a=5, b=6;
printf("%d", sum(a,b));
printf("%d", cube(n));
getch();
}
```

Output

11

27

2.13.3. Conditional Inclusion

It is also called conditional compilation. By using various conditional statements, special preprocessors allow certain portion of the source code to be complied.

The following are the conditional directives

```
#if
#else
#elif
#endif
#ifdef
#ifndef
```

Syntax:

```
#if constant expression1
______________
______________
Sequence of statements
#elif constant expression2
______________
______________
Sequence of statements
#else
______________
______________
Sequence of statements
#endif
```

Example program

```
#include<stdio.h>
#include<conio.h>
#define a 8
#define b 1
void main()
{
#if(a==7)
printf("Good morning");
#elif(b==9)
```

```
printf("Good afternoon");
#else
printf("Good evening");
#endif
getch();
}
```

Output:

```
Good evening
```

#ifdef : It is true for defined macros

#ifndef: It is true for undefined macros

Syntax:

```
#ifdef macroname
_______________
//Sequence of statements
#endif
#ifndef macroname
_______________
//Sequence of statements
#endif
```

Example program

```
#include<stdio.h>
#include<conio.h>
#define gane "welcome"
void main()
{
#ifdef gane
printf("#ifdef is true");
#endif
#ifndef vina
printf("#ifndef is true");
#endif
getch();
```

}

Output:

#ifdef is true

#ifndef is true

2.14. Compilation and Linking Process

The source code written is saved with the .c extension before compiling it.

Compilation

The compiler does the compilation process. The compiler takes the file containing the source code and translates the code to the machine code. The compiler then places that machine code into an output file called an object file and has the file extension .obj. The process of translating the source code into an object file is called C*ompiling*.

Linking

After the compiler has created all the object files, another program is called to bundle them into an executable program file. That program is called *Linker* and the process of bundling them into the executable file is called *Linking.*

The linker assembles two lists after looking at all the object files.

- The list of publics: items found in the object file.
- The list of unresolved externals: items not in the object file but required for processing.

The linker finds the publics and places their addresses into unresolved externals until the needs are satisfied. Now, the binary file is created containing the whole program.

This binary file is the executable file with the extension .exe. the compilation and linking process is given in the figure 2.3 below.

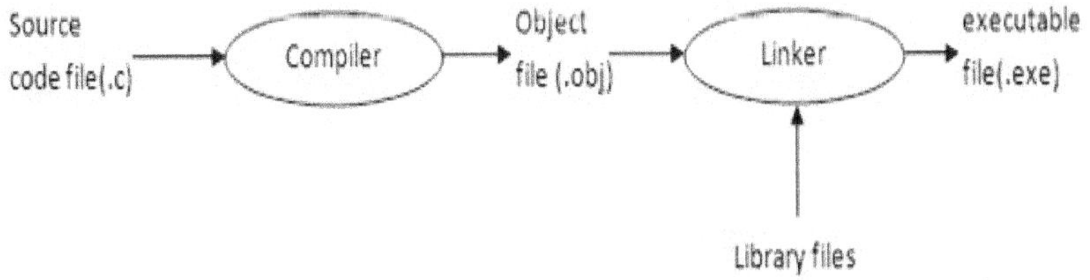

Figure 2.3: Compiling and Linking Process

2.15. Basic Example Programs

1. **To find whether the given number is even or odd.**

```
#include<stdio.h>
void main()
{
        int no;
        printf("Enter the number..\n");
        scanf("%d",&no);
    if(no% 2 ==0)
                printf("It is an even number");
    else
                printf("It is an odd number");
}
```

Output

Enter the number.

20

It is an even number

2. **To find greatest of three numbers.**

```
#include<stdio.h>
void main()
{
    int a, b, c;
    printf("\n Enter the three numbers \n");
    scanf("%d%d%d",&a,&b,&c);
    if(a > b)
    if (a>c)
                print("a=%d is greatest", a);
    else
                print("c=%d is greatest", c);
    else if(b>c)
                print("b=%d is greatest", b);
    else
                print("c=%d is greatest", c);
}
```

Output

```
Enter the three numbers 12 21 39
39 is greatest
```

3. **To perform arithmetic operations using switch case**

```
#include<stdio.h>
void main( )
{
    int n;
    printf("Enter two numbers");
    scanf("%d%d",&a,&b);
    printf("1.Addition\n2.Subtraction\n3.Multiplication\n4.Division\n5.Modulus\n");
    printf("Enter your choice :");
    scanf("%d",&n);
    switch(n)
    {
        case 1: printf("Sum=%d",a+b); break;
        case 2: printf("Difference=%d",a-b");break;
        case 3: printf("Product==%d",a*b");break;
        case 4: printf("Quotient=%d",a/b");break;
        case 5: printf("Reminder=%d",a%b");break;
        default: printf("please enter the right choice");
    }
}
```

Output

```
Enter two numbers 3 2
1.Addition
2.Subtraction
3.Multiplication
4.Division
5.Modulus
Enter your choice 2
Difference=1
```

4. **Armstrong number**

```
#include<stdio.h>
void main()
{
long int i, c=0, a, no;
printf("\nEnter a Number\n");
scanf("%d", &a);
e = a;
while(a>0)
{
    b = a % 10;
    c = c + b *b *b;
    a = a / 10;
}
if(e==c)
    printf("\nThe Given Number is an Armstrong Number");
else
    printf("\nThe Given Number is NOT an Armstrong Number");
}
```

Output: Enter a Number: 153

The Given Number is an Armstrong Number

5. **Area and Circumference of the circle**

```
#include<stdio.h>
void main()
{
    float r, area, circum;
    printf("Enter the value of the radius of the circle");
    scanf("%f",&r);
    area=3.14*r*r;
    circum=2*3.14*r
    printf("The area of circle is %f \n, area);
    printf("The circumference of the circle %f ", circum);
}
```

Output:

Enter the value of the radius of the circle 4

The area of circle is 50.240002

The circumference of the circle 25.120001

6. Program to accept a single digit and print it in words

```
#include<stdio.h>
void main()
{
    int n;
    printf("Enter a number :");
    scanf("%d",&n);
    switch(n)
    {
    case 0: printf("ZERO"); break;
    case 1: printf("ONE");break;
    case 2: printf("TWO");break;
    case 3: printf("THREE");break;
    case 4: printf("FOUR");break;
    case 5: printf("FIVE");break;
    case 6: printf("SIX");break;
    case7: printf("SEVEN");break;
    case 8: printf("EIGHT");break;
    case 9: printf("NINE");break;
    default: printf("please enter the number between 0 and 9");
    }
}
```

Output:

Enter a number : 5

FIVE

7. **Factorial of a number**

```
#include<stdio.h>
void main()
{
    int n,f=1, i=1;
    printf("Enter the no for which u want factorial of");
    scanf("%d",&n);
    while(i<=n)
    {
        f*=i;
        i++;
    }
    printf(" factorial of %d = %d ",n,f);
}
```

Output :

Enter the no for which u want factorial of 4

factorial of 4 = 24

8. **Fibonacci series**

```
#include<stdio.h>
void main()
{
    int n, first = 0, second = 1, next, c;
    printf("Enter the number of terms\n");
    scanf("%d",&n);
    printf("First %d terms of Fibonacci series are :-\n",n);
    for ( c = 0 ; c < n ; c++ )
    {
        if ( c <= 1 )
                next = c;
        else
     {
             next = first + second; first = second;
             second = next;
     }
```

```
        printf("%d\n",next);
    }
    getch();
    }
```

Output:

Enter the no of terms 10

First 10 terms of Fibonacci series are:-0 1 1 2 3 5 8 13 21 34 55

9. Leap year or not

```
#include<stdio.h>

void main()

{

    int year;

    printf("Enter the year..\n);

    scanf("%d",&year);

    if ((year % 4 ==0)&&(year%100 != 0))

      printf("it is a leap year");

     else

     {

      if (year%400==0)

                printf("it is a leap year");

      else

                printf("it is not a leap year");

     }

}
```

Output

Enter the year.

2014

It is not a leap year

10. Program to Swap two numbers with and without third variable

```
#include<stdio.h>
void main()
{
    int a,b,c;
    printf("Enter two numbers\n");
    scanf("%d%d",&a,&b);
    printf("Swapping With third variable\n");
    c=a;
    a=b;
    b=c;
    printf("a=%d\tb=%d",a,b);
    printf("Swapping Without third variable\n");
    a=a+b;
    b=a-b;
    a=a-b;
    printf("a=%d\tb=%d",a,b);
}
```

Output

```
Enter two numbers
3 2
Swapping With third variable
a=2   b=3
Swapping Without third variable
a=2   b=3
```

11. Program to find roots of quadratic equation

```
#include<stdio.h>
#include<math.h>
void main()
{
    float a, b, c, d, x1, x2;
    printf("Enter the coefficients\n");
    scanf("%f%f%f",&a,&b,&c);
    d=(b*b)-(4*a*c);
```

```
    if(d>=0)
    {
      x1=(-b-sqrt(d))/(2*a);
      x2=(-b+sqrt(d))/(2*a);
      printf("the sol is %f and %f",x1,x2);
    }
    else
    {
     x1=-b/(2*a);
     x2=sqrt(-d)/(2*a);
     printf("The solution is %f + i%f and %f  -%f",x1,x2,x1,x2);
    }
}
```

Output

```
Enter the coefficients
1 1 1
The solution is -0.50000 + i0.866025 and -0.500000 – i0.866025
```

12. Temperature conversion–centigrade to Fahrenheit

```
#include<stdio.h>
void main()
{
float C,T;
printf("Enter the value of the temperature in Celsius scale");
scanf("%f",&C);
F=9*C/5+32;
printf("The value of temperature in Fahrenheit scale is %f ",F);
}
```

Output:

```
Enter the value of the temperature in Celsius scale 45
The value of temperature in Fahrenheit scale is 113.000000
```

13. Prime number or not

```
#include <stdio.h>
void main()
{
    int n, i, flag=0;
    printf("Enter a positive integer: ");
    scanf("%d",&n);
    for(i=2;i<=n/2;++i)
    {
            if(n%i==0)
            {       flag=1;
                    break;
            }
    }
    if (flag==0)
        printf("%d is a prime number.",n);
    else
        printf("%d is not a prime number.",n);
}
```

Output:

Enter a positive integer: 26

26 is not a prime number

14. Biggest of three numbers using ternary operator

```
# include <stdio.h>
void main()
{
    int a, b, c, big ;
    printf("Enter three numbers : ");
    scanf("%d %d %d", &a, &b, &c);
    big = a > b ? (a >c ? a : c) : (b > c ? b : c);
    printf("\nThe biggest number is : %d", big) ;
}
```

Output: Enter three numbers: 5 8 9

The biggest number is : 9

15. Program to find largest digit in a number and sum of digits of a number

```
#include<stdio.h>
void main()
{
    int n, max=0, rem, sum=0;
    printf("\n enter a number");
    scanf("%d",&n);
    while(n!=0)
    {
        rem=n%10;
        n=n/10;
        sum=sum+rem;
    if(rem>max)
        {
        max=rem:
        }
    }
printf("\n the largest digit is: %d",max);
printf("\n the sum of the digit is: %d",sum);
}
```

Output:

```
enter a number 532
the largest digit is: 5
the sum of the digits is: 10
```

Exercise

1. **What is the output of the program**

```
#include<stdio.h>
int main()
{
enum result {pass, fail, withheld};
enum result student1, student2, student3;
student1=pass;
student2=fail;
student3=withheld;
```

```
printf("%d\t,%d\t,%d\n",student1,student2,student3);
return 0;
}
```

2. **Which of the following statements is true?**
   a. Range of float id -2.25e+38 to 2.25e+38
   b. A float is 4 bytes wide, whereas a double is 10 bytes wide
   c. Size of short integer and long integer can be verified using the sizeof() operator.
   d. Range of double is -1.7e-38 to 1.7e+38
3. **Trace the error in the program**

```
#include<stdio.h>
int main()
{
    display();
    return 0;
}
void display()
{
     printf("Hello");
}
```

4. **How many times hello will be printed?**

```
#include<stdio.h>
void main()
{
int x;
for(x=-1;x<=10;x++)
{
if(x<5)
continue;
else
break;
printf("Hello");
}
return 0;
}
```

5. **What is the output of the program?**

```
#include<stdio.h>
int main()
{
int i=0;
for(;i<=5;i++);
    printf(%d",i);
return 0;
}
```

UNIT III

ARRAYS AND STRINGS

3.1. Introduction to Arrays

An Array is a collection of similar data items of the same type accessed under a common name.

Data items are stored in continuous memory allocations.

Example: Name list(collection of names of the type string), Mark list(collection of marks of the type integer)

The variable that is discussed so far can hold a single value but when we want to store 3 integers(not only integers all data types) numbers we need 3 variables, for 5 integers 5 variables, 10 integers 10 variables, 1000 integers 1000 variables. Therefore it is difficult to introduce and manage those number of variables in the programming language.

For example consider the following situation:

```
#include <stdio.h>
void main()
{
int var1=10;
int var2=11;
int var3=12;
int var4=13;
int var5=14;
...
...
...
...
...
}
```

In the above example it is difficult to introduce n variables in the program. Here the solution is to use arrays, within an array n data items can be placed. An array is a data structure to store fixed-size collection of data or elements of the similar type.

Therefore the above example can be written as

```
#include <stdio.h>
void main()
{
int a[1000];
}
```

- int is the data type
- a specifies the array name which holds 1000 data items
- [ ] specifies the size of the array and size must be a constant value

3.2. Types of Array

There are two types of array–One Dimensional Array and Multi-Dimensional Array. Multi Dimensional includes Two Dimensional and Three Dimensional Array. The types are explained in detail below.

3.2.1. One Dimensional Array

One Dimensional array is represented using a single subscript and stored in continuous memory allocation.

3.2.1.1. Array Declaration

Like declarations for variables of other types, an array declaration has the array's type, array's name and brackets with or without size. The declaration does not actually create an array, it simply tells the compiler that this variable will hold an array of the specified type. Therefore an array should be declared first and then defined.

where array's *type* is the data type of the contained elements

array's name can be any valid user defined name.

brackets are special symbols indicating that this variable holds an array.

Syntax

<data-type><array-name> [size]

Example:

float price[5]

float→ data type

price→ array name

[5]→ maximum number of elements in the array

An index variable or subscript is required to access any element stored in array.

Subscript starts with 0 and ends with arraysize-1.

price[0]	price[1]	price[2]	price[3]	price[4]
430.50	560.70	360.05		

Here the index variable starts at 0th position and ends at 4th position of the array(5-1=4). price[0] has the first element and price[2] has the last element. Total Number of elements in the current price array is 3, maximum 5 elements can be stored into it

3.2.1.2. Array Initialization

After an array is declared, it's elements must be initialized.

Array Initialization can be done in the following ways.

1. Compile time: values are known in advance ie., before compilation
2. Run time: values are known during runtime ie., during execution of the program

1. Compile Time

Initial values should be known in advance and arrays can be initialized at the time of declaration

data-type array-name[size]={list of values};

Using an assignment expression, it is not possible to assign to all elements of an array at once, therefore some or all elements of an array can be initialized when the array is defined. Example :

int a[10] = {10,1 1, 12,13, 14, 15, 16, 17, 18,19};

Full Array Initialization

int a[5] = {12, 16, 8, 4, 2};

a[0]	a[1]	a[2]	a[3]	a[4]
12	16	8	4	2

Partial Array Initialization

Here the array is initialized with partial elements or a few elements, so the remaining elements are automatically initialized to 0.

For example,

a) int a[5] = {12, 16};

a[0]	a[1]	a[2]	a[3]	a[4]
12	16	0	0	0

b) int a[2]=8;

a[0]	a[1]	a[2]	a[3]	a[4]
12	16	8	0	0

Initialization Without Size

If the size is not mentioned inside the array dimension, then the compiler considers the number of initialized elements into account.

float b[ ] = {10.2, 2.2, 6.4, 3.0, 9.0,8.8};

Here the size is omitted

b[0]	b[1]	b[2]	b[3]	b[4]	b[5]
10.2	2.2	6.4	3.0	9.0	8.8

2. *Run Time*

An array can also be explicitly initialized at run time(ie., array values are obtained explicitly through keyboard during execution time). In the run time initialization of the arrays looping statements are almost compulsory. Looping statements are used to initialize the values of the arrays one by one by using assignment operator or through the keyboard by the user.

int a[5];

scanf("%d%d%d%d%d", &a[0],&a[1],&a[2],&a[3],&a[4]); //suitable for simple applications

if suppose array a has 100 elements, then it is difficult to do above syntax. Better solution is Looping

or

for(int i=0; i<5;i++)

scanf("%d", &a[i]);

i=0; 0< 5; true

a[0]=12 (user input during run time)

i++

i=1; 1< 5; true

a[1]=16 (user input during run time)

i++

i=2; 2< 5; true

a[2]=8 (user input during run time)

i++

i=3; 3< 5; true

a[3]=4 (user input during run time)

i++

i=4; 4< 5; true

a[4]=2 (user input during run time)

i++

i=5; 5< 5; false

a[0]	a[1]	a[2]	a[3]	a[4]
12	16	8	4	2

3.2.2. Two-dimensional Array

A two-dimensional array is a type of multi-dimensional array. It contains a list of one-dimensional arrays that is two subscripts,one representing the row and the other representing the column.

If we want to prepare a mark sheet of n students, then we need to select two dimensional array instead of one dimensional array. The reason is, we need to store marks of n subjects for n students. Whenever we want to store multiple data for n items then multidimensional array is the best choice.

3.2.2.1. Array Declaration

The array can be declared by giving the two subscript values ie., the number of rows and number of columns. Given below is the syntax of a two dimensional array.

Syntax

```
<data-type><array-name> [ row_size ] [column_size]
```

Example

a[3][3] → A two dimensional array a has 3 rows and 3 columns

datatype → any valid c datatype

m → number of rows

n→number of columns

Representation of Two-dimensional Array

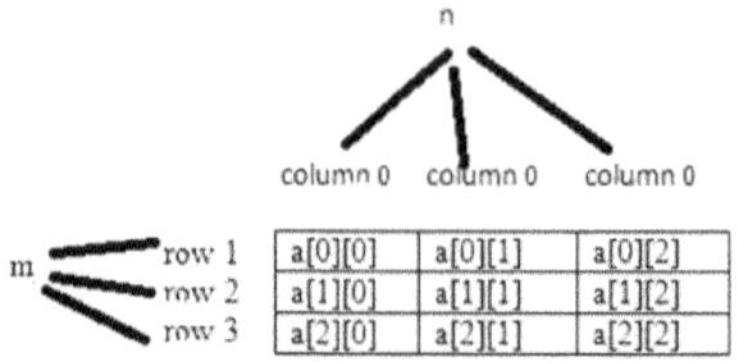

Two index variables or subscripts say i and j are required to access any element stored in the two dimensional array.

3.2.2.2. Array Initialization

Initializing Two-Dimensional Arrays

1) int a[3][4] = { {10, 17, 12, 2} , {15, 8, 9, 24} , {2, 5, 66, 51} };

   or

   int a[3][4] = {10,17,12,2,15,8,9,24,2,5,66,51};

	a[0]	a[1]	a[2]	a[3]
a [0]	10 a[0][0]	17 a[0][1]	12 a[0][2]	2 a[0][3]
a[1]	15 a[1][0]	8 a[1][1]	9 a[1][2]	24 a[1][3]
a[2]	2 a[2][0]	5 a[2][1]	66 a[2][2]	51 a[2][3]

printf("%d", a[2][3]);

/* output will be 9, [2][3] means third element of the second row of the array */

2)int a[3][2]={ {10} , {15,3} , {2,} };

	a[0]	a[1]
a[0]	10	0
a[1]	15	3
a[2]	2	0

If elements are not initialized, default value 0 is used.

Accessing Two-Dimensional Array Elements

- Use two index variables or subscripts say i and j to access the elements stored in 2D array, where index variable i is used to represent row and j is used to represent column.
- Use two for loops to process rows and columns

Eg.,

```
int a[3][4];
for( i =0; i <3; i++){
for( j =0; j <4; j++){
printf("a[%d][%d] = %d\n", i,j, a[i][j]);
}
}
```

3.3. Example Programs

Computing Mean, Median and Mode

```
#include<stdio.h>
#include<conio.h>
void main()
{
int a[50],n,i,sum=0,j,temp=0,mid,count=0,maxCount=0,maxValue=0;
clrscr();
printf("Enter the count\n");
scanf("%d",&n);
printf("Enter the values\n");
for(i=0;i<n;i++)
{
scanf("%d",&a[i]);
sum+=a[i];
}
printf("Mean=%d\n",sum/n);
for(i=0;i<n;i++)
{
for(j=i+1;j<n;j++)
{
if(a[i]>a[j])
{
temp=a[i];
a[i]=a[j];
a[j]=temp;
}
```

```
} }
mid=n/2;
if((n%2)!=0)
printf("Median=%d\n",a[mid]);
else
printf("Median=%d\t%d\n",a[mid-1],a[mid]);
for (i = 0; i < n; ++i) {
        int count = 0;
        for (j = 0; j < n; ++j) {
            if (a[j] == a[i])
            ++count;
        }
        if (count > maxCount) {
            maxCount = count;
            maxValue = a[i];
        }
    }
 if(maxCount<=1)
 printf("No Mode");
 else
    printf("Mode=%d",maxValue);
getch();
}
```

Output

Enter the count

4

Enter the values

3

2

3

1

Mean=2

Median=2 3

Mode=3

To find the largest and smallest of the given array

```
#include<stdio.h>
#include<conio.h>
void main()
{
int a[10],i,small,large,n;
printf("Enter the number of elements to be inserted");
scanf("%d",&n);
printf("Enter the elements\n");
for(i=0;i<n;i++)
scanf("%d",&a[i]);
printf("\narray elements are");
for(i=0;i<n;i++)
printf("\n%d",a[i]);
small=a[0];
large=a[0];
for(i=1;i<n;i++)
{
if(a[i]>large)
large=a[i];
else if(a[i]<small)
small=a[i];
}
printf("\nThe largest of the given array is %d",large);
printf("\nThe smallest of the given array is %d",small);
getch();
}
```

Output

```
Enter the number of elements to be inserted 5
Enter the elements
12 34 56 87 43
array elements are
12
34
```

56

87

43

The largest of the given array is 87

The smallest of the given array is 12

To insert an element to an array in the given position

```
#include<stdio.h>
#include<conio.h>
void main()
{
int a[10],n,i,pos,x;
printf("Enter the number of elements to be inserted");
scanf("%d",&n);
printf("Enter the elements");
for(i=0;i<n;i++)
scanf("%d",&a[i]);
printf("\narray elements are \n");
for(i=0;i<n;i++)
printf ("%d", a[i]);
printf("\nEnter the new element and its position in the array");
scanf("%d\n%d",&x,&pos);
for(i=n;i>pos;i--)
a[i]=a[i-1];
a[pos]=x;
printf("\n");
n++;
printf("\nArray after the insertion");
for(i=0;i<n;i++)
printf("\n%d",a[i]);
getch();
}
```

Output

Enter the number of elements to be inserted

5

Enter the elements

32 46 12 78 23

array elements are

32 46 12 78 23

Enter the new element and its position in the array44 3

Array after the insertion

32

46

12

44

78

23

Matrix Operations

Matrix Addition

```
#include<stdio.h>
#include<conio.h>
void main()
{
int a[3][3],b[3][3],c[3][3],i,j,m,n;
printf("Enter the rows and columns of two matrices\n");
scanf("%d %d",&m,&n);
printf("Enter the elements of A matrix");
for(i=0;i<m;i++)
{
for(j=0;j<n;j++)
scanf("%d",&a[i][j]);
}
printf("Enter the elements of B matrix");
for(i=0;i<m;i++)
{
```

```
for(j=0;j<n;j++)
scanf("%d",&b[i][j]);
}
printf("The elements of A matrix");
for(i=0;i<m;i++)
{
printf("\n");
for(j=0;j<n;j++)
printf ("\t%d",a[i][j]);
}
printf("\nThe elements of B matrix");
for(i=0;i<m;i++)
{
printf("\n");
for(j=0;j<n;j++)
printf ("\t%d",b[i][j]);
}
printf("\nThe addition of two matrices");
for(i=0;i<m;i++)
{
printf("\n");
for(j=0;j<n;j++)
{
c[i][j]=a[i][j]+b[i][j];
printf ("\t%d",c[i][j]);
}
}
getch();
}
```

Output

Enter the rows and columns of two matrices

3 3

Enter the elements of A matrix 1 2 3 4 5 6 7 8 9

Enter the elements of B matrix 1 2 3 4 5 6 7 8 9

The elements of A matrix

```
1  2  3
4  5  6
7  8  9
```

The elements of B matrix

```
1  2  3
4  5  6
7  8  9
```

The addition of two matrices

```
2   4   6
8   10  12
14  16  18
```

Matrix Multiplication

```
#include<stdio.h>
#include<conio.h>
void main()
{
int a[3][3],b[3][3],c[3][3],i,j,k,r,s;
int m,n;
printf("\nEnter the rows and columns of A matrix");
scanf("%d %d",&m,&n);
printf("Enter the rows and columns of B matrix");
scanf("%d %d",&r,&s);
if(m!=r)
printf("\nThe matrix cannot multiplied");
else
{
printf("Enter the elements of A matrix");
for(i=0;i<m;i++)
{
for(j=0;j<n;j++)
scanf("%d",&a[i][j]);
}
printf("Enter the elements of B matrix");
```

```
for(i=0;i<m;i++)
{
for(j=0;j<n;j++)
scanf("%d",&b[i][j]);
}
printf("The elements of A matrix");
for(i=0;i<m;i++)
{
printf("\n");
for(j=0;j<n;j++)
printf ("\t%d",a[i][j]);
}
printf("\nThe elements of B matrix");
for(i=0;i<m;i++)
{
printf("\n");
for(j=0;j<n;j++)
printf ("\t%d",b[i][j]);
}
for(i=0;i<m;i++)
{
printf("\n");
for(j=0;j<n;j++)
{
c[i][j]=0;
for(k=0;k<m;k++)
c[i][j]=c[i][j]+a[i][k]*b[k][j];
}
}
}
printf ("The multiplication of two matrices");
for(i=0;i<m;i++)
{
printf("\n");
```

```
for(j=0;j<n;j++)
printf("\t%d",c[i][j]);
}
getch();
}
```

Output

```
Enter the rows and columns of two matrices
3 3
Enter the elements of A matrix 1 1 1 2 2 2 3 3 3
Enter the elements of B matrix 1 1 1 2 2 2 3 3 3
The elements of A matrix
        1   1   1
        2   2   2
        3   3   3
The elements of B matrix
        1   1   1
        2   2   2
        3   3   3
The multiplication of two matrices
        6   6   6
        12  12  12
        18  18  18
```

Transpose of a Matrix

```
#include<stdio.h>
#include<conio.h>
void main()
{
int a[3][3],i,j,m,n;
clrscr();
printf("\nEnter the rows and columns:");
scanf("%d%d",&m,&n);
{
printf("\nEnter the matrix elements:");
for(i=0;i<m;i++)
```

```
{
for(j=0;j<n;j++)
{
scanf("%d",&a[i][j]);
}
}
printf("\nThe given matrix is:");
for(i=0;i<m;i++)
{
printf("\n");
for(j=0;j<n;j++)
{
printf("%d",a[i][j]);
}
}
printf("\nThe transpose of matrix is:");
for(i=0;i<m;i++)
{
printf("\n");
for(j=0;j<n;j++)
printf("%d",a[j][i]);
}
}
getch();
}
```

Output

```
Enter the rows and columns:2 2
Enter the matrix elements:
2
3
4
5
The given matrix is:
23
```

45

The transpose of matrix is:

24

35

Matrix Scaling

```
#include<stdio.h>
void main()
{
int sx=0,sy=0,i,j,k,m=0,n=0,a[10][10],scal[10][10],sum,result[10][10];
printf("Enter the order of the matrix");
scanf("%d",&n);
printf("Enter the matrix");
for(i=0;i<n;i++)
        {
        for(j=0;j<n;j++)
                {
                scanf("%d",&a[i][j]);
                }
        }
if(n==2)
{
printf("Enter the ratio of scaling, sx=");
scanf("%d",&sx);
scal[0][0]=sx;
scal[1][1]=1;
}
if(n==3)
{
printf("Enter the ratio of scaling, sx=");
scanf("%d",&sx);
printf("Enter the ratio of scaling, sy=");
scanf("%d",&sy);
scal[0][0]=sx;
scal[1][1]=sy;
```

```
scal[2][2]=1;
}
printf("The scaling matrix is");
for(i=0;i<n;i++)
{
        for(j=0;j<n;j++)
                {
                        if(i!=j)
                        scal[i][j]=0;
                        printf("scal[%d][%d]=%d\n",i,j,scal[i][j]);
                }
        }
for(i=0; i<n; i++)
                for(j=0; j<n; j++)
                        result[i][j] = 0;
        for(i=0; i<n; i++) {
                for(j=0; j<n; j++){
                sum=0;
                                for(k=0; k<n; k++)
                                {
                                        sum+=a[i][k]*scal[k][j];
                                        result[i][j]=sum;
                                }
                        }
                }
        printf("\nScaled Matrix:\n");
        for(i=0; i<n; i++)
                for(j=0; j<n; j++)
                {
                                printf("result[%d][%d]=%d  ", i,j,result[i][j]);
                                printf("\n\n");
                }
        }
```

Output

```
Enter the order of the matrix2
Enter the matrix1
2
3
4
Enter the ratio of scaling, sx=2
The scaling matrix isscal[0][0]=2
scal[0][1]=0
scal[1][0]=0
scal[1][1]=1

Scaled Matrix:
result[0][0]=2

result[0][1]=2

result[1][0]=6

result[1][1]=4
```

Determinant of a Matrix

```
#include<conio.h>
#include<stdio.h>
int a[20][20],m;
int determinant(int f[20][20],int a);
int main()
{
 int i,j;
 printf("\n\nEnter order of matrix : ");
 scanf("%d",&m);
 printf("\nEnter the elements of matrix\n");
 for(i=1;i<=m;i++)
 {
 for(j=1;j<=m;j++)
 {
 printf("a[%d][%d] = ",i,j);
 scanf("%d",&a[i][j]);
 }
 }
 printf("Matrix A is\n");
 for(i=1;i<=m;i++)
```

```
	{
				printf("\n");
				for(j=1;j<=m;j++)
				{
						printf("\t%d \t",a[i][j]);
				}
	}
 printf("\n \n");
 printf("\n Determinant of Matrix A is %d .",determinant(a,m));
 getch();
}

int determinant(int f[20][20],int x)
{
 int pr,c[20],d=0,b[20][20],j,p,q,t;
 if(x==2)
 {
	d=0;
	d=(f[1][1]*f[2][2])-(f[1][2]*f[2][1]);
	return(d);
	}
 else
 {
	for(j=1;j<=x;j++)
	{
		int r=1,s=1;
		for(p=1;p<=x;p++)
		 {
			for(q=1;q<=x;q++)
				{
				 if(p!=1&&q!=j)
				 {
					b[r][s]=f[p][q];
					s++;
```

```
                                        if(s>x-1)
                                        {
                                               r++;
                                               s=1;
                                               }
                                        }
                                 }
                        }
            for(t=1,pr=1;t<=(1+j);t++)
            pr=(-1)*pr;
            c[j]=pr*determinant(b,x-1);
    }
            for(j=1,d=0;j<=x;j++)
    {
                  d=d+(f[1][j]*c[j]);
     }
            return(d);
  }
}
```

Output

```
Enter order of matrix : 3

Enter the elements of matrix
a[1][1] = 1
a[1][2] = 1
a[1][3] = 1
a[2][1] = 2
a[2][2] = 1
a[2][3] = 2
a[3][1] = 3
a[3][2] = 3
a[3][3] = 2
Matrix A is

        1                1                1
        2                1                2
        3                3                2


 Determinant of Matrix A is 1 .
```

Sum of Diagonal Elements in a Matrix

```
#include <stdio.h>
#include <conio.h>
void main()
{
int a[3][3],i,j,m,n,sum=0;
clrscr();
printf("\nEnter the no. of rows in the matrix A");
scanf("%d",&m);
printf("\nEnter the no. of columns in the matrix A");
scanf("%d",&n);
printf("\nEnter the elements in the matrix A");
for(i=0;i<m;i++)
{
for(j=0;j<n;j++)
{
scanf("%d",&a[i][j]);
}
}
printf("\nThe Addition of diagonal elements in the matrix is\n");
for(i=0;i<m;i++)
{
sum=sum+a[i][i];
}
printf("%d",sum);
getch();
}
```

Output

```
Enter the no. of rows in the matrix A 2
Enter the no. of columns in the matrix A 2
Enter the elements in the matrix A
1
1
1
```

1

The Addition of diagonal elements in the matrix is

2

Sum of Elements in a Matrix

```
#include<stdio.h>
#include<conio.h>
void main()
{
int i,j,rs,cs,a[10][10],sum=0;
printf("Enter the order of matrix:");
scanf("%d%d",&rs,&cs);
printf("Enter the elements of matrix:");
for(i=0;i<rs;i++)
{
for(j=0;j<cs;j++)
{
scanf("%d",&a[rs][cs]);
}
}
for(i=0;i<rs;i++)
{
for(j=0;j<cs;j++)
{
sum+=a[rs][cs];
}
}
printf("Sum of Elements of the matrix is%d",sum);
getch();
}
```

Output

Enter the order of matrix:2 2

Enter the elements of matrix:1 1 1 1

Sum of Elements of the matrix is 4

3.4. String

Definition: A String is an array of characters, terminated by delimiter '\0' or null. %s is used to print a string

Declaring Strings: C language does not support string as a data type. It represents strings as character arrays.

Syntax

char string_name[size];

The size determines the number of characters in the string_name array.

Eg.,char name[9];

String Initialization

a)char name[]= {'N','a','l','a','y','i','n','i','\0'};

name[0]	name[1]	name[2]	name[3]	name[4]	name[5]	name[6]	name[7]	
N	a	l	a	y	i	n	i	\0

b)char name[]= "Nalayini" ; // Always string ends with null character

name[0]	name[1]	name[2]	name[3]	name[4]	name[5]	name[6]	name[7]	name[8]
N	a	l	a	y	i	n	i	\0

c)char name[9]= "Nalayini" ; // Always string ends with null character

name[0]	name[1]	name[2]	name[3]	name[4]	name[5]	name[6]	name[7]	name[8]
N	a	l	a	y	i	n	i	\0

d)char name[8]= "Nalayini" ; //wrong

How to Display Strings

char name[]= "Nalayini"

1. printf("%s",name); → the full string is displayed (Nalayini)
2. printf("%.3s",name); → only 3 characters are displayed (Nal)

Limitations

- No Explicit support for strings in C
- String Input and Output operations are implemented in <stdio.h>
- String manipulation functions are implemented in string library <string.h>

3.5. String Operations

There are various string operations that can be performed with or without built in function. The built in function of string length, copy, compare and concatenate in shown in the table 3.1 below.

FUNCTION NAME	PROTOTYPE	INPUT	OUTPUT	ROLE/USE	EXAMPLE
Strlen	int strlen(const char *s);	string constant (or) character array (or) pointer pointing to string	length of the string (excluding null character)	calculates the length of the string s	I/P:Raju O/P:4
Strcpy	char *strcpy(char *dest,const char *src);	source string and destination memory location (not a constant)	after copying, it returns a pointer to the destination string	copies the source string 'src' to the destination string 'dest'.	I/P: src:Raju O/P: dest:Raju
Strcat	char *strcat(char *dest,const char *src);	source string and destination string(not a constant)	a pointer to the destination string after concatenation	appends a copy of the string 'src' to the end of the string 'dest'	I/P:src:Raj dest:Kumar O/P: dest:RajKumar
Strcmp	int strcmp(const char *s1,const char *s2);	two strings	ASCII difference of first dissimilar character or zero if the characters are same.	compares two strings	I/P: s1:Raj s2:Ram O/P:3

Table 3.1: String Operations

Example Programs

Program Using gets() and puts()

```
#include<stdio.h>
void main()
{
 char name[30];
  printf("Enter name: ");
  gets(name);//Function to read string from user.
  printf("Name: ");
  puts(name);//Function to display string.
}
```

Output

Enter name: Nalayini

Nalayini

String Manipulation Program

```
#include <stdio.h>
#include <string.h>
void main ()
{
  char str1[12] = "good";
  char str2[12] = "morning";
  char str3[12];
  int len ;
  strcpy(str3, str1); /* copy str1 into str3 */
  printf("strcpy( str3, str1) : %s\n", str3 );
  strcat( str1, str2); /* concatenates str1 and str2 */
  printf("strcat( str1, str2): %s\n", str1 );
  len = strlen(str1); /* calculates length of the string*/
  printf("strlen(str1) : %d\n", len );
}
```

Output

```
strcpy( str3, str1) : good
strcat( str1, str2): goodmorning
strlen(str1) : 11
```

Source Code to Find the Frequency of Characters

```
#include <stdio.h>
void main()
{
  char name[10],ch;
  int i,count=0;
  printf("Enter a string: ");
  gets(name);
  printf("Enter a character to find frequency: ");
  scanf("%c",&ch);
  for(i=0;name[i]!='\0';++i)
  {
    if(ch==name[i])
```

```
        ++count;
    }
    printf("Frequency of %c = %d", ch, count);
}
```

Output

Enter a string: nalayini

Enter a character to find frequency: a

Frequency of a = 2

String Operations Using Predefined Functions

```
#include <stdio.h>
#include <conio.h>
#include <string.h>
void str_len();
void str_comp();
void str_con();
void str_cpy();
char a[25],b[25],c[50];
void main()
{
int choice;
clrscr();
printf("1. finding the length of the string");
printf("\n2. string comparison");
printf("\n3. string copy");
printf("\n4. String concatenate");
printf("\nEnter ur choice");
scanf("%d",&choice);
switch(choice)
{
case 1:
str_len();
break;
case 2:
```

```
str_comp();
break;
case 3:
str_cpy();
break;
case 4:
str_con();
break;
default:
exit(1);
}
getch();
}
void str_len()
{
int n;
fflush(stdin);
printf("\n Enter the string");
gets(a);
n=strlen(a);
printf("\nThe length of the string is %d",n);
}
void str_comp()
{
fflush(stdin);
printf("\n Enter the I string");
gets(a);
printf("\nEnter the II String");
gets(b);
if(strcmp(a,b)==0)
printf("\n The two strings are identical");
else
printf("\nThe strings are different");
}
```

```
void str_cpy()
{
fflush(stdin);
printf("\n Enter the  string");
gets(a);
strcpy(b,a);
printf("\nThe copied string  :");
puts(b);
}
void str_con()
{
fflush(stdin);
printf("\n Enter the I string");
gets(a);
printf("\nEnter the II String");
gets(b);
strcat(a,b);
printf("\nThe concatenated string is  : ");
puts(a);
}
```

Output

```
1. finding the length of the string
2. string comparison
3. string copy
4. String concatenate
Enter ur choice 1
 Enter the string  computer
The length of the string is 9
```

String Operations without Using Pre-defined Functions

```
#include <stdio.h>
#include <conio.h>
#include <string.h>
void str_len();
```

```
void str_con();
void str_cpy();
char a[25],b[25],c[50];
void main()
{
int choice;
clrscr();
printf("1. finding the length of the string");
printf("\n2. string copy");
printf("\n3. String concatenate");
printf("\nEnter ur choice");
scanf("%d",&choice);
switch(choice)
{
case 1:
str_len();
break;
case 2:
str_cpy();
break;
case 3:
str_con();
break;
default:
exit(1);
}
getch();
}
void str_len()
{
int n=0,i;
fflush(stdin);
printf("\n Enter the string");
gets(a);
```

```
for(i=0;a[i]!='\0';i++)
n++;
printf("\nThe length of the string is %d",n);
}
void str_cpy()
{
int i;
fflush(stdin);
printf("\n Enter the  string");
gets(a);
for(i=0;a[i]!='\0';i++)
b[i]=a[i];
printf("\nThe copied string  :");
puts(b);
}
void str_con()
{
int n=0,i;
fflush(stdin);
printf("\n Enter the I string");
gets(a);
printf("\nEnter the II String");
gets(b);
for(i=0;a[i]!='\0';i++)
{
n++;
}
for(i=0;b[i]!='\0';i++)
{
a[n++]=b[i];
}
printf("\nThe concatenated string is  : ");
puts(a);
}
```

Output

1. finding the length of the string

2. string copy

3. String concatenate

Enter ur choice 2

Enter the string computer

The copied string : computer

Program to Display Character Array & their Addresses

```
#include <stdio.h>
void main()
{
char a[]={'A','B','C','D'};
int i;
clrscr();
for(i=0;a[i]!='\0';i++)
{
printf("\nThe array elements are : %c",a[i]);
printf("\nThe memory location is %u",&a[i]);
}
getch();
}
```

Output

The array elements are : A

The memory location is 65522

The array elements are : B

The memory location is 65523

The array elements are : C

The memory location is 65524

The array elements are : D

The memory location is 65525

String Array

A string is an array of characters. Therefore an array of strings is an array of arrays of characters.

Syntax:

char names[MAX][SIZE];

names→ an array of character arrays

MAX→ maximum number of strings

SIZE→ number of characters in the string

Two Dimensional Character Array

A character array can be a two dimensional array. A collection of strings can be stored in a two dimensional array.

The syntax is:

char a[5][10];

Here, The array a accommodates 5 strings with 9 characters long. The last location is allotted for storing the NULL character. A NULL character must terminate each character string.

a[0]	L	O	H	I	T	H	'\0'			
a[1]	N	I	S	W	A	T	H	'\0'		
...										
...										
a[MAX-1]										

Example Programs

```
#include<stdio.h>
void main()
{
char a[4][10],i,j,n;
clrscr();
printf("\nEnter the number of names to be stored in the array");
scanf("%d",&n);
printf("\nEnter the names one by one\n");
for(i=0;i<n;i++)
```

```
{
fflush(stdin);
gets(a[i]);
}
printf("\nThe names are\n");
for(i=0;i<n;i++)
{
puts(a[i]);
printf("\n"); }
getch();
}
```

Output:

```
Enter the number of names to be stored in the array 3
Enter the names one by one
arthi
archana
kanimozhi
The names are
arthi
archana
kanimozhi
```

Program to sort the given strings alphabetically

```
#include<stdio.h>
#include<conio.h>
#include<string.h>
void main()
{
char names[20][20],temp[10],c;
int i,j,k,n=0;
clrscr();
printf("\nEnter Names to stop type keyword END ......\n");
scanf("%s",&names[n]);
while(strcmp(names[n],"END")>0)
```

```
{
n++;
scanf("%s",names[n]);
}
printf("\n");
for(i=0;i<n;i++)
printf("%10s",names[i]);
printf("\n");
printf("\n");
printf("Number of  Names...... %d\n",n);
for(i=0;i<n-1;i++)
for(j=i+1;j<n;j++)
{
if(strcmp(names[i],names[j])>0)
{
strcpy(temp,names[i]);
strcpy(names[i],names[j]);
strcpy(names[j],temp);
}
}
printf("After Sorting the Names are .....\n");
for(i=0;i<n;i++)
printf("%10s",names[i]);
printf("\n");
getch();
}
```

Output

```
Enter Names to stop type keyword END ......
suji lak muni anil durga anil chiru babu END
suji  lak  muni  anil  durga  anil  chiru  babu
Number of Names......8
After Sorting the Names are.....
anil  anil  babu  chiru  durga  lak  muni  suji
```

3.6. Sorting

Sorting is a mechanism to organize or arrange the unsorted elements either in ascending or descending order.

Types of Sorting

1. Internal Sort
2. External Sort

1. Internal Sort

It is suitable for small collection of data. This method uses only the primary memory during sorting process. All data items are held in main memory and no secondary memory is required in this sorting process. If all the data that is to be sorted can be accommodated at a time in memory is called internal sorting.

Types of Internal Sort

1. Insertion sort
2. Selection sort
3. Bubble Sort
4. Heap Sort
5. Shell Sort
6. Quick sort

2. External Sort

External sorting is required when the large data set being **sorted** do not fit into the main memory of a computing device (usually RAM) and instead they must reside in the slower external memory (usually a hard drive).All external sorts are based on process of merging

Types of External Sort

1. Merge sort
2. Two-way merge
3. Multi-way merge

Internal sort	External sort
It is suitable for small collection of data	It is suitable for large data set
It fits into the main memory itself	It resides in the external memory
Execution is faster than External sort	It is slower

Table 3.2: Difference between Internal and External Sort

3.6.1. *Internal Sort Algorithms*

Bubble Sort

It proceeds by looking at the list from left to right. Each adjacent pair of elements is compared. Whenever a pair is found not be in order, the elements are exchanged such that the larger number bubbles upto the right end. It is also called a sinking sort meaning that the elements sink down in the list to their proper position.

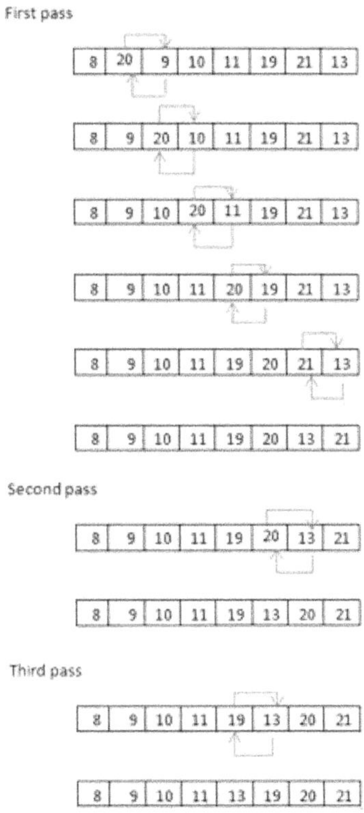

To print the ascending and descending order of the given array using bubble sort

```
#include<stdio.h>
#include<conio.h>
void main()
{
int x[10],n,i,j,k;
```

```
printf("Enter the number of elements to be inserted");
scanf("%d",&n);
printf("Enter the elements");
for(i=0;i<n;i++)
scanf("%d",&x[i]);
for(i=0;i<n-1;i++)
{
for(j=i+1;j<n;j++)
{
if(x[i]<x[j])
{
k=x[i];
x[i]=x[j];
x[j]=k;
}
}
}
printf("\n Descending order ");
for(i=0;i<n;i++)
printf("\n%d",x[i]);
printf("\n Ascending order ");
for(j=n-1;j>=0;j--)
printf("\n%d",x[j]);
getch();
}
```

Output

```
Enter the number of elements to be inserted
5
Enter the elements
10 30 50 60 20
Descending order
60
50
30
```

20

10

Ascending order

10

20

30

50

60

Selection Sorting

It is very simple and natural way of sorting a list. It finds the smallest element in the list and exchanges it with the element present at the head of the unsorted list. Selection and exchange are important in selection sort. For n number of elements, n-1 passes are made.

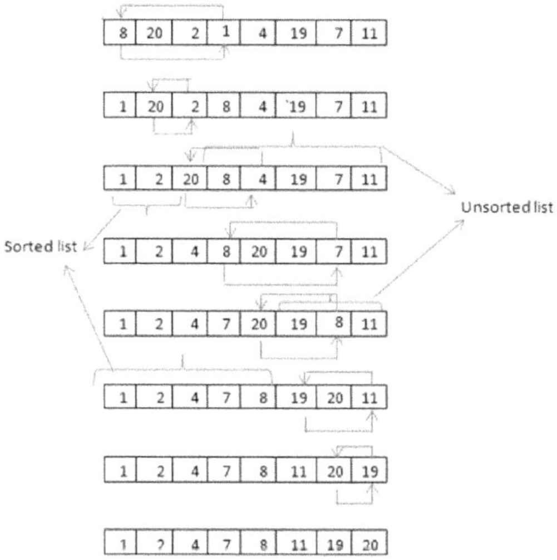

Program to sort n elements using selection sort

```
#include<stdio.h>
void main()
{
int list[20];
int small, pos, n, i, j, temp;
printf("Enter the  number of elements of the list:\n");
```

```
scanf("%d", &n);
printf("Enter the elements of the list:\n");
for(i=0;i<n;i++)
scanf("%d", &list[i]);
for(i=0;i<n-1;i++)
{
small=list[i];
pos=i;
for(j=i+1;j<n;j++)
{
If(small>list[j])
{
small=list[j];
pos=j;
}
}
If(pos!=i)
{
temp=list[i];
list[i]=list[pos];
list[pos]=temp;
}
}
printf("\n the sorted list is");
for(i=0;i<n;i++)
printf("%d",list[i]);
}
```

Insertion Sort

This algorithm resembles the process of arranging a pack of playing cards. The first two numbers are put in correct relative order. The third number is inserted at correct place relative to the first two numbers. The fourth number is inserted at the correct place relative to the first three numbers and so on... Given a list, it is divided into two parts sorted and unsorted part. The first element becomes the sorted part and rest becomes unsorted part.

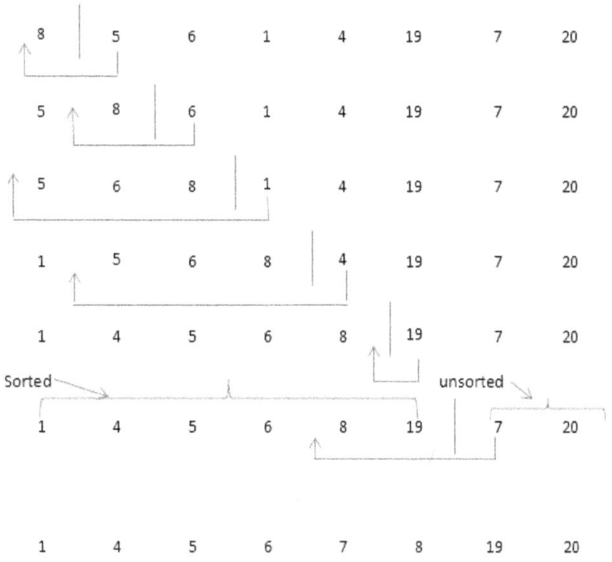

Program to sort n elements using insertion sort

```
#include<stdio.h>
void main()
{
int list[50];
int n,i,j,temp;
printf(" enter the number of elements of the list");
scanf("%d",&n);
printf("Enter the elements of the list");
for(i=0;i<n;i++)
scanf("%d", &list[i]);
for(i=1;i<n;i++)
{
temp=list[i];
j=i-1;
while((temp<list[j]) && (j>=0))
{
list[j+1]=list[j];
```

```
j=j-1;
}
list[j+1]=temp;
}
printf("the sorted list is......");
for(i=0;i<size;i++)
{
printf("%d", list[i]);
}
}
```

3.6.2. External Sort Algorithms

Merge Sort

It follows Divide and Conquer algorithm. Merge can happen only when the inputs are in sorted order.

Divide the problem into a number of sub-problems(ie., divide the array of elements until it becomes indivisible).**Conquer** the sub-problems by solving the it recursively. **Combine or Merge** the solutions(sorted order) of the sub-problems in order to obtain the solution for the original problem

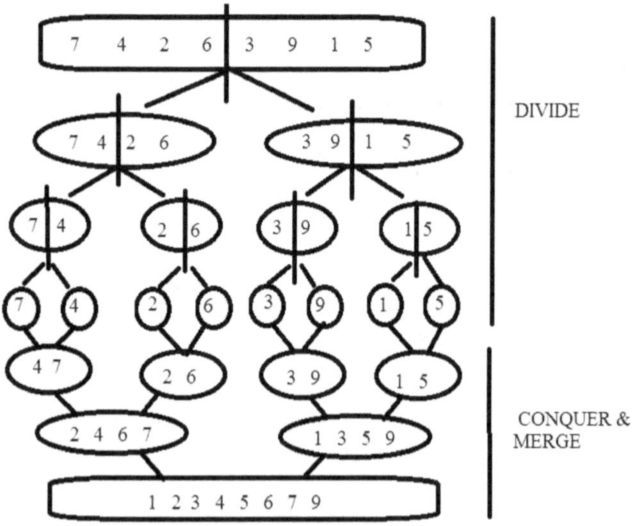

Two-way Merge

Algorithm: Assume unsorted data is on disk at start

Repeat:

1. Read M records into main memory & sort internally.(M = maximum number of records that can be stored at one time)
2. Write this sorted sub-list onto disk. (This is one "run").

Until all data is processed into runs

Repeat:

1. Merge two runs into one sorted run twice as long
2. Write this single run back onto disk

Until all runs processed into runs twice as long

Merge runs again as often as needed until only one large run: the sorted list

Unsorted Data on Disk

23 67 34 12 7 46 3

Assume M = 3 (M would actually be much larger, of course.) First step is to read 3 data items at a time into main memory, sort them and write them back to disk as runs of length 3. Next step start merging runs until we get one run.

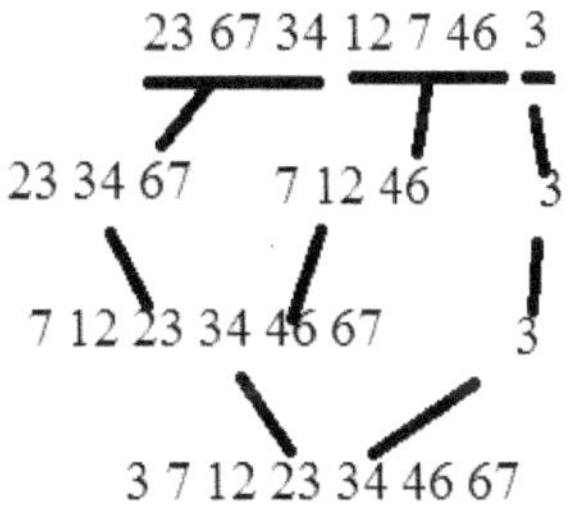

3.7. Searching

It is to find whether the given item(number, character, string) present in the array or not. If present, a successful search otherwise unsuccessful search.

Types of Searching

1. Linear search
2. Binary search

3.7.1. *Linear Search*

It searches the given element one by one in a sequential way until the element is found.

```
#include <stdio.h>
#include<conio.h>
void main()
{
int a[10];
int i, n, ele, f = 0;
printf("Enter the no of elements to be inserted \n");
scanf("%d", &n);
printf("Enter the elements\n");
for (i = 0; i <n; i++)
{
scanf("%d", &a[i]);
}
printf(" array elements are \n");
for (i = 0; i <n; i++)
{
printf("%d\n", a[i]);
}
printf("Enter the element to be searched \n");
scanf("%d", &ele);
/* Linear search */
for (i = 0; i <n ; i++)
{
if (ele == a[i] )
{
f = 1;
break;
}
}
```

```
if (f == 1)
printf("search is successful\n");
else
printf("search is unsuccessful\n");
getch();
}
```

Output

```
Enter the no of elements to be inserted
5
Enter the elements
12
43
67
23
89
array elements are
12
43
67
23
89
Enter the element to be searched
67
search is successful
```

3.7.2. Binary Search

Binary search saves searching time than linear search. Input should be the sorted array. Divide the sorted array into two halves (Binary) by finding the middle position. If the element to be searched is less than the middle one, do search in the first half otherwise in the second half. If the element is found stop searching otherwise again divide the respective sub array into two half and find the middle one ,compare the value of the element to be searched with the middle one, if it is lesser then do search in the first half else in the second half, if element is found stop searching otherwise repeat the same till the element if found or the array becomes indivisible.

```
#include<stdio.h>
#include<conio.h>
void main()
{
    int a[10];
    int i, j, n, temp, ele;
    int low, mid, high;
    clrscr();
    printf("Enter the elements to be inserted\n");
    scanf("%d", &n);
    printf("Enter the elements\n");
    for (i = 0; i < n; i++)
    {
    scanf("%d", &a[i]);
    }
    printf("array elements are \n");
    for (i = 0; i < n; i++)
    {
    printf("%d\n", a[i]);
    }
    /* Bubble sort */
    for (i = 0; i < n; i++)
    {
    for (j = 0; j < (n - i - 1); j++)
    {
    if (a[j] > a[j + 1])
    {
    temp = a[j];
    a[j] = a[j + 1];
    a[j + 1] = temp;
    }}
    }
    printf("Sorted array is...\n");
    for (i = 0; i < n; i++)
```

```
{
printf("%d\n", a[i]);
}
printf("Enter the element to be searched \n");
scanf("%d", &ele);
/* Binary search */
low = 0;
high = n-1;
do
{
mid = (low + high) / 2;
if (ele< a[mid])
high = mid - 1;
else if (ele> a[mid])
low = mid + 1;
} while (ele != a[mid] && low <= high);
if (ele == a[mid])
{
printf("search is successful \n");
}
else
{
printf("search is unsuccessful \n");
}
getch();
}
```

Output

Enter the elements to be inserted

5

Enter the elements

30

56

23

78

66

array elements are

30

56

23

78

66

Sorted array is...

23

30

56

66

78

Enter the element to be searched

78

search is successful

Exercise

1. **What will be the output of the program?**

```
#include<stdio.h>
int main()
{
int arr[1]={10};
printf("%d\n",0[arr]);
return 0;
}
```

2. **Trace the output if array begins at 64480.**

```
#include<stdio.h>
int main()
{
int arr[]={1,2,3,4,5};
printf("%u %u\n",arr,&arr);
return 0;
}
```

3. **What will be the output of the program?**

```
#include<stdio.h>
int main()
{
float array[]={10.1,11.2,12.3,14.5};
printf("%d\n",sizeof(array)/sizeof(array[0]));
return 0;
}
```

4. **What does strcmp() function returns if two strings are identical?**
5. **What will be the output of the program?**

```
#include<stdio.h>
#include<string.h>
int main()
{
char str1[20]="Hello",str2[20]="World";
printf("%s\n",strcpy(str2,strcat(str1,str2)));
return 0;
}
```

UNIT IV

FUNCTIONS AND POINTERS

4.1. Introduction to Functions

Definition

A function is a group of statements that together perform a task. Every C program has at least one function, which is main() function and all other additional functions that can be defined by the user.

Syntax:

```
return_type function_name(parameter_list)
{
        Body of the function;
}
```

Explanation:

Return_type: The type of the value that the function returns as the result of the execution is called as return type of the function. If no value is returned by the function, then the return type of the function is *void.* Void means nothing.

Function_name: The actual name of the function. The name should be meaningful without any space or special characters in it. The name should not be a predefined keyword.

Parameter_list: When the function is invoked, it needs some data to process the task. So the data can be passed to the function as parameters which are optional. The parameter list refers to the type, order and the number of the parameters of the function.

Function body: The collection of statements inside the curly braces to perform a particular task.

Example:

```
int maximum(int num1,int num2)
{
    if(num1>num2)
      return num1;
    else
      return num2;
}
```

4.2. Function Prototype (or) Declaration

A function declaration tells the compiler about a function's name, return type and parameters. Function declaration is a statement and hence terminated by a semicolon(;). The function definition contains the actual body of the function which is discussed in detail in the later sections. The function declaration should be done before the main() function if the function definition is written after the main() function. If the function definition is written before the main() function, then the function declaration statement is not required.

In the function declaration statement, the parameter names are optional whereas the data type of the parameters, order and the number of parameters is mandatory.

Syntax:

```
return_type function_name(parameter_list);
```

Example:

```
int maximum(int num1,int num2);
(or)
int maximum(int,int);
```

4.3. Function Definition

The function definition contains the actual body of the function. It tells the compiler exactly what task has to be done and how can it be done.

Syntax:

```
return_type function_name(parameter_list)
{
        //body of the function
}
```

Example:

```
int maximum(int num1,int num2)
{
    if(num1>num2)
              return num1;
    else
              return num2;
}
```

The difference between function declaration and function definition is shown in the table 4.1 below.

FUNCTION DECLARATION	FUNCTION DEFINITION
A function declaration tells the compiler about a function's name, return type and parameters.	A function definition tells the compiler exactly what task has to be done and how it is to be done.
The parameter name is optional	The parameter name is mandatory.
It has to be declared only before the main() function	Function definition can be written before or after the main() function.
It is terminated by a semicolon(;)	It is not terminated by a semicolon(;)

Syntax: return_type function_name(parameter_list);	Syntax: return_type function_name(parameter_list)
	{
	Body of the function;
	}

Example: int maximum(int,int);	Example: int maximum(int num1,int num2)
	{
	if(num1>num2)
	return num1;
	else
	return num2;
	}

Table 4.1: Difference between Function Declaration and Definition

Calling a Function

To use a function, a call has to be made. When a program calls a function, program control is transferred from the calling function to the called function. The called function performs the defined task and when the return statement is executed or when its function-end closing braces is reached, it returns the program control back to the called function.

Example Program

```
#include<stdio.h>
int maximum(int ,int); /*function declaration or prototype*/
void main()
{
        int a=100,b=200,res;
        res=maximum(a,b); /*function call*/
        printf("The maximum number is %d",res);
}
/*function definition*/
int maximum(int num1, int num2)
{
        if(num1>num2)
```

```
            return num1;
    else
            return num2;
}
```

Advantages of Function

1. Reduction in code redundancy.
2. Enabling code reuse.
3. Better readability.
4. Information hiding.
5. Improved debugging and testing.
6. Improved maintainability.

4.4. Classification of Functions

Functions can be classified based on two criteria.

1. Based upon who develops the function
2. Based upon the input/output (or) arguments and return type.

Based upon who develops the function:

There are two types of function based on the developer. They are:

1. User defined function
2. Library function (or) Predefined function

1. User Defined Function

User defined functions are defined by the user while writing a program. The user can develop any number of functions based on his/her need. Each function is defined for a particular purpose/functionality written in the body of the function. These functions are also called as *programmer defined functions.* There are three elements of a user defined functions. They are:

1. Function declaration (or) prototype
2. Function definition (or) implementation
3. Function call (or) use (or) invocation

1. Function Declaration

All identifiers (except labels) need to be declared before they are used. As function names are also identifiers, they are declared in the form as follows.

return_type function_name(parameter_list);

- The name of the function is also called as *function designator.*
- The parameter list is separated by comma (,).
- If only the type of the parameter is given, then the function declaration is said to have *abstract parameter declaration.*
- If the function declaration consists of the valid names of the parameters with its data types(parameter list), then it is said to have a *complete parameter declaration.*
- No two parameters can have the same name.
- Function declaration should be terminated by a semicolon(;).
- A function need not be declared if it is defined before it is called.

2. Function Definition

The definition part has two sections namely:

1. Header of the function and
2. Body of the function
    1. Header of the function:

       The syntax is

       return_type function_name(parameter_list)

       - It can have only complete parameter declaration.
       - The return type, the number and the type of parameters in the function header should exactly match the corresponding return type, the number and the types of parameters in the function declaration if present.
       - The header should not have a semicolon.
       - It is not mandatory to have the same names for the parameters in the function declaration and in the function definition.
    2. Body of the function:
       - It consists of a set of statements enclosed within braces. They can be non-executable (or) executable statements.
       - The non-executable statements declare the local variable in the function and the executable statements determine its functionality.

3. Function Call

The function call is done using the function name in the source program with the parameters if present. The function call does not contain the data type for the parameter list and the return type for the function. It contains only the parameter name and function name. if the function returns any value, then the function call is assigned to a variable similar to the data type of the return value.

The syntax is

function_name(parameter_list);

Example:

maximum(a,b); /*no value id returned*/

(or)

Result=maximum(a,b); /*an integer value is returned. Result is also of int type*/

2. *Predefined Function*

The standard functions are defined in the C compiler which need not be written again. The inbuilt functions are grouped together and placed in a common place called library (or) pre-processor directives. The function declaration, function definition, input and output of these functions are predefined in the pre-processor with the predefined syntax. Only call is used in the program.

Example: strlen() is predefined in string.h header file to find the length of the string. In order to use strlen(), #include<string.h> has to be added in the pre-processor part.

Based upon the input/output (or) arguments and return type:

The function prototype can be given in the following forms:

1. Function with no arguments and no return type
2. Function with arguments and no return type
3. Function with arguments and with return type
4. Function with no arguments and with return type.

The explanation of all the four types with example is given below. The dashed arrow in the syntax represents only the control flow and the solid arrows represents both data and control flow.

- Function with no arguments and no return type
    - No data transfer takes place between the calling function and the called function.
    - The called function does not receive any data from the calling function and does not send back any value to the calling function.
    - It is also called as *No Way Communication*

Syntax:

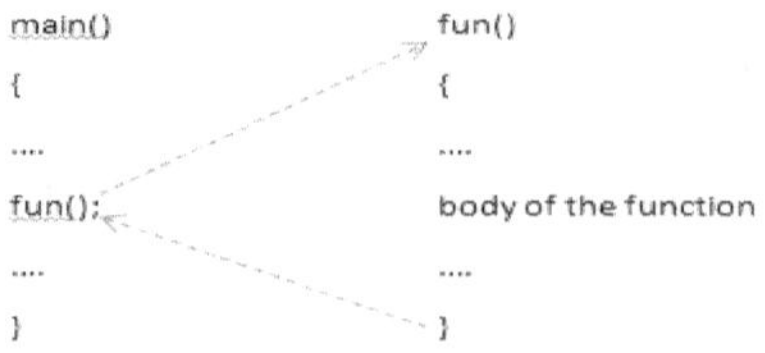

Example:

```
#include<stdio.h>
void add(void);
void main()
{
    add();
}
void add()
{
    int a,b;
    printf("Enter two numbers\n");
    scanf(%d%d",&a,&b);
    printf("Sum=%d\n",a+b);
}
```

- Function with arguments and no return type
  - Data is transferred from calling function to called function.
  - The called function receives some data from the calling function and does not send back any values to calling function.
  - It is also called as *One Way Communication*

Syntax:

```
main()                      fun(argument list)
{                           {
....                        ....
fun(argument list);                     body of the function
....                        ....
}                           }
```

Example:

```
#include<stdio.h>
void add(int,int);
void main()
{
        int a,b;
        printf("Enter two numbers\n");
        scanf("%d%d",&a,&b);
        add(a,b);
```

```
}
void add(int x,int y)
{
        printf("Sum=%d\n",x+y);
}
```

- Function with arguments and with return type
  - Data transfer takes place between the calling and called function
  - The called function receives data from the calling function and sends back a value to the calling function.
  - It is also called as *Two Way Communication*

Syntax:

```
main()                              return_type fun(argument list)
{                                   {
....                                ....
variable=fun(argument list);                      body of the function
....                                return var;
}                                   }
```

Example:

```
#include<stdio.h>
int add(int,int);
void main()
{
        int a,b,c;
        printf("Enter two numbers\n");
        scanf("%d%d",&a,&b);
        c=add(a,b);
        printf("Sum=%d",c);
}
int add(int x,int y)
{
        int z;
        z=x+y;
        return z;
}
```

- Function with no arguments and with return type.
    - The calling function does not pass any arguments to the called function but the called function returns a value to the calling function.
    - It is also called as *One Way Communication*

Syntax:

```
main()                              return_type fun()
{                                   {
....                                ....
variable=fun();                     body of the function
....                                return var;
}                                   }
```

Example:

```
#include<stdio.h>
int add();
void main()
{
        int c;
        c=add();
        printf("Sum=%d",c);
}
int add()
{
        int x,y,z;
        printf("Enter two numbers\n");
        scanf("%d%d",&x,&y);
        z=x+y;
        return z;
}
```

4.5. Built-in Functions

String Functions

FUNCTION NAME	PROTOTYPE	INPUT	OUTPUT	ROLE/USE	EXAMPLE
Strlen	int strlen(const char *s);	string constant (or) character array (or) pointer pointing to string	length of the string (excluding null character)	calculates the length of the string s	I/P:Raju O/P:4
Strcpy	char *strcpy(char *dest,const char *src);	source string and destination memory location (not a constant)	after copying, it returns a pointer to the destination string	copies the source string 'src' to the destination string 'dest'.	I/P: src:Raju O/P: dest:Raju
Strcat	char *strcat(char *dest,const char *src);	source string and destination string(not a constant)	a pointer to the destination string after concatenation	appends a copy of the string 'src' to the end of the string 'dest'	I/P:src:Raj dest:Kumar O/P: dest:RajKumar
Strcmp	int strcmp(const char *s1,const char *s2);	two strings	ASCII difference of first dissimilar character or zero if the characters are same.	compares two strings	I/P: s1:Raj s2:Ram O/P:3
Strrev	char *strrev(char *s);	a string	pointer to the reversed string	reverses the content of a string s	I/P:Raj O/P:jaR
Strlwr	char *strlwr(char *s);	a string	pointer to the converted string	converts the string to lowercase	I/P:RAJ O/P:raj
Strupr	char *strupr(char *s);	a string	pointer to the converted string	converts the string to uppercase	I/P:raj O/P:RAJ
Strset	char *strset(char *s, char ch);	a string and a character	pointer to string where all the characters in the string is replaced by the given character	set all characters in a string s to the character ch	I/P: s:raj ch=i O/P:iii
Strchr	char *strchr(const char *s, char c);	a string and a character	scans the input in the forward direction. If character is found, it returns a pointer to the first occurrence of the character. If not found, it returns NULL.	scans the string for the first occurrence of a given character	I/P: s:raman c=a O/P:aman
Strrchr	char *strrchr(const char *s,char c);	a string and a character	scans the input in the reverse direction. If character is found, it returns a pointer to the first occurrence of the character. If not found, it returns NULL.	finds the last occurrence of a character c in the string s	I/P: s:raman c=a O/P:an

Strstr	char *strstr(const char *s1,const char *s2);	two strings	if string s2 is found, it returns a pointer to the position from where the string starts else returns NULL	finds the occurrence of a substring s2 in another string s1	I/P: s1:raman s2=am O/P:aman
Strncpy	char *strncpy(char *dest,const char *src,int n);	a source string to be copied. An integer value represents the number of characters to be copied. A destination memory where the source to be copied.	returns a pointer the destination string where n characters from the source string is copied.	copies at the most n characters of string 'src' to the string 'dest'	I/P: src:Raju n=3 O/P: dest:Raj
Strncat	char *strncat(char *dest,const char *src,int n);	a source string to be appended. A destination string where the src string to be appended and the number of characters	a pointer to the deststr where at most n characters of source string is appended	appends at the most n characters of the string src to the string dest.	I/P:src:Raj dest:Kumar n=3 O/P: dest:RajKum
Strcmpi	int strcmpi(const char *s1,const char *s2);	two strings	returns the ASCII difference of the first different character or zero if both the strings are same	compares two strings without case sensitivity	I/P: s1:RAj s2:Ram O/P:3
Strncmp	int strncmp(const char *s1,const char *s2,int n);	two strings and n number of characters	compares both the string for n characters and returns ASCII difference of the first dissimilar corresponding characters or zero if both strings are same	compares at most n characters of two strings s1 and s2	I/P: s1:Raj s2:Ram n=2 O/P:0
Strncmpi	int strncmpi(const char *s1,const char *s2,int n);	two strings and n number of characters	returns the ASCII difference of the first different character or zero if both the strings are same	compares at most n characters of two strings s1 and s2 without case sensitivity	I/P: s1:RAj s2:Ram n=2 O/P:0
Strnset	char *strnset(char *s,charch,int n);	a string, a character and integer value n	a pointer to the string where first n characters in the string are replaced by the given character	sest the first n characters of the string s to character ch	I/P: s:raj ch=t n=1 O/P:taj

Table 4.2: String Functions

Math Functions

The header file math.h defines various mathematical functions and one macro. The basic library functions present in math.h header file are listed in the table below. The return type of the functions are mostly "double", but when the result of the function cannot be represented as the floating decimal or when the magnitude is too large to represent then HUGE_VAL macro is used. It returns zero if the magnitude is too small.

FUNC NAME	PROTOTYPE	INPUT	OUTPUT	ROLE/USE	EXAMPLE
acos	double acos(double x)	A floating point value in the interval [-1,+1]	The arc cosine in the range [0,π] radians	Computes the principal value of arc cosine in x	i/p:0.9 o/p:25.855040
asin	double asin(double x)	A floating point value in the interval [-1,+1]	The arc sine in the range [-π/2,+π/2] radians	Computes the principal value of arc sine in x	i/p:0.9 o/p:64.158067
atan	double atan(double x)	A floating point value	The arc tangent in the range [-π/2,+π/2] radians	Computes the principal value of arc tangent in x	i/p:1.0 o/p:45.0000
atan2	double atan2(double y, double x)	x & y are floating point values representing x- and y-coordinate respectively	The arc tangent of y/x in the range [-π,+π] radians	Computes the principal value of arc tangent in y/x	i/p: x:-7.000 y:7.000 o/p:135.0000
cos	double cos(double x)	Floating point value representing angle in radians	Cosine of x	Computes the cosine of x	i/p:60.000 o/p:0.500
cosh	double cosh(double x)	Floating point value	Hyperbolic Cosine of x. Returns range error if the magnitude of x is too large	Computes the hyperbolic cosine of x	i/p:1.000 o/p:1.543081
sin	double sin(double x)	Floating point value representing angle in radians	sine of x	Computes the sine of x	i/p:45.000 o/p:0.707107
sinh	double sinh(double x)	Floating point value	Hyperbolic sine of x. Returns range error if the magnitude of x is too large	Computes the hyperbolic sine of x	i/p:0.500 o/p:0.521095
tanh	double tanh(double x)	Floating point value	Hyperbolic tangent of x.	Computes the hyperbolic tangent of x	i/p:0.500 o/p:0.462117
exp	double exp(double x)	Floating point value	Exponential value of x. Returns range error if the magnitude of x is too large	Computes the value of **e** raised to the **xth** power	i/p:0.000 o/p:1.0000
frexp	double frexp(double x, int *exp)	x-Floating point value, exp-pointer to an int object	If x is not zero, the normalized fraction is **x** times a power of two, and its absolute value is always in the range 1/2 to 1. If **x** is zero, then the normalized fraction is zero and zero is stored in exp.	Computes the normalized fraction where x=mantissa*2^exp	i/p: x:1024.00 o/p: 0.50*2^11
ldexp	double ldexp(double	Floating point value	returns **x** multiplied by 2 raised to the power of **exponent**.	Computes x*2^{exp}	i/p: x:0.65 exp:3

	x, int exp)	representing the significand. exp-value of exponent			o/p: 5.2000
log	double log(double x)	Floating point value	Natural logarithm of x	Computes the base-e logarithm of x	i/p:2.7000 o/p:0.993252
log10	double log10(double x)	Floating point value	common logarithm of x for x>0	Computes the base-10 logarithm of x	i/p:10000.00 o/p:4.0000
modf	double modf(double x, double *y)	x-Floating point value, y-pointer to an object where integral part is stored.	the fractional part of x, with the same sign stored in y.	Computes the fractional component and sets integer to the integer component	i/p: x:8.0000 o/p: 0.123456
pow	double pow(double x, double y)	x-floating point base value y- floating point power value	returns x^y	Computes **x** raised to the power of **y**	i/p:x:3.05 y:1.98 o/p:9.097324
sqrt	double sqrt(double x)	Floating point value	Returns square root of x	Computes $\sqrt{x}$	i/p:5.000 o/p:2.236068
ceil	double ceil(double x)	Floating point value	Returns the smallest integral value not less than x	Computes the smallest integer value greater than or equal to **x**.	i/p:1.6 o/p:2.0
fabs	double fabs(double x)	Floating point value	Returns the absolute value of x	Computes the absolute value of x	i/p:-344 o/p:344.000
floor	double floor(double x)	Floating point value	returns the largest integral value not greater than x	Computes the largest integer value less than or equal to **x**.	i/p:1.6 o/p:1.0
fmod	double fmod(double x, double y)	x & y are the floating point value with the division numerator & denominator respectively	returns the remainder of dividing x/y	Computes the remainder of **x** divided by **y**	i/p:x:9.200 y:2.00 o/p:1.200

Table 4.3: Math Functions

4.6. Recursion

Recursion is a powerful programming technique that can be used to solve the problem that can be expressed in terms of similar problems of smaller size. A function that calls itself is known as *Recursive function.* This phenomenon is called as *Recursion.* Recursion is classified according to the following criteria.

1. Whether the function calls itself directly (*direct recursion*) or indirectly (*indirect recursion*).
2. Whether there is any pending operation on return from a recursive call. If the recursive call is the last operation of a function, the recursion is known as *tail recursion.*
3. According to the pattern of recursive calls.

   3.1. Linear recursion

   3.2. Binary recursion

   3.3. N-ary recursion

   Every recursive problem consists of two cases.

   - Base case: Base case is the smallest instant of problem, which can be easily solved and need not be expressed in terms of itself (no recursive call).
   - Recursive case: The problem is defined in terms of itself, while reducing the problem size.

4.6.1. Linear Recursion

The simplest form of recursion is linear recursion which makes only one recursive call. During the execution of the function call, a number of new activation records are created and piled up on the run time stack. This is called winding of recursion. When memory space is available winding terminates as the terminating condition is reached. If no memory space is available, it terminates abnormally.

Example:

```
// Factorial of a number using recursion.
#include<stdio.h>
#include<conio.h>
long factorial(int);
void main()
{
        int n;
        long f;
        clrscr();
        printf("Enter the number\n");
        scanf("%d",&n);
        f=factorial(n);
```

```
        printf("Factorial of %d=%ld",n,f);
        getch();
}
long factorial(int n)
{
        if(n==0)
                return 1;
        else
                return (n*factorial(n-1));
}
```

Output

Enter the number

5

Factorial of 5 = 120

4.6.2. Binary Recursion

A binary recursive function calls itself twice. In the binary recursion, the tree of recursive calls is called a binary tree. Binary recursion is used in solving problems like:

- Tower of Hanoi
- Sorting by Merge sort
- Searching by Binary search
- Fibonacci series generation

Example:

```
//finding a number in a Fibonacci series given the location in the series
#include<stdio.h>
#include<conio.h>
int binaryfib(int);
void main()
{
        int n, int b;
        printf("Enter the location\n");
        scanf("%d",&n);
        b=binaryfib(n);
        printf("%dth Fibonacci number is %d",n,b);
```

```
        getch();
}
int binaryfib(int n)
{
        if(n==1)
                return 0;
        if(n==2)
                return 1;
        else
                return binaryfib(n-1)+binaryfib(n-2);
}
```

Output

Enter the location

4

4th Fibonacci number is 2

//program to generate Fibonacci series using recursion.//

```
#include<stdio.h>
#include<conio.h>
int binaryfib(int);
void main()
{
        int n, int b;
        printf("Enter the number of terms\n");
        scanf("%d",&n);
        for(i=1;i<n;i++)
                printf("%d\t",binaryfib(i));
        getch();
}
int binaryfib(int n)
{
        if(n==1)
                return 0;
```

```
        if(n==2)
                return 1;
        else
                return binaryfib(n-1)+binaryfib(n-2);
}
```

Output

Enter the number of terms

6

0 1 1 2 3 5

Working Principle

Tree of recursive calls for binaryfib(4)

The solid arrows represent the function call and the dashed arrows represent the return value as the result of the call.

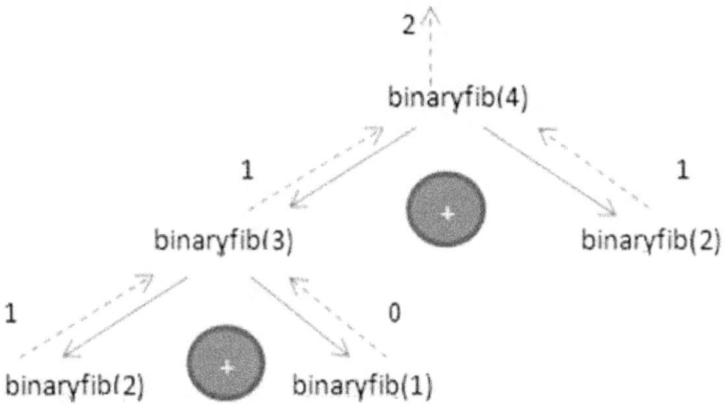

Advantages:

- The length of the program is reduced compared to iterative version.
- The code is more concise, clear and easier to understand.

Disadvantage:

- It requires extra storage i.e., large amount of memory if the depth of recursion is very large.
- It is not efficient in execution speed and time.

4.7. Example Program

Computation of Sine Series

```
#include<stdio.h>
#include<conio.h>
void main()
{
        int i, n;
        float x, sum, t;
        clrscr();
        printf(" Enter the value for x : ");
        scanf("%f",&x);
        printf(" Enter the value for n : ");
        scanf("%d",&n);
        x=x*3.14159/180;
        t=x;
        sum=x;
        /* Loop to calculate the value of Sine */
        for(i=1;i<=n;i++)
        {
                t=(t*(-1)*x*x)/(2*i*(2*i+1));
                sum=sum+t;
        }
        printf(" The value of Sin(%f) = %.4f",x,sum);
        getch();
}
```

Output

```
Enter the value for x : 30
Enter the value for n : 5
The value of Sin(0.523598) = 0.5000_
```

Scientific Calculator Using Built-in Functions

```
#include <stdio.h>
#include <math.h>
void main()
{
 float x,y,answer;
 int n;
printf("What do you want to do?\n");
printf("1.sin 2.cos 3. tan 4. sinh 5.cosh 6.tanh 7.1og10 8. square root. 9.exponent 10.power.");
scanf ("%d",&n);
        if (n<10 && n>0)
        {
                printf("\n What is x? ");
                scanf("%f",&x);
                switch (n)
                {
                                case 1: answer = sin(x); break;
                                case 2: answer = cos(x);  break;
                                case 3: answer = tan(x);   break;
                                case 4: answer = sinh(x); break;
                                case 5: answer = cosh(x);  break;
                                case 6: answer = tanh(x);  break;
                                case 7: answer = log10(x); break;
                                case 8: answer = sqrt(x); break;
                                case 9: answer = exp(x); break;
                }
        }
        if (n==10)
        {
                printf("What is x and y?\n");
                scanf("%f%f",&x,&y);
                answer = pow(x,y);
        }
```

```
if (n>0 && n<11)
                printf("%f",answer);
        else
                printf("Wrong input.\n");
}
```

Output

```
What do you want to do?
 1.sin
 2.cos
 3. tan
 4. sinh
 5.cosh
 6.tanh
 7.log10
 8. square root
 9.exponent
 10.power
8

 What is x? 8
2.828427
```

Binary Search Using Recursive Functions

```
#include<stdio.h>
int binarysearch(int[],int,int,int,int);
int main()
{

        int a[10],i,n,m,c,l,u;
        printf("Enter the size of an array: ");
        scanf("%d",&n);
        printf("Enter the elements of the array: " );
        for(i=0;i<n;i++)
        {
                scanf("%d",&a[i]);
        }
        printf("Enter the number to be search: ");
        scanf("%d",&m);
        l=0,u=n-1;
        c=binarysearch(a,n,m,l,u);
```

```
        if(c==0)
                printf("%d is not found.",m);
        else
                printf("%d is found.",m);

        return 0;
}
int binarysearch(int a[],int n,int m,int l,int u)
{
        int mid,c=0;
        if(l<=u)
        {
                mid=(l+u)/2;
                if(m==a[mid])
                {
                        c=1;
                }
                else if(m<a[mid])
                {
                        return binarysearch(a,n,m,l,mid-1);
                }
                else
                        return binarysearch(a,n,m,mid+1,u);
        }
        else
                return c;
}
```

Output

```
Enter the size of an array: 5
Enter the elements of the array: 67
43
56
12
88
Enter the number to be search: 56
56 is found.
```

4.8. Introduction to Pointers

Definition of Pointer

A pointer is a variable that holds the address of another variable or a function. A pointer is a powerful feature that adds enormous power and flexibility to C language. Asterisk(*) is the pointer operator used to represent a pointer.

Syntax:

A pointer variable can be declared as

type_specifier *identifier;

In the syntax, * is called as the punctuator and read from right to left.

Example:

int *age;

It is read as age is a pointer to an integer.

- Every pointer variable takes the same amount of memory space irrespective of whether it is pointer to int, float, char or any other type.
- Pointer holds address. The address of a variable is assigned to the pointer variable using the address of operator as shown in the fig. below
- For pointer variable %p is used as the format specifier.
- The data type of the pointer is the data type of the variable which it is pointing to.

int *ptr=&age;

The address used in the representation below is only for understanding purpose and not the fixed values.

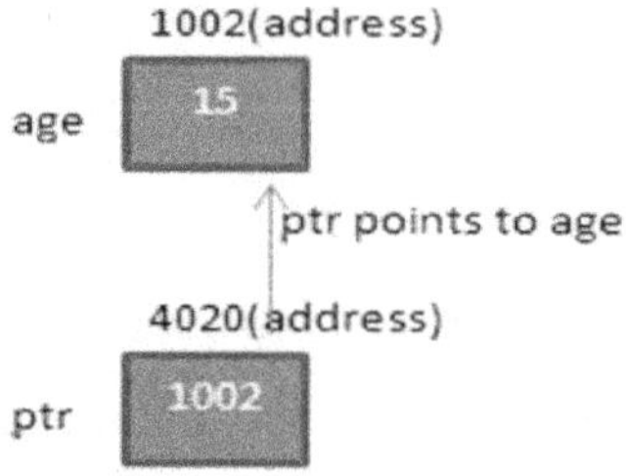

Pointer to Pointer:

Pointer to Pointer is a level of indirection added to the concept of pointers. The first pointer contains the address of the second pointer. The second pointer contains the address of the variable.

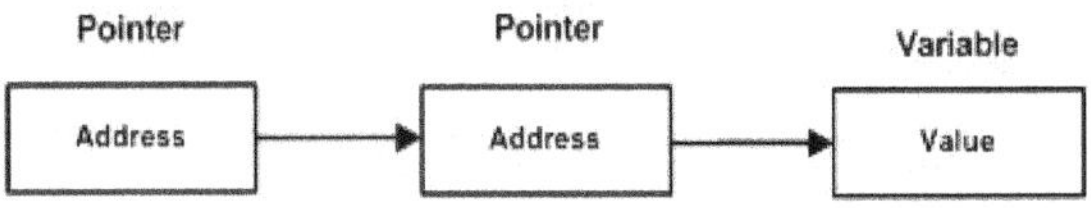

Example:

int val=12;

int *ptr=&val;

int **pptr=&ptr;

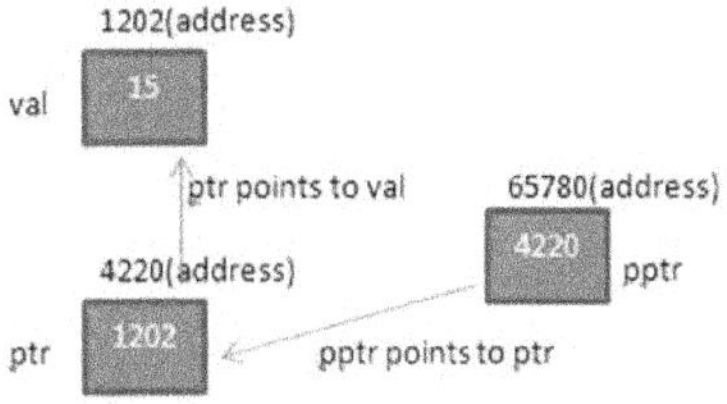

Void Pointer:

Void is a data type which means nothing or not known. Void pointer is a generic pointer and can point to any type of object.

Example: void *ptr;

NULL Pointer:

A null pointer is a special pointer that does not point any object. It does not hold the address of any object or function. It has numeric value 0 (zero). The following declaration statement declares nptr as a null pointer.

Example:

int *nptr=0;

(or)

int *nptr=NULL;

Dereferencing is not possible in a null pointer.

4.9. Initialization of Pointer Variable

Pointer initialization is the process of assigning address of a variable to pointer variable. It contains address of a variable of same data type. The address operator (&) is used to determine and return the address of the variable associated with it. Pointer can only be assigned with l-value.

Example:

```
int a=10;
int *ptr;        /*pointer declaration*/
ptr=&a;          /*pointer initialization*/
                                  (or)
int *ptr=&a;  /*pointer declaration and initialization together*/
```

4.10. Operations on Pointers

The operations that can be done on a pointer are

1. Referencing operation
2. Dereferencing a pointer

Referencing Operation:

A pointer variable is made to refer to an object. This reference is made using the reference operator (or) address of operator (&).

Example:

```
float fval=12.5;
float *fptr=&fval;
          ↖Reference operator
```

Dereferencing a Pointer:

The referenced object by a pointer can be indirectly accessed by dereferencing the pointer. It is done using dereference operator (*) which is also called as indirection operator.

Example:

```
#include<stdio.h>
#include<conio.h>
void main()
{          int val=12;
           int *ptr=&val;
           int **pptr=&ptr;
           printf("Value=%d\n",val);
           printf("Value by dereferencing ptr=%d\n",*ptr);
           printf("Value by dereferencing pptr=%d\n",**pptr);
           printf("Value of ptr=%p\n",ptr);
           printf("Value of pptr=%p\n",pptr);
}
```

Output

Value=12

Value by dereferencing ptr=12

Value by dereferencing pptr=12

Value of ptr=FFF0

Value of pptr=FFF2 **/*The value of the pointers are addresses.*/**

4.11. Pointer Arithmetic

Arithmetic operations can be applied to pointers in a restricted form. When arithmetic operators are applied on pointers, the outcome of the operation is governed by pointer arithmetic.

The operations are:

1. Addition operation
2. Increment operation
3. Subtraction operation
4. Decrement operation
5. Comparison operation

1. Addition Operation

- Addition of two pointers is not allowed.
- An integer value can be added to the pointer variable which is commutative i.e., ptr+1 is same as 1+ptr.

Example:

```
int n=10,*ptr;
ptr=&n;
printf("%p\n",ptr);
printf("%p\n",ptr+1);
```

Output:

```
FFF2    //base value
FFF4    //final value
```

The final value=(base address)+(number *size of the data type)

If the value is float n=10,*ptr;

```
Then output would be FFF2    //base value
                     FFF6    //final value
```

2. *Increment Operation*

- Increment operator is applied to the operand of pointer type. It can be pre or post increment.

Example:

Pre-increment

```
int n=10,*ptr,*pptr;
ptr=&n;
pptr=++ptr;
printf("%p\n",ptr);
printf("%p\n",pptr);
```

Output:

```
FFF6
FFF6
```

Post-increment

```
int n=10,*ptr,*pptr;
ptr=&n;
pptr=ptr++;
printf("%p\n",ptr);
printf("%p\n",pptr);
```

Output:

```
FFF6
FFF4
```

3. *Subtraction Operation*

- A pointer and an integer can be subtracted where the operation is not commutative i.e., ptr-1 is not same as 1-ptr.
- Two pointers can also be subtracted when it points to the elements of the same array.

Example 1:

```
int n=10,*ptr;
ptr=&n;
printf("%p\n",ptr);
printf("%p\n",ptr-2);
```

Output:

```
FFF4
FFF0
```

Example 2:

```
int n[3]={10,2,4},*ptr,*pptr;
ptr=&n[0];
pptr=&n[1];
printf("%p\n",pptr-ptr);
printf("%d\n",pptr-ptr);
```

Output:

```
0002
2
```

4. *Decrement Operation*

- The decrement operator can be applied to an operand of pointer type. It can be pre-decremented or post-decremented.

Pre-decrement

```
int n=10,*ptr,*pptr;
ptr=&n;
pptr=--ptr;
printf("%p\n",ptr);
printf("%p\n",pptr);
Output:
        FFF2
        FFF2
```

Post-decrement

```
int n=10,*ptr,*pptr;
ptr=&n;
pptr=ptr--;
printf("%p\n",ptr);
printf("%p\n",pptr);
Output:
        FFF2
        FFF4
```

5. *Comparison Operation*

- A pointer can be compared with a pointer of the same type or with zero.
- A comparison of pointer is meaningful only when they point to the elements of the same array.
- The relative comparison is shown in the table 4.4 below. The resultant value will be 1 if the condition holds true or 0 if the condition holds false.

OPERAND 1	OPERAND 2	RESULT TYPE	EXAMPLE	INITIAL VALUE	FINAL VALUE
float *	float *	int	r=p1!=p2	p1=2002 p2=2008	1
float *	float *	int	r=p1<p2	p1=2002 p2=2008	1
int *	int *	int	r=p1>p2	p1=2002 p2=2008	0
float *	float *	int	r=p1==p2	p1=2002 p2=2008	0

Table 4.4: Relative Comparison of Pointers

Illegal pointer operation:

- Addition of two pointers is not allowed.
- Only integer can be added to pointers. Float and double are not allowed.
- Multiplication, division, and bitwise operators can't be applied to pointers.
- A pointer of one type can't be assigned to the pointer of another type.
- A pointer variable cannot be assigned a non-address value (except zero).

4.12. Pointers and Arrays

In C language, arrays and pointers are so closely related that cannot be studied in isolation. They are often used interchangeably. The relationships are

1. The name of an array refers to the address of the first element of the array i.e., a expression of array type decomposes to pointer type. The name of an array refers to the address of the first element of the array with two exceptions
    a. When an array name is operand of size of operator it does not decompose to the address of its first element.
    b. When an array name is an operand of reference or address-of operator it does not decompose to the address of its first element.
2. Any operation that invokes array subscripting is done by using pointers. The expression of form E1[E2] is automatically converted into an equivalent expression of form *(E1+E2).
3. A pointer variable can take different addresses as value whereas in array the address is fixed.

Consider an array: int arr[4];

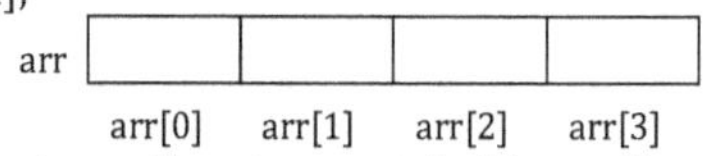

- The name of the array points to first element and address of it.
- The name of the array = arr.
- Address of the first element = &arr[0].
- Hence arr is equivalent to &arr[0].
- The value at &arr[0] is given by arr[0].
- The value at arr is given by *arr.
- Hence arr[0] is equivalent to *arr.

Example Program

```
#include<stdio.h>
void main()
{
        int array[3]={10,15,20};
        printf("Elements are %d %d %d\n", array[0], array[1], array[2]);
        printf("Elements are %d %d %d\n", *(array+0), *(array+1), *(array+2));
        printf("Elements are %d %d %d\n", 0(array), 1(array),2(array));
}
```

Output:

Elements are 10 15 20

Elements are 10 15 20

Elements are 10 15 20

Advantages of Pointers:

- Function cannot return more than one value but when the same function can modify many pointer variables and function as if it is returning more than one variable.
- In the case of arrays, we can decide the size of the array at runtime by allocating the necessary space.

Disadvantages of pointers:

- If sufficient memory is not available during runtime for the storage of pointers, the program may crash.
- If the programmer is not careful and consistent with the use of pointers, the program may crash.

Passing pointers to function:

The pointer can be passed as an argument to the function. This is similar to the pass by reference concept explained in the function section. Refer to pass by reference for explanation.

4.13. Array of Pointers

Pointers and arrays are explained in detail and compared in the previous topics. Now let me show you how to represent an array of pointers. As we all know, pointer contains the address of another variable. If an array stores those pointers that points to the address of variable of any type, then that is named as array of pointers. To be simpler, look at the example below.

Example:

```
int var[3]={1,2,3};
int *ptr[3];
for(i=0;i<3;i++)
ptr[i]=&var[i]; //assign the address of integer
```

In the above example, the variable var is an array of size 3 and ptr is a pointer that contains the address of the array var. so, ptr is called as the array of pointers.

This concept is more useful to store array of characters called strings.

For example,

```
char *week[]={"Sunday","Monday","Tuesday","Wednesday","Thursday","Friday","Saturday"};
```

Example Program

Sorting of Names

```
#include<stdio.h>
#include<conio.h>
#include<string.h>
#include<alloc.h>
void main()
{
        char *x[20],t[20];
        int i,j,n=0;
        clrscr();
        printf("Enter no. of names : ");
        scanf("%d",&n);
        printf("\n");
        for(i=0;i<n;i++)
        {
                printf("Enter the names %d : ",i+1);
                x[i]=(char *)malloc(20*sizeof(char));
                scanf("%s",x[i]);
        }
        for(i=0;i<n-1;i++)
            for(j=i+1;j<n;j++)
                if(strcmp(x[i],x[j])>0)
                {
                        strcpy(t,x[j]);
                        strcpy(x[j],x[i]);
                        strcpy(x[i],t);
                }
        printf("\nSorted list is :  \n");
        for(i=0;i<n;i++)
        {
        printf("%d %s\n",i+1,x[i]);
        }
getch(); }
```

Output

```
Enter no. of names : 4

Enter the names 1 : pavi
Enter the names 2 : arun
Enter the names 3 : abi
Enter the names 4 : sasi

Sorted list is :
1 abi
2 arun
3 pavi
4 sasi
```

4.14. Parameters

Parameter provides data communication between the calling function and the called function. There are two types of parameters. They are

1. Actual parameters
2. Formal parameters.

1. Actual Parameters

The parameters transferred from the calling to the called function are called as actual parameters.

2. Formal Parameters

The parameters transferred from the called to the calling function are called as formal parameters.

Example:

```
main()                          int func(int x,int y)
{                               {
        .....                           .....
        C=fun(a,b);                     ......
        ......                  }
}
```

In the example above, *a*and *b* are the *actual parameters.*

x and *y* are the *formal parameters.*

4.14.1. Parameter Passing Methods

There are two ways of passing parameters in a function. They are:

1. Call by value (or) pass by value
2. Call by reference (or) pass by reference

1. *Pass by Value*

The method of passing arguments by value is also called as call by value. In this method, the values of actual arguments are copied to the formal parameters of the function. If the arguments are passed by value, the changes made in the values of formal parameters inside the called function are not reflected back to the calling function.

Example:

//program to swap two numbers.

```
#include<stdio.h>
#include<conio.h>
void swap(int,int);
void main()
{     int a,b;
      clrscr();
      printf("Enter two numbers\n");
      scanf("%d%d",&a,&b);
      swap(a,b);
      printf("In main function,a=%d,b=%d",a,b);
      getch();
}
void swap(int x,int y)
{
          int z;
          printf("Before swapping:x=%d,y=%d",x,y);
          z=x;
          x=y;
          y=z;
          printf("After swapping:x=%d,y=%d",x,y);
}
```

Output

```
Enter two numbers
2 3
Before swapping:x=2,y=3
After swapping:x=3,y=2
In main function:a=2,b=3
```

The values of x and y swapped in the user defined function is not reflected in the values of a and b in the main() function. The formal arguments are copies of actual parameters and are stored in a different memory location. The disadvantage of call by value is wastage of memory by copying the arguments to a different memory location.

2. *Pass by Reference*

The method of passing arguments by address or reference is also called as call by reference or call by address. In this method, the addresses of the actual argument are passed to the formal parameters of the function. If the arguments are passed by reference, the changes made in the values pointed to by the formal parameters in the called function are reflected back to the calling function.

Example:

//program to swap two numbers.

```
#include<stdio.h>
#include<conio.h>
void swap(int*,int*);
void main()
{
    int a,b;
    clrscr();
    printf("Enter two numbers\n");
    scanf("%d%d",&a,&b);
    swap(&a,&b);
    printf("In main function,a=%d,b=%d\n",a,b);
    getch();
}
void swap(int *x,int *y)
{
    int z;
    printf("Before swapping:x=%d,y=%d\n",*x,*y);
    z=*x;
    *x=*y;
    *y=z;
    printf("After swapping:x=%d,y=%d\n",*x,*y);
}
```

Output

```
Enter two numbers
2 3
Before swapping:x=2,y=3
After swapping:x=3,y=2
In main function:a=3,b=2
```

The actual and formal parameters are pointing to the values in the same memory location. Only the memory location is passed as arguments and not the values. The changes made are in the original values and not in its copies. The advantage of call by reference is avoids wastage of memory.

// changing the value of the variable using pass by reference

```
#include<stdio.h>
#include<conio.h>
void change(int*);
void main()
{
    int a;
    clrscr();
    printf("Enter the number\n");
    scanf("%d",&a);
    change(&a);
    printf("In main function,a=%d\n",a);
    getch();
}
void change(int *x)
{
        int z;
        printf("Enter the new number\n");
        scanf("%d",&z);
        printf("Before changing:x=%d\n",*x);
        *x=z;
        printf("After changing:x=%d\n",*x);
}
```

Output

```
Enter the number
3
In main function,a=3
Enter the new number
6
Before changing:x=3
After changing:x=6
```

4.15. Example Programs

All simple programs can be written using function. Few examples for function and pointer are given below.

1. **Simple calculator using function**

```
#include<stdio.h>
#include<conio.h>
#include<stdlib.h>
void add(int a,int b)
{
    printf("Addition of %d and %d is %d \n",a,b,a+b);
}
void sub(int a,int b)
{
    printf("Subtraction of %d and %d is %d \n",a,b,a-b);
}
void mult(int a,int b)
{
    printf("Multiplication of %d and %d is %d \n",a,b,a*b);
}
void div1(int a,int b)
{
    printf("Division of %d and %d is %d \n",a,b,a/b);
}
```

```
void main()
{
    int a,b,c;
    int n=0; clrscr();
    printf("************* Calculator program ***************\n");
    printf("\n Enter two numbers");
    scanf("%d%d",&a,&b);
    do
    {
        printf("______________________");
        printf("\n1.addition\n");
        printf("2.subtraction\n");
        printf("3.multiplication \n");
        printf("4.division\n");
        printf("5.exit \n");
        printf("______________________");
        printf("\nenter your choice \n");
        scanf("%d",&c);
        switch(c)
        {
            case 1: add(a,b); break;
            case 2:sub(a,b); break;
            case 3: mult(a,b); break;
            case 4:div1(a,b); break;
            case 5:exit(0);
            default:printf("wrong choice \n");
        }
        printf("you want to continue press 1");
        scanf("%d",&n);
        }while(n==1);
    getch();
}
```

Output

```
************* Calculator program ***************
Enter two numbers 6 3
_______________________
1.addition
2.subtraction
3.multiplication
4.division
5.exit
_______________________
enter your choice 1
Addition of 6 and 3 is 9
you want to continue press 1 1
_______________________
1.addition
2.subtraction
3.multiplication
4.division
5.exit
_______________________
enter your choice 2
Subtraction of 6 and 3 is 3
you want to continue press 1 1
_______________________
1.addition
2.subtraction
3.multiplication
4.division
5.exit
_______________________
enter your choice 3
Multiplication of 6 and 3 is 18 you want to continue press 1 1
_______________________
1.addition
```

2.subtraction

3.multiplication

4.division

5.exit

---

enter your choice 4

Division of 6 and 3 is 2

you want to continue press 1 1

1.addition

2.subtraction

3.multiplication

4.division

5.exit

---

enter your choice 6

Wrong choice

you want to continue press 1 1

1.addition

2.subtraction

3.multiplication

4.division

5.exit

---

enter your choice 5

2. **Reverse the sentence using function**

```
#include <stdio.h>
void reverse();
void main()
{
    printf("Please enter a sentence: ");
    reverse();
    getch();
```

```
    }
    void reverse()
    {
        char c;
        scanf("%c",&c);
        if(c != '\n')
        {
                reverse();
                printf("%c",c);
        }
    }
```

Output

```
I am an Indian
naidnI na ma I
```

3. Addition of two numbers using pointers

```
#include<stdio.h>
#include<conio.h>
void main()
{
    int *ptr1, *ptr2;
    int num;
    printf("\nEnter two numbers : ");
    scanf("%d %d", ptr1, ptr2);
    num = *ptr1 + *ptr2;
    printf("Sum = %d", num);
}
```

Output

```
Enter two numbers: 2 3
Sum = 5
```

4. **Program to read an array and reverse its content**

```
#include<stdio.h>
#include<conio.h>
#define MAX 30
void main() {
   int size, i, arr[MAX];
   int *ptr;
   clrscr();
   ptr = &arr[0];
   printf("\nEnter the size of array : ");
   scanf("%d", &size);
   printf("\nEnter %d integers into array: ", size);
   for (i = 0; i < size; i++) {
     scanf("%d", ptr);
     ptr++;
   }
   ptr = &arr[0];
   printf("\nElements of array in reverse order are :");
   for (i = size - 1; i >= 0; i--)
   {
      printf("\nElement %d is : %d  ", i, *ptr);
      ptr++;
   }
getch();
}
```

Output:

```
Enter the size of array : 5
Enter 5 integers into array: 10 20 30 40 50
Elements of array in reverse order are :
Element 4 is : 10
Element 3 is :20
Element 2 is :30
Element 1 is :40
Element 0 is :50
```

Exercise

1. **What is the output of the program?**

```
#include<stdio.h>
int main()
{
    int fun();
    int i;
    i = fun();
    printf("%d\n", i);
    return 0;
}
int fun()
{
    int year = 2017;
}
```

2. **What will be the output of the program?**

```
#include<stdio.h>
void fun(int*, int*);
int main()
{
    int i=2, j=3;
    fun(&i, &j);
    printf("%d, %d", i, j);
    return 0;
}
void fun(int *i, int *j)
{
    *i = *i**i;
    *j = *j**j;
}
```

3. **Try running the code**

```
#include<stdio.h>

int reverse(int);

int main()

{

  int no=5;

  reverse(no);

  return 0;

}

int reverse(int no)

{

  if(no == 0)

    return 0;

  else

    printf("%d,", no);

  reverse (no--);

}
```

4. **Find the error.**

```
#include<stdio.h>

int main()

{

  int a=10;

  void f();

  a = f();

  printf("%d\n", a);

  return 0;

}
```

```
void f()
{
   printf("Hi");
}
```

5. **What will be the output?**

```
#include<stdio.h>
int main()
{
   int i=3, *j, k;
   j = &i;
   printf("%d\n", i**j*i+*j);
   return 0;
}
```

UNIT V

STRUCTURES

5.1. Introduction

Structure is a user-defined data type in which different data items of different data types can be stored under a common template. It helps us to construct a complex data type. But in arrays we can store collection of similar datatypes only. For example if we want to store different information like book_name, book_id, author_name, publisher_name, price into a book record, use structure to store these different data items. Structure combines many related data of different type under single name.

5.1.1. Structure Definition

Structure is a collection of dissimilar elements or data items of different data type stored under a single name.

Syntax:

```
struct<structure_name>
{
data_member 1;
data_member 2;
...........
............
data_member n;
};
```

where struct is the keyword, <structure_name> is any user defined name to identify the structure, data_member 1,...,data_member n are called as data members of the structure.

5.1.2. Need for Structure Data Type

Array is not suitable to store different data under common roof. Therefore whenever we want to store different data of different type, we need to go for structure data type.

Suppose, if we want to store details of an employee like name, age, address, phone _no, salary etc under common template, use structure to hold this information rather than arrays

Example:

```
struct employee
{
  char ename[10];
  int age;
  char address[15];
  int phone_no;
  int salary;
};
```

Array	Structure
Collection of similar data items of the same type	Collection of dissimilar data items of different type
It allocates static memory	It allocates dynamic memory
Data access by subscript or index	Data access by operator(either . or →)
Data access takes less time	Data access takes more time
Derived data type	User defined data type

Table 5.1: Difference between Array and Structure

5.1.3. Characteristics of Structure

1) Data members can't be initialized inside the structure
2) A structure variable is required to access the data members of the structure. If the declared structure variable is a normal variable then dot(.) operator also called period or member access operator is used to access the data members. If the declared structure variable is a pointer variable then reference operator(→) is used.
3) Contents of all structure elements of different data types can be copied to another structure variable of its type using assignment operator.
4) Nesting of structure is possible.

5.2. Structure Declaration

A structure can be declared in the following ways

1. within the structure definition
2. within the main function

1. within the structure definition

```
struct<structure_name>
{
data_member 1;
```

data_member 2;

…………

…………

data_member n;

}structure_variable1, structure_variable2,………structure_variable n;

where structure_variable1, structure_variable2,……….structure_variable n are the structure variables

2. within the main function

```
struct<structure_name>
{
data_member 1;
data_member 2;
…………
…………
data_member n;
};
void main()
{
/* declaring structure variables */
Struct structure_name structure_variable1, structure_variable2,…..,structure_variable n;
}
```

5.3. Structure Initialization

Inside the main() function, it can be done in the following ways

```
1)struct book_details
  {
  char book_name[15];
  char author_name[15];
  char publisher_name[15];
  float price;
  };
  void main()
  {
  struct book_details b1 = {"DataStructures", "Nalayini", "Tata", 195.75 }; //initialization
  }
```

```
2)struct book_details
   {
     char book_name[15];
     char author_name[15];
     char publisher_name[15];
     float price;
   };
   void main()
   {
   struct book_details b1;
   b1. book_name= "DataStructures";
   b1.author_name="Nalayini"
   b1. publisher_name= "Tata";
   b1.price= 195.75;
   }
3) struct book_details
   {
     char book_name[15];
     char author_name[15];
     char publisher_name[15];
     float price;
   };
   void main()
   {
   struct book_details  b1;
   scanf(" %s ", b1.book_name);
   scanf(" %s ", b1.author_name);
   scanf(" %d ",b1.publisher_name);
   scanf(" %f ", &b1.price);
   }
```

If we want to store details of n books we can use **Array of Structure**

```
   struct book_details
   {
     char book_name[15];
```

```
    char author_name[15];
    char publisher_name[15];
    float price;
  }b1[5];
  void main()
  {
  int i;
  for(i=0;i<5;i++)
  {
  scanf(" %s ", b1[i].book_name);
  scanf(" %s ", b1[i].author_name);
  scanf(" %d ",b1[i].publisher_name);
  scanf(" %f ", &b1[i].price);
  }
  }
```

5.4. Nested Structure

It is nothing but structure within structure. A structure can be declared as a data member inside other structure.

In this example address structure is declared as one of the data member inside the employee structure. Structure variable is used to access the address structure data members and e is used to access the employee structure data members. Since address structure is one of the data members of employee structure, the following syntax can be used to access the respective data.

```
struct address
{
char city[10];
int pincode;
}a;
struct employee
{
char ename[10];
int age;
struct address a;
```

```
   }e;
   e.ename="nila";
   e.age=21;
   e.a.city="chennai";
   e.a.pincode=600066;
```

Structure Within Structure Using Normal Variable

```
#include<stdio.h>
#include<string.h>
struct address
{
   char city[10];
   int pincode;
};
struct employee
{
 char  ename[10];
int age;
struct address a; // Nested structure
}e;
void main()
{
struct employee e={ "nila", 21, "chennai", 666};
printf("Employee name is:%s \n", e.ename );
printf("Employee age is:%d \n", e.age);
printf("Employee city is:%s \n", e.a.city );
printf("Employee pincode is:%d \n", e.a.pincode );
getch();
}
```

Output

Employee name is: 1

Employee age is: Niswath

Employee city is: chennai

Employee pincode is:666

5.5. Array of Structures

Array of Structures is used to store different information of different datatype for n objects.

```
#include<stdio.h>
struct student_details
{
char student_name[20];
int roll_no;
int marks;
};
void main()
{
struct student_details s[10];
int i;
printf("Enter student details:\n");
for(i=0;i<10;i++)
{
s[i].roll_no=i+1;
printf("Enter student name: ");
scanf("%s",s[i].student_name);
printf("Enter student marks: ");
scanf("%d",&s[i].marks);
printf("\n");
}
printf("students details:\n\n");
for(i=0;i<10;i++)
{
printf("%d",s[i].roll_no);
puts(s[i].student_name);
printf("%d",s[i].marks);
}
getch();
}
```

Output

Enter student details

Enter student name: Parimelazhagan

Enter student marks: 88

Enter student name:Niswath

Enter student marks: 99

.

.

.

students details

1

Parimelazhagan

Marks: 88

2

Niswath

99

.

.

.

Example Program Using Structures and Pointers

Structure Within Structure Using Pointer Variable

```
#include<stdio.h>
#include<string.h>
struct address
{
char city[10];
int pincode;
};
struct employee
{
char  ename[10];
int age;
struct address a; // Nested structure
```

```
}e1,*e;
void main()
{
struct employee e1={"nila", 21, "chennai", 666};
e=&e1;
printf("Employee name is:%s \n", e→ename );
printf("Employee age is:%d \n", e→age);
printf("Employee city is:%s \n", e→a.city );
printf("Employee pincode is:%d \n", e→a.pincode );
getch();
}
```

Output

Employee name is: 1

Employee age is: Niswath

Employee city is: chennai

Employee pincode is:666

5.6. Structure and Functions

- A structure can be passed(by value or by address(reference)) from main() or any sub function to any function.
- Make the structure visible to all functions by declaring its structure variable as global.

```
#include<stdio.h>
struct student
{
char student_name[15];
int roll_no;
};
void Display(struct student stu);
void main()
{
struct student s1;
printf("Enter student name: ");
scanf("%s",s1.student_name);
printf("Enter roll number:");
scanf("%d",&s1.roll_no);
```

```
Display(s1);// passing structure variable s1 as argument
getch();
}
void Display(struct student stu)
{
printf("Student Name: %s",stu.student_name);
printf("\n Student Rollno: %d",stu.roll_no);
}
```

Output

Enter student name: Lohith

Enter roll number: 19

Student Name: Lohith

Student Rollno: 19

5.6.1. Passing Array of Structure to Function

Array of structures is the collection of structures, in which different information of different types can be stored. Pass Array of Structure as a parameter either by value or address (reference) to function.

```
#include<stdio.h>
#include<conio.h>
struct book_details
{
char book_name[20] ;
int price;
}b[3];
void  accept(structbook_detailsb1[], int n)
{
int i;
for(i=0;i<n;i++)
{
printf("enter book name and price");
scanf("%s", b1[i].book_name);
scanf("%d", &b1[i].price);
}
```

```
for(i=0;i<n;i++)
{
printf("%s", b1[i].book_name);
printf("%d", b1[i].price);
}
}
void main()
{
clrscr();
accept(b,3);
getch();
}
```

Output :

```
enter book name and price
dbms
500
enter book name and price
ds
400
enter book name and price
oops
300
dbms
500
ds
400
oops
300
```

Advantages:

- More than one data member can be accessed at a time.
- Most of the applications make use of structures eg. To send output to printer

Disadvantages

- Consumes more memory when compared to union
- Execution is slower when compared to union

5.7. Self Referential Structure

A self referential structure is a dynamic structure that contains a pointer member that points to another structure that is of same structure type (pointing to them self).

For example:

Syntax:

```
struct name
{
member 1;
member 2;
......
member n;
struct name *pointer;
};
```

Example:

```
struct node
{
int data;
struct node *nextptr;
};
```

In the above example, the nextptr is a self referential structure–a pointer that is a member of structure node and points to the same type(node).

Diagrammatic representation

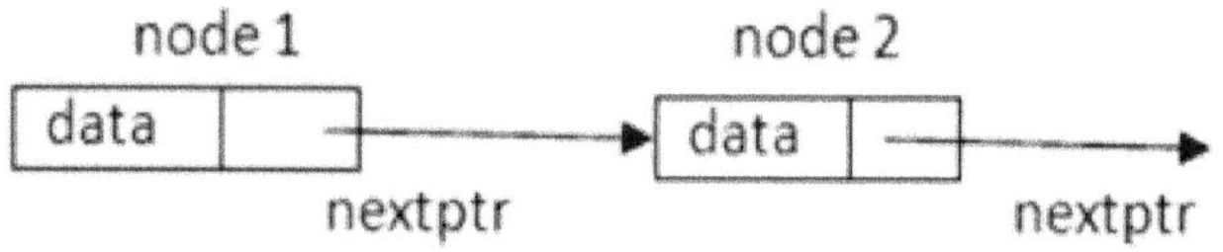

Application and Advantages:

- Self referential structures are more useful for applications that involve linked data structures like list, tree, stack, queue and so on.
- Self referential structure can be expanded or contracted dynamically.
- Operations like insertion or deletion of nodes can be done by simple and straight forward alteration of pointers.

5.8. Union

Union is a user defined data type in which all its data members share a common memory location. Therefore the starting address is same for all its data members. The data member which has largest size is taken as the entire size of the union. To overcome the disadvantages of structures, union concept is used. The syntax is as follows:

union<union_name>

{

data_member 1;

data_member 2;

…………

…………

data_member n;

};

Example:

union book_details

{

char book_name[15];

float price ;

}b1;

Here the size of the union is 15.

S.No	Structure	Union
1.	The keyword is struct.	The keyword is union.
2.	Memory allocation is done for all the data members in the structures. **Example.** struct student { int rollno; char name[5]; }s1; The memory allocation is 7 Bytes.	Memory allocation is done for the data member which requires maximum allocations. **Example:** union student { int rollno; char name[5]; }s1; The memory allocation is 5 Bytes
3.	All the data members are available in the primary memory at any time of execution.	Only the last stored data element is available in the primary memory at any time of execution.
4.	Since memory is allocated for all the data members, no data is deleted in the primary memory	Since memory is not allocated for all the data member, only one data is available and other data is deleted from the primary memory

Table 5.2: Difference between Structure & Union

Example:

```
#include<stdio.h>
union employee
{
char emp_name[20];
int emp_id;
float emp_salary;
}e1;
struct department
{
char dept_name[10];
int dno;
char dept_location[30];
}d1;
void  main()
{
printf("size of union = %d",sizeof(e1));
printf("\nsize of structure = %d",sizeof(d1));
getch();
}
```

Output

```
size of union = 20 // Union considers the data member which has the largest memory size
size of structure = 42 // Structure adds all its data members size
```

Advantages:

- Effective memory utilization
- Execution is faster

Disadvantages:

- Only one data member can be accessed at a time

5.9. Dynamic Memory Allocation

When the size of the variable is not known until the compile time, we go for the concept of dynamic memory allocation. More over to handle dynamic data structures, we need to use dynamic memory allocation. The memory is created dynamically during the run-time and can be released after use that is no longer needed. This avoids overflow and underflow of memory and enables the program to obtain more memory space at the execution time to hold new dynamically created nodes. The memory limit can be as large as the amount of available physical memory in the computer or the amount of virtual memory in the virtual memory system. When the memory is small, it can be shared by more users.

Static memory allocation	Dynamic memory allocation
Memory is allocated at compile time.	Memory is allocated at run time.
Memory can't be increased while executing program.	Memory can be increased while executing program.
Used in array.	Used in linked list.

Table 5.3: Difference between Static and Dynamic Memory Allocation

The library functions to handle dynamic memory allocation are

Function	Description/Use	Syntax
malloc()	Allocates requested size of bytes and returns a pointer first byte of allocated space	ptr=(cast-type*)malloc (byte_size);
calloc()	Allocates space for an array elements, initializes to zero and then returns a pointer to memory	ptr=(cast-type*)calloc (number, byte_size);
free()	deallocate the previously allocated space	realloc (pointer_name, new_size);
realloc()	Change the size of previously allocated space	free (pointer_name);

Table 5.4: Dynamic Memory Allocation Functions

malloc():

malloc() stands for memory allocation.

The malloc() function allocates single block of requested memory.

It doesn't initialize memory at execution time, so it has garbage value initially. The number of arguments is 1.

It returns NULL if memory is not sufficient.

calloc():

calloc() stands for contiguous allocation.

The calloc() function allocates multiple block of requested memory.

It initially initializes all bytes to zero. The number of arguments is 2.

It returns NULL if memory is not sufficient.

Example Program

```
//sum of n numbers using malloc() and free()
#include <stdio.h>
#include <stdlib.h>
int main()
{
        int num, i, *ptr, sum = 0;
        printf("Enter number of elements: ");
        scanf("%d", &num);
        ptr = (int*) malloc(num * sizeof(int));  //memory allocated using malloc
        if(ptr == NULL)
        {
                printf("Error! memory not allocated.");
                exit(0);
        }
        printf("Enter elements of array: ");
        for(i = 0; i < num; ++i)
        {
                scanf("%d", ptr + i);
                sum += *(ptr + i);
        }
        printf("Sum = %d", sum);
        free(ptr);
        return 0;
}
```

Output

```
Enter number of elements: 4
Enter elements of array: 2
34
12
5
Sum = 53
```

//find maximum number using calloc()

```
#include <stdio.h>

#include <stdlib.h>

int main()

{

        int num, i, *ptr, max = 0;

        printf("Enter number of elements: ");

        scanf("%d", &num);

        ptr = (int*) calloc(num, sizeof(int));

        if(ptr == NULL)

        {

                printf("Error! memory not allocated.");

                exit(0);

        }

        printf("Enter elements of array: ");

        for(i = 0; i < num; ++i)

        {

                scanf("%d", ptr + i);

                if(*(ptr+i)>max)

                max= *(ptr + i);

        }

        printf("Sum = %d", max);

        free(ptr);

        return 0;

}
```

Output

```
Enter number of elements: 5
Enter elements of array: 12
23
45
8
99
Sum = 99
```

//using realloc()

```
#include <stdio.h>
#include <stdlib.h>
int main()
{
        int *ptr, i , n1, n2;
        printf("Enter size of array: ");
        scanf("%d", &n1);
        ptr = (int*) malloc(n1 * sizeof(int));
        printf("Address of previously allocated memory: ");
        for(i = 0; i < n1; ++i)
                printf("%u\t",ptr + i);
        printf("\nEnter new size of array: ");
        scanf("%d", &n2);
        realloc(ptr, n2);
        for(i = 0; i < n2; ++i)
                printf("%u\t", ptr + i);
        return 0;
}
```

Output

```
Enter size of array: 2
Address of previously allocated memory: 246     248
Enter new size of array: 4
246     248     250     252
```

//Matrix multiplication using dynamic memory allocation

```
#include <stdio.h>
#include <stdlib.h>
void main()
{
        int **mat1,**mat2,**mat3,i,j,k,m1,m2,n1,n2;
        printf("Enter the order of matrix 1(m1*n1): ");
        scanf("%d%d", &m1,&n1);
        printf("Enter the order of matrix 2(m2*n2): ");
        scanf("%d%d", &m2,&n2);
        if(m1!=n2)
```

```
{
        printf("Multiplication not possible");
        exit(0);
}
else
{
/* Allocating memory for three matrix rows. */
        mat1 = (int **) malloc(sizeof(int *) * m1);
        mat2 = (int **) malloc(sizeof(int *) * m2);
        mat3 = (int **) malloc(sizeof(int *) * m1);
/* Allocating memory for the col of three matrices. */
for(i=0; i<m1; i++)
        mat1[i] = (int *)malloc(sizeof(int) * n1);
for(i=0; i<m2; i++)
        mat2[i] = (int *)malloc(sizeof(int) * n2);
for(i=0; i<m1; i++)
        mat3[i] = (int *)malloc(sizeof(int) * n2);
printf("Enter the elements of matrix 1: ");
for(i = 0; i < m1; i++)
for(j = 0; j < n1; j++)
{
        printf("mat1[%d][%d]=",i,j);
        scanf("%d",&mat1[i][j]);
}
printf("Enter the elements of matrix 2: ");
for(i = 0; i < m2; i++)
for(j = 0; j < n2; j++)
{
        printf("mat2[%d][%d]=",i,j);
        scanf("%d",&mat2[i][j]);
}
if(mat1==NULL||mat2==NULL||mat3==NULL)
{
        printf("Error! Memory not allocated");
```

```
            exit(0);
        }
        for(i=0;i<m1;i++)
            for(j=0;j<n2;j++)
                {
                 mat3[i][j]=0;
                for(k=0;k<n1;k++)
                        mat3[i][j]+=mat1[i][k]*mat2[k][j];
                }
        printf("Resultant matrix is\n");
         for(i=0;i<m1;i++)
            for(j=0;j<m2;j++)
            {
                printf("mat3[%d][%d]=",i,j);
                printf("%d\n",mat3[i][j]);
            }
            }
                printf("\n");
    }
```

Output

```
Enter the order of matrix 1(m1*n1): 2
2
Enter the order of matrix 2(m2*n2): 2
2
Enter the elements of matrix 1: mat1[0][0]=1
mat1[0][1]=2
mat1[1][0]=1
mat1[1][1]=2
Enter the elements of matrix 2: mat2[0][0]=1
mat2[0][1]=3
mat2[1][0]=3
mat2[1][1]=1
Resultant matrix is
mat3[0][0]=7
mat3[0][1]=5
mat3[1][0]=7
mat3[1][1]=5
```

5.10. Typedef

Typedef is a keyword used in C to give a new name to any previously defined data type. It gives synonyms or aliases to data types. For example,

```
typedef unsigned int integer;
```

Where the type 'unsigned int' can be named as 'integer' and can be accessed as follows.

integer a,b; //the term unsigned int is replaced by integer.

Where a and b are of type unsigned integers.

Similarly in structure, typedef can be used to name a user defined data type. Consider the example program below.

```
#include <stdio.h>
#include <string.h>
typedef struct Books {
      char title[50];
      char author[50];
      char subject[100];
      char book_id[20];
      int publish_year;
} Book;
int main( ) {
      Book book;
      strcpy( book.title, "C Programming");
      strcpy( book.author, "Rajeswari");
      strcpy( book.subject, "C Programming Tutorial");
      strcpy(book.book_id,"BK1210");
      book.publish_year=2017;
      printf( "Book title : %s\n", book.title);
      printf( "Book author : %s\n", book.author);
      printf( "Book subject : %s\n", book.subject);
      printf( "Book book id : %s\n", book.book_id);
      printf( "Book book published year : %d\n", book.publish_year);
      return 0;
}
```

Output

```
Book title : C Programming
Book author : Rajeswari
Book subject : C Programming Tutorial
Book book id : BK1210
Book book published year : 2017
```

In the above example, the user defined data type 'struct Books' is named as 'Book'.

So, the variables for the structure is declared as

Book book;

Instead of

Struct Books book;

Typedef	#define
It is performed by the compiler.	It is processed by the preprocessor
It can give symbolic names to predefined data type only.	It can define values as well.
Ex: typedef unsigned char letter;	Ex: #define TRUE 1

Table 5.5: Difference between typedef and #define

5.11. Introduction to Data Structure

Definitions

- A Data structure represents the logical relationship that exists between individual elements of data to carry out certain task.
- A Data Structure defines a way of organizing all data items that consider not only the elements stored but also stores the relationship between the elements.

Why do you need data structure?

Data structure allows you to achieve an important goal – Component Reuse. Component reuse says once each data structure has been implemented, it can be used over and over again in various applications.

5.11.1. Classification of Data Structure

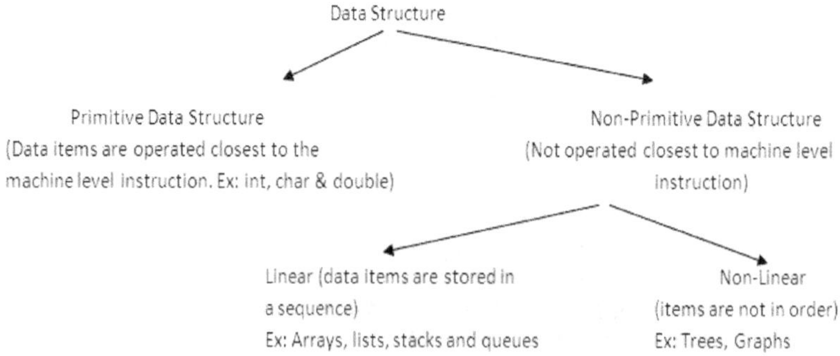

5.11.2. ADT

ADT stands for Abstract Data Type. ADT is a mathematical specification whose behavior is given by a set of operations and set of values. It gives you only the set of operations to be performed and not how it can be implemented. It is called "abstract" since it gives an implementation independent view.

Example:

```
//to check empty condition
int isempty(struct node *head)
{
  if(head==NULL)
  return 0; //list is empty
  else
  return 1; //list contains elements
}
```

5.12. List

A list is a ordered sequence of elements $a_1,a_2...a_{n-1},a_n$. The elements of the list are all of same type. The operations performed on a list are

- Creation
- Insertion
  - Insert first
  - Insert middle
  - Insert last
- Deletion
  - Delete first
  - Delete middle
  - Delete last
- Search
- Find-previous, next, first, last, kth.
- Isempty
- Islast
- Display
- Count

5.12.1. Implementation of List

- Array implementation
- Linked list implementation
- Cursor based implementation

Now let me explain the linked list type of implementation in detail.

5.12.2. Types of Linked List

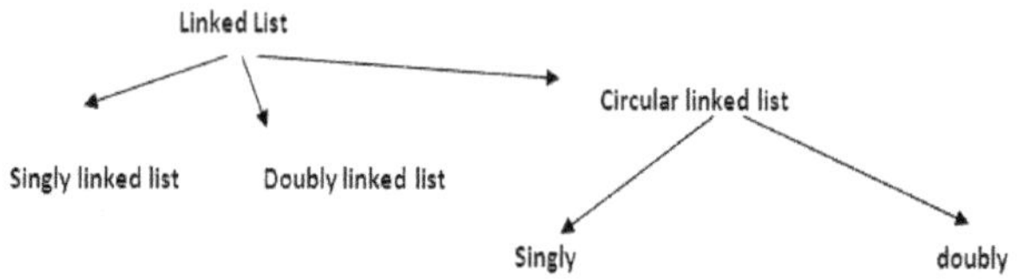

5.13. Singly Linked List

Linked list is a collection of nodes or structures. Each element in a list is a Node. In singly linked list, each node contains two fields in which first one stores the data or content and the second field contains the pointer or reference to the next node in the list. The first node is called head. It is called singly linked list as each node contains only single link to the next node.

General Representation

Data field	Link/next/address field

Difference between Array and Linked List

Array	Linked List
Array is a contiguous static memory allocation where the size of the array should be fixed.	Linked list has dynamic memory size and involves dynamic memory allocation
Inserting a new element in an array of elements is expensive.	Ease of insertion and deletion
The elements can be accessed randomly. Binary search can be done.	Random access is not possible. Elements should be accessed sequentially from the first node. Binary search can't be performed.

Table 5.6: Difference between Array and Linked List

Procedure for the creation of a node

1. Define a structure with two fields-data and next pointer.
2. Each node can be created as follows.
   2.1. Allocation of memory for a node
   2.2. Assign the data
   2.3. Assign the link

3. Repeat step 2 for n nodes and assign the last nodes next pointer to NULL to represent the end of the list.

ADT for singly linked list

```
//structure definition
struct node
{
 int data;
 struct node *next;
}*head;
//creation of a node
void create(struct node *head, int num)
{
  struct node *p;
  head=(struct node*)malloc(sizeof(struct node));
  head->data=num;
  head->next=NULL;
  p=head;
  scanf("%d",&num);
  do
  {
        p->next=(struct node*)malloc(sizeof(struct node));
        p=p->next;
        p->data=num;
        scanf("%d",&num);
  }while(num!=0);
  p->next=NULL:
}
```

Initially, head is NULL. Now, as per the create ADT above a list is created. Head node is first created and it is also named as p. p is used for traversal in the list when it has more than one element.

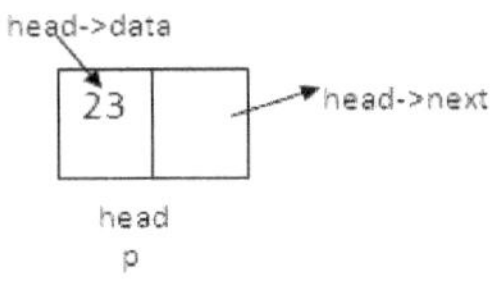

Now, the elements are added to the head in the list and the last node's next pointer is assigned NULL to denote the end of the list.

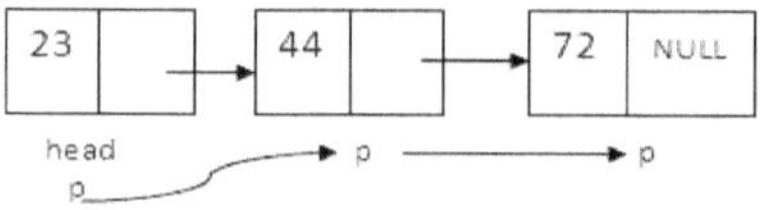

//insertion of a node

```
void insertfirst(struct node *head, int num)
{
  struct node *newnode;
  newnode=(struct node*)malloc(sizeof(struct node));
  newnode->data=num;
  newnode->next=head;
  head=newnode;
}
void insertmiddle(struct node *head, int num, int pos)
{
  struct node *newnode,*temp;
  temp=head;
  while(temp->data!=pos)
          temp=temp->next;
  newnode=(struct node*)malloc(sizeof(struct node));
  newnode->data=num;
  newnode->next=temp->next;
  temp->next=newnode;
}
void insertlast(struct node *head, int num)
{
  struct node *newnode,*temp;
  temp=head;
  while(temp->next!=NULL)
          temp=temp->next;
  newnode=(struct node*)malloc(sizeof(struct node));
  newnode->data=num;
```

```
    temp->next=newnode;
    newnode->next=NULL;
}
```

Insertion is carried out in the list created above. A node can be inserted in the beginning by moving the head pointer to the newly created node.

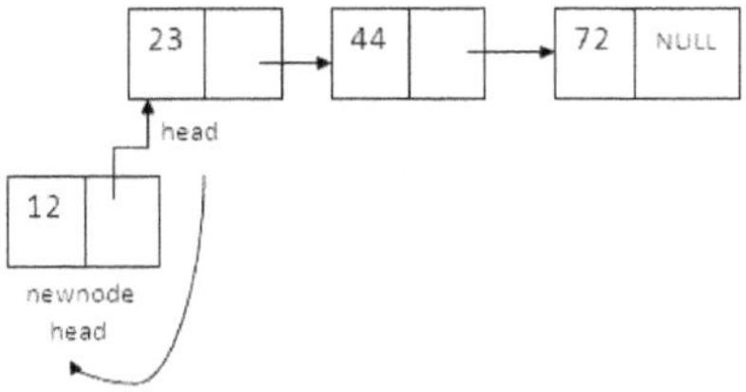

A node can be inserted at any position by getting the value after which it can be inserted. In the above example if you want to insert a node after 23, then it is done by shifting the pointer as shown in the diagram below. The values at the top of the nodes are dummy addresses given to make better understanding of the concept.

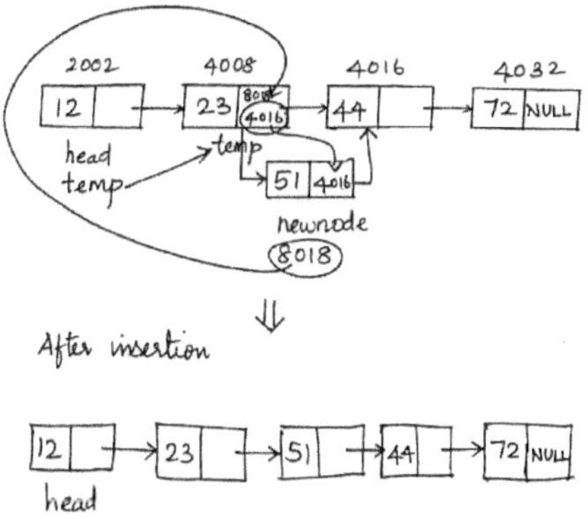

A node can be inserted at the last by shifting the NULL values to the newnode and the next pointer of the last node to newnode.

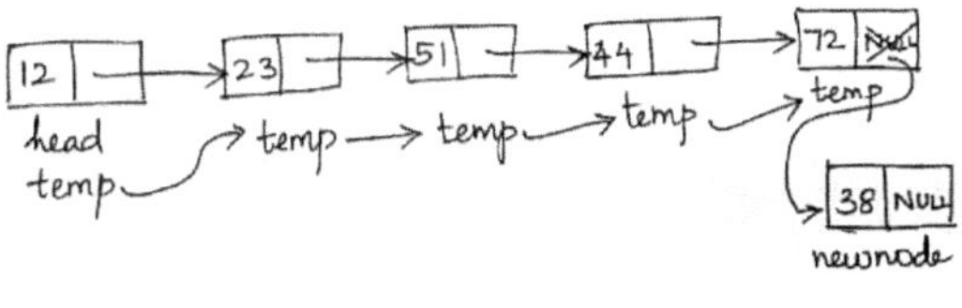

//deletion of a node

```
void deletefirst(struct node *head)
{
  struct node *temp;
  temp=head;
  temp->next=head;
  free(temp);
}
void deletemiddle(struct node *head, int value)
{
  struct node *temp,*t;
  temp=head;
  while(temp->data!=value)
  {
        t=temp;
        temp=temp->next;
  }
  t->next=temp->next;
  free(temp);
}
void deletelast(struct node *head)
{
  struct node *temp,*t;
  temp=head;
  while(temp->next!=NULL)
  {
        t=temp;
        temp=temp->next;
  }
  t->next=NULL;
  free(temp);
}
```

Now, the last updated list contains -12,23,51,44,72 and 38. Deletion can be performed by adjusting the pointers as shown below.

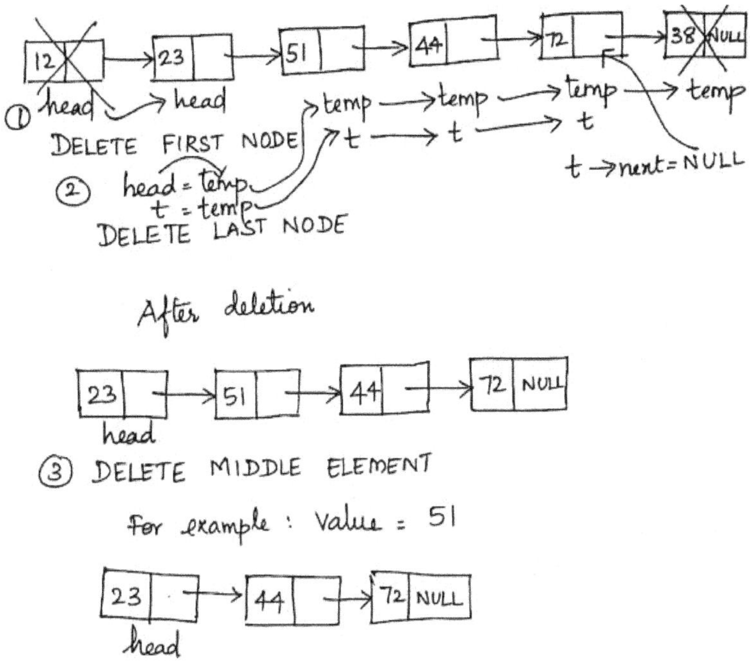

//search a value in the list

```
int search(struct node *head,int value)
{
    struct node *temp;
    int flag=0;
    temp=head;
    while(temp->next!=NULL)
    {
        If(temp->data==value)
        return 1;
        temp=temp->next;
    }
  if(flag==0)
  return 0; //value not found
}
```

//To count the elements in the list

```
int count(struct node *head)
{
  int count=0;
  struct node *temp;
  temp=head;
  while(temp->next!=NULL)
  {
          count++;
          temp=temp->next;
  }
  return count;
}
```

//to check empty condition

```
int isempty(struct node *head)
{
  if(head==NULL)
  return 0; //list is empty
  else
  return 1; //list contains elements
}
```

//To display the entire elements of the list in order

```
void display(struct node *head)
{
  struct node *temp;
  temp=head;
  while(temp->next!=NULL)
  {
          printf("%d",temp->data);
          temp=temp->next;
  }
  printf("%d",temp->data);
}
```

Example Programs

//Implement singly linked list

```
#include<stdio.h>
#include<conio.h>
void insert(int);
void modify(int,int);
void del(int);
void disp();
struct node *find(int);
struct node *findprev(int);
struct node
{
int data;
struct node *next;
}*head=NULL;
void main()
{
int ch,n,a,b;
clrscr();
printf("1.insert2.delete3.modify4.disp 5.exit");
do
{
printf("enter choice");
scanf("%d",&ch);
switch(ch)
{
 case 1:
printf("entr no to insert");
scanf("%d",&n);
insert(n);
break;
case 2:
printf("enter no to delete");
scanf("%d",&n);
```

```
del(n);
break;
case 3:
printf("enter no to modify");
scanf("%d",&a);
printf("enter new numb");
scanf("%d",&b);
modify(a,b);
break;
case 4:
disp();
break;
case 5:
exit(0);
default:
printf("enter valid choice");
}
}while(ch!=6);
}
void insert(int n)
{
int ch,a,b;
struct node *x,*y;
x=(struct node *)malloc(sizeof(struct node));
x->data=n;
if(head==NULL)
{
head=x;
x->next=NULL;
}
else
{
printf("insert at 1.first 2.end 3.inbetween");
scanf("%d",&ch);
```

```
switch(ch)
{
case 1:
x->next=head;
head=x;
break;
case 2:
y=head;
while(y->next!=NULL)
y=y->next;
y->next=x;
x->next=NULL;
break;
case 3:
printf("enter prev element");
scanf("%d",&a);
y=find(a);
x->next=y->next;
y->next=x;
break;
default:
printf("enter valid choice");
}
}
}
void disp()
{ struct node *x;
x=head;
while(x!=NULL)
{
printf("\n%d",x->data);
x=x->next;
}
}
```

```
struct node *find(int q)
{
struct node *x;
x=head;
while(x!=NULL&&x->data!=q)
x=x->next;
return(x);
}
void del(int n)
{
struct node *x,*y;
x=head;
if(x->data==n)
{
head=x->next;
free(x);
}
else
{
x=find(n);
y=findprev(n);
y->next=x->next;
free(x);
}
}
struct node *findprev(int n)
{
struct node *x;
x=head;
while(x->next!=NULL&&x->next->data!=n)
x=x->next;
return(x);
}
```

```
void modify(int a,int b)
{
struct node *x;
x=find(a);
x->data=b;
}
```

Output:

```
1.insert
2.delete
3.modify
4.display
5.exit
Enter choice 1
Enter no to insert
5
Enter choice 1
Enter no to insert
4
Insert at 1.first 2.end 3.inbetween
1
Enter choice 1
Enter no to insert
6
Insert at 1.first 2.end 3.inbetween
3
Enter previous element
5
Enter choice 1
Enter no to insert
7
Insert at 1.first 2.end 3.inbetween
2
Enter choice 4
4
```

5

6

7

Enter choice1

Enter no to insert

2

Insert at 1.first 2.end 3.inbetween

3

Enter previous element

5

Enter choice4

4

5

2

6

7

Enter choice2

Enter no to delete

4

Enter choice4

5

2

6

7

Enter choice2

Enter no to delete

7

Enter choice4

5

2

6

Enter choice3

Enter no to modify

6

```
Enter new numb
8
Enter choice4
5
2
8
```

//display student details using singly linked list

```
#include<stdio.h>
#include<stdlib.h>
#include<conio.h>
struct node
{
int reg_no, Aggregate;
char name[30];
struct node *next;
};
typedef struct node* List;
typedef struct node* Position;
void create(List);
void display(List start);
int main()
{
List start=(Position)calloc(1,sizeof(struct node));
create(start);
printf("Students above 8 Aggregate\n");
display(start);
getch();
return 0;
}
void create(List start)
{
int no;
```

```
printf("Enter no. of students: ");
scanf("%d",&no);
while(no--)
{
printf("Enter name: ");
scanf("%s",start->name);
printf("Enter register number: ");
scanf("%d",&(start->reg_no));
printf("Enter Aggregate: ");
scanf("%d",&(start->Aggregate));
if(no != 0)
{
start->next=(Position)calloc(1,sizeof(struct node));
start=start->next;
}
}
start->next=NULL;
}
void display(List start)
{
while(start != NULL)
{
if(start->Aggregate > 8)
{
printf("Name: %s",start->name);
printf(" register number: %d",start->reg_no);
printf(" Aggregate: %d\n",start->Aggregate);
}
start=start->next;
}
}
```

Output:

```
Enter no. of students: 4
Enter name: Jack
Enter register number: 101
Enter Aggregate: 7
Enter name: Jim
Enter register number: 102
Enter Aggregate: 9
Enter name: Tim
Enter register number: 103
Enter Aggregate: 9
Enter name: Sachin
Enter register number: 104
Enter Aggregate: 5
Students above 8 Aggregate
Name: Jim register number: 102 Aggregate: 9
Name: Tim register number: 103 Aggregate: 9
```

//string operations using singly linked list

```
#include<stdio.h>
#include<stdlib.h>
struct node{
char c;
struct node *next;
};
typedef struct node* List;
typedef struct node* Position;
List create();
void concat(List X,List Y);
int str_length(List X);
void display(List X);
void findchar(List X,List Y);
int main()
{
List X, Y;
X=create();
Y=create();
printf("\nThe first string is : ");
display(X);
printf("\nThe second string is : ");
display(Y);
findchar(X,Y);
```

```
printf("First string length = %d Second String length = %d",
str_length(X) , str_length(Y));
concat(X,Y);
printf("\nthe concat string is: ");
display(X);
getch();
return 0;
}
List create()
{
int i;
char str[100];
Position temp=(List)malloc(sizeof(struct node)), X;
X=temp;
printf("\nEnter string: ");
scanf("%s",str);
for(i=0;str[i]!='\0';i++)
{
temp->c=str[i];
temp->next=(List)malloc(sizeof(struct node));
temp=temp->next;
}
temp->c='\0';
temp->next=NULL;
return X;
}
void concat(List X,List Y)
{
List z=X;
while(z->next->c != '\0')
z=z->next;
z->next=Y;
}
```

```
int str_length(List X)
{
int len=0;
while(X->c != '\0')
{
len++;
X=X->next;
}
return len;
}
void display(List X)
{
while(X->c != '\0')
{
printf("%c",X->c);
X=X->next;
}
}
void findchar(List X,List Y)
{
Position temp1=X, temp2;
int flag;
while(temp1->c != '\0')
{
temp2=Y; flag=1;
while(temp2->c != '\0')
{
if(temp1->c == temp2->c)
{
flag=0;
break;
}
temp2=temp2->next;
}
```

```
if(flag == 1)
{
printf("\nThe first character in the string X which does not occur
in string Y is %c\n",temp1->c);
return;
}
temp1=temp1->next;
}
printf("\n no such character found\n");
}
```

Output

```
Enter string: work

Enter string: run

The first string is : work
The second string is : run
The first character in the string X which does not occur in string Y  is w
First string length = 4 Second String length = 3
the concat string is: workrun
```

Exercise

1. **What will be the output of the program?**

```
#include<stdio.h>
int main()
{
  union var
  {
    int a, b;
  };
  union var v;
  v.a=10;
  v.b=20;
  printf("%d\n", v.a);
  return 0;
}
```

2. What will be the output?

```
#include<stdio.h>
int main()
{
    struct value1
    {
        int bit1;
        float bit3;
        int bit4;
    }bit1;
    union value2
    {
        int bit1;
        float bit3;
        int bit4;
    }bit2;
    printf("%d\n", sizeof(bit1));
    printf("%d\n", sizeof(bit2));
    return 0;
}
```

3. Find the output

```
#include<stdio.h>
#include<stdlib.h>
int main()
{
  int *p;
  p = (int *)malloc(20);
  printf("%d\n", sizeof(p));
  free(p);
  return 0;
}
```

4. **Assume integer is 2 bytes wide. How many bytes will be allocated for the following code?**

```
#include<stdio.h>
#include<stdlib.h>
#define MAXROW 3
#define MAXCOL 4
int main()
{
  int (*p)[MAXCOL];
  p = (int (*) [MAXCOL])malloc(MAXROW *sizeof(*p));
  return 0;
}
```

5. **Point out the error in the program**

```
#include<stdio.h>
int main()
{
  int i;
  #if A
    printf("Enter any number:");
    scanf("%d", &i);
  #elif B
    printf("The number is odd");
  return 0;
}
```

UNIT VI

FILE PROCESSING

6.1. Why Files?

It is difficult to manage large volume of data by main memory (volatile), after the programs are executed, the data will be lost because they are stored in the temporary variables and arrays. Therefore it is necessary to store our data permanently in some place. Files are the solution for the permanent retention of data and it is viewed as a stream of characters. In C language, files are stored inside the disk or secondary storage devices, so that the data can be stored permanently and retrieved when required.

6.2. Definition

A file is a collection or group of related records, placed on the disk or secondary storage devices.

A record is the collection or group of related fields, Use structure or class to represent the record.

A Field is the group of characters which contains the actual data

Eg. employee(name, id, age, designation, address)

Here the employee record has 5 fields, and each field can have the meaningful values. The name field has the value nala, id field has the value 11, age field has the value 32, designation field has the value lecturer, and address field has the value puzhal

6.3. Types of Files

1. Text Files

It consists of text related information such as special symbols, alphabets and digits. It stores the ASCII value of the characters into the file and uses only 7 bits for character and last bit(8th bit) has 0. Text files are easily readable. Each text file should be properly saved with extensions such as, .txt, .c, etc

2. Binary Files

It is the combination of all type of data such as text, image, audio, video, etc. It stores all complex type data and uses entire byte(8 bits) to store the information. Binary files are not in a readable format. It can be saved with .mp3, .doc, etc depending on the type of data.

Note: Text file stores the ASCII values into the file that in turn called as binary file. Therefore all text files are also called binary but reverse case is not true

Difference between Text File and Binary File

Text File	Binary File
It consists of text related information such as special symbols, alphabets and digits	It contains custom data(text, audio, video, images, etc)
Uses only 7 bits for character and last bit(8th bit) has 0	Uses entire byte(8 bits) to store the information
Easily readable	Unreadable for humans
Time taken to access data is more	Takes less time to access the data
Handling of newline(end of line) character occupies an extra space in memory since it is converted into carriage return while writing into the disk and converted back into newline while reading. Therefore text files occupies more space compared to binary files	It requires less space compared to text file and there are no conversions taken place
It uses a special character to denote the EOF(end of file), that special character is stored with the ASCII 26 into the file, as soon as it is encountered in the file, immediately it returns EOF to the program	It does not require any special character to denote the end of file
Each character occupies 1 byte(but only 7 bits) in text file. For example, the integer value 5040 will occupy 2 bytes in the memory but 5 bytes in the text files	Here the integer value 5040 occupies the same 2 bytes in both memory and the binary file

Table 6.1: Difference between Text File and Binary File

6.4. Files and Streams

In C language each file is viewed as a sequential stream of bytes and ends with an EOF. Always a stream is associated with the file process, if a file opens, its associated stream is also opened automatically. Whenever a program starts its execution, the following files and their associated streams are also opened automatically:

1. Standard Input (stdin)
2. Standard Output (stdout)
3. Standard Error (stderr)

Streams

It is also a file or any physical device such as monitor or printer or keyboard. It provides communication between the programs and the files. Reading characters from the file and writing characters into the file are also said to be sequence of streams. It allows the user to access any files conveniently and efficiently. Every file object contains the stream information such as the error status, EOF status, buffer status and the current position details. File functions in 'C'

Category	File Function	Prototype	Role
File access	fopen()	FILE *fopen(const char* filename, const char *mode);	opens a file
	fclose()	int fclose(*stream);	closes a file
Unformatted input/output	fgetc()	int fgetc(*stream);	reads character from a file stream
	fputc()	int fputc(int ch, FILE *stream);	writes character to a file stream
	fgets()	char *fgets(char *str, int count, FILE *stream);	reads strings from a file stream
	fputs()	int fputs(const char *str, FILE *stream);	writes string into a file stream
Formatted input/output	fscanf()	int fscanf(FILE *stream, const char *format, ...);	Reads the data from the file stream
	fprintf()	int fprintf(FILE *stream, const char *format, ...)	Writes data into the file stream
Block Input/output	fread()	int fread(void *buffer, int size, int count, FILE *stream);	reads the no of objects stored from a file. Applicable for binary file
	fwrite()	int fwrite(const void *buffer, int size, int count, FILE *stream);	writes specified no of objects to a file. Applicable for binary file
File positioning	ftell()	long ftell(FILE *stream);	returns the current file position indicator
	fseek()	int fseek(FILE *stream, long offset, int origin);	moves the file position indicator to a specific location in a file
	rewind()	void rewind(FILE *stream);	moves the file position indicator to the beginning of the file
Error handling	feof()	int feof(FILE *stream);	checks for the end-of-file
	ferror()	int ferror(FILE *stream);	checks for a file error
Operations on files	remove()	int remove(const char *fname);	erases a file
	rename()	int rename(const char *old_filename, const char *new_f ilename);	renames a file
File handling functions	putw()	int putw(int number, FILE *fp);	write an integer value into a file
	getw()	int getw(FILE *fp);	read integer value from a file

Table 6.2: File Functions in C

6.4.1. File Declaration

To declare a file, use FILE structure as the base ,which is the predefined structure available in stdio.h and then declare a file variable as pointer to it.

Prototype

FILE *fp; // fp is the file pointer that points to a FILE structure.

6.4.2. File Pointer

It is a pointer to a FILE structure and contains the following file information

1. file name
2. its current position
3. status about read and write process
4. error and EOF status.

6.5. File Operations (for Both Text and Binary Files)

1. Open the file
2. Read from or Write into the file
3. Close the file

Opening a File

6.5.1. fopen()

The **fopen()** function opens the specified file name in the specified file access mode. The file can be opened either in text or binary mode. if fopen() encounters error at opening the file, returns null pointer otherwise file pointer associated with the file

The prototype for the fopen() function is

FILE *fopen(const char* filename, const char *mode);

"filename" is the pointer to a string of characters. The filename should be valid and also contains a path specification.

"mode" is a pointer to a string and decides the file access mode.

Example

FILE *fp;

fp=fopen("g.txt","r");

Here fopen() opens the "g.txt" file in read mode and returns the file pointer to fp.

File Access Modes

File Access Mode	Description	Action
"r"	Read mode	If file exists start reading, otherwise returns null
"rb"	Read in binary mode	If file exists start reading, otherwise returns null
"w"	Write mode	If file exists content is overwritten, otherwise new file is created
"wb"	Write in binary mode	If file exists content is overwritten, otherwise new file is created
"a"	Append mode	If file exists data is appended at the end of the file, otherwise new file is created to append the data
"ab"	Append in binary mode	If file exists data is appended at the end of the file, otherwise new file is created to append the data
"r+"	Both for reading and writing	If file exists start reading, otherwise returns null
"rb+"	Both for reading and writing in binary mode	If file exists start reading, otherwise returns null
"w+"	Both for writing and reading	If file exists content is overwritten, otherwise new file is created
"wb+"	Both for writing and reading in binary mode	If file exists content is overwritten, otherwise new file is created
"a+"	Both for appending and reading	If file exists data is appended at the end of the file, otherwise new file is created to append the data
"ab+"	Both for appending and reading in binary mode	If file exists data is appended at the end of the file, otherwise new file is created to append the data

Table 6.3: File Access Modes

Difference between Write and Append Mode

Write mode	Append mode
If an existing file is opened in the write mode, its contents are overwritten.	If an existing file is opened in the append mode, pointer is moved to end of the file and starts adding or appending data at the end. It does not overwrite the already existing data
FILE *fp; fp=fopen("g.txt", "w");	FILE *fp; fp=fopen("g.txt", "a");

Table 6.4: Difference between Write and Append Mode

Closing the File

6.5.2. fclose()

fclose(): It closes the given file stream. If the file is closed successfully, returns 0 otherwise EOF

The prototype for closing the file is

int fclose(FILE *stream);

"stream" file pointer closes the file //where stream is the file pointer closes the file

Example:

FILE *fp;

fp=fopen("g.txt","r");

fclose(fp); // fp closes the file g.txt

Reading from and writing into the file

Reading from and writing to a text file

For reading and writing in a text file, use the functions fprintf() and fscanf(). They are similar to

printf() and scanf() but requires a pointer to the FILE structure.

6.5.3. fprintf()

fprintf(): It writes the formatted data to the file through file pointer. If the string is written successfully into the file returns positive otherwise a negative number

int fprintf(FILE *stream, const char *format, ...)

"stream" file pointer pointing to the given file

"format" it's a string type contains the data to be written to the file and the format specifiers.

Example

fprintf(fp,"%s%d",m,n); // fp is the file pointer and m is the string variable and n is the integer variable. Any format specifiers can be used like printf.

6.5.4. *fscanf()*

fscanf(): It reads formatted data from the file through the file pointer. It data is read successfully returns the data otherwise EOF.

int fscanf(*stream, const char *format, ...);

"stream" file pointer pointing to the given file

"format" it's a string type contains the data read from the file along with the format specifiers

Example

fscanf(fp,"%d",&n); // fp is the file pointer and n is the integer variable. Any format specifiers can be used like scanf().

Example: To read a number from the text file using fscanf() and print it on the screen

First save a number into the text file d.txt, say

12

```
#include<stdio.h>
#include<conio.h>
void main()
{
int n;
FILE *fp;
clrscr();
if ((fp = fopen("d.txt","r")) == NULL)  //fp is the file pointer pointing to the text file "d.txt"
{
printf("file Open error");
exit(1); // if file does not exists returns NULL.
}
fscanf(fp,"%d", &n);        //with the help of fscanf() the value is read from the text file "d.txt"
printf("The value of n read from file is=%d", n);
fclose(fp);
getch();
}
```

Output

The value of n read from file is=12

Example: To write a number into the text file using fprintf()

```
#include<stdio.h>
#include<conio.h>
void main()
{
int n;
FILE *fp;
clrscr();
fp = fopen("b3.txt","w"); //fp is the file pointer pointing to the text file "b3.txt"
if(fp== NULL)
{
printf("no file");
exit(1);
}
printf("enter the number to be written: ");
scanf("%d",&n);
fprintf(fp,"%d",n); //value is written to the file using fprintf()
fclose(fp);
getch();
}
```

Output

enter the number to be written:13

Open the file b3.txt and view the number

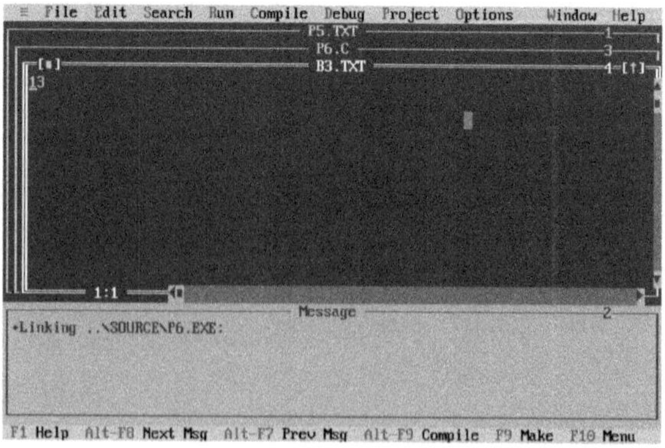

Reading and Writing to a Binary File

Functions fread() and fwrite() are used for reading from and writing to a Binary file

Writing to a Binary File

6.5.5. fwrite()

fwrite(): To write data into the binary file. It consists of 4 arguments, the data to be written, size of the data, number of data to be written and the file pointer. It returns the number of data successfully written otherwise error. If size is 0, it returns 0.

int fwrite(const void *buffer, int size, int count, FILE *stream);

"**buffer**" contains the data to be written

"**size**" represents the size of the data

"**count**" the number of data

"**stream**" file pointer points to the output file

Example

fwrite(&e, sizeof(struct employee),1,fp); //it writes data into the file f.dat

e contains the employee data, size of employee data, number of employee records to write, file pointer

Reading from a Binary File

6.5.6. fread()

fread(): To read data from the binary file. It consists of 4 arguments, the data to be read and stored in the buffer in the same order, size of the data, number of data to be read and the file pointer. It returns the number of data successfully read otherwise error. If size is 0, it returns 0.

int fread(void *buffer, int size, int count, FILE *stream);

"**buffer**" contains the data to be read and stored in the order in it read the data

"**size**" represents the size of the data

"**count**" the number of data

"**stream**" file pointer points to the input file

Example

fread(&e,sizeof(struct employee),1,fp);   //it reads data from the file f.dat

e contains the employee data, size of employee data, number of employee records to read, file pointer

Example: Program to write and read of an employee using fwrite() and fread()

```
#include<stdio.h>
#include<conio.h>
struct employee
{
int eid;
char *ename;
char *eaddress;
};
void main()
{
int i;
struct employee e;
FILE *fp;
clrscr();
if ((fp=fopen("f.dat","wb")) == NULL) //file pointer fp points to the f.dat file in write binary
mode
{
printf("file Error");
exit(1);
}
printf("enter employee details\n");
scanf("%d", &e.eid);
scanf("%s",e.ename);
scanf("%s",e.eaddress);
fwrite(&e, sizeof(struct employee),1,fp); //it writes data into the file f.dat
fread(&e,sizeof(struct employee),1,fp);    //it reads data from the file f.dat
printf("\nemployee id is: %d\nemployee name is: %s\nemployee address is:
%s\n",e.eid,e.ename,e.eaddress);
fclose(fp);
getch();
}
```

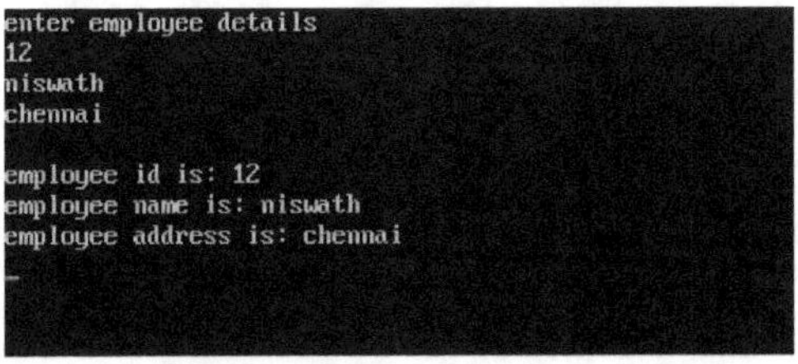

Note: Binary file can contain all combinations of data, .dat is the generalized file to store all type of data

Example: Program to write and read the details of n employees using fwrite() and fread()

```
#include<stdio.h>
#include<conio.h>
struct employee
{
int eid;
char *ename;
};
void main()
{
int i;
struct employee e[4];
FILE *fp;
clrscr();
if ((fp=fopen("g.txt","wb")) == NULL){
printf("file Error");
exit(1);
}
printf("enter employee details\n");
for(i=1; i<5;i++)
{
printf("enter employee id: ");
scanf("%d", &e[i].eid);
printf("enter employee name: ");
scanf("%s",e[i].ename);
```

```
fwrite(&e, sizeof(struct employee),1,fp); //it writes employee record one by one into the file
}
fp=fopen("g.txt","rb");
for(i=1;i<5;i++)
{
fread(&e,sizeof(struct employee),1,fp); //it reads employee record one by one from the file
printf("\nemployee id is: %d\nemployee name is: %s\n",e[i].eid,e[i].ename);
}
fclose(fp);
getch();
}
```

```
enter employee details
enter employee id: 1
enter employee name: nala
enter employee id: 2
enter employee name: kala
enter employee id: 3
enter employee name: niswath
enter employee id: 4
enter employee name: parimelazhagan

employee id is: 1
employee name is: nala

employee id is: 2
employee name is: kala

employee id is: 3
employee name is: niswath

employee id is: 4
employee name is: parimelazhagan
```

6.5.7. fgets()

fgets(): It reads the string of characters from the input file and stores it in a string. It has three arguments, a string to read and stores the characters, length of the string and the file pointer.It returns the string on success and null on failure. Always the string is null terminated.

char *fgets(char *str, int count, FILE *stream);

"str" reads and stores the characters

"count" length of the string

"stream" file pointer points to the input file

Example

fgets(book,80,fp); //book is the string reads and stores the set of characters, 80 the length of the string, fp is the file pointer

6.5.8. fputs()

fputs(): It writes the string of characters into the output file. It has two arguments, a string contains the characters to be written and the file pointer. It returns the positive integer on success and EOF on failure. Always the string is null terminated.

int fputs(const char *str, FILE *stream);

"str" contains the string to be written

"stream" file pointer points to the output file

Example

fputs(book,fp);   //writes book data into the file

book is a string has the data to be written, fp is the file pointer

Example: Program to write and read the book names using fputs() and fgets()

```
#include<stdio.h>
#include<conio.h>
void main()
{
FILE *fp;
char book[80];
clrscr();
fp=fopen("a.txt", "w+"); // a.txt is opened both for writing and reading
printf("Enter book names into file (type end to stop)\n");
gets(book);
while(strcmp(book, "end")!=0)
{
fputs(book,fp);   //writes book name one by one into the file
fputs("\n",fp);
gets(book);
} //fp is pointing to the last record
rewind(fp); //it brings back fp to the beginning of the file
printf("Reading data from file\n");
fgets(book,80,fp);  //reads first book data from the file
while(feof(fp)==0) //feof() It checks whether the EOF is reached or not.
{
```

```
puts(book);            //prints the book data one by one
fgets(book,80,fp);  //reads next next book data from the file
}
fclose(fp); // to close the file
getch();
}
```

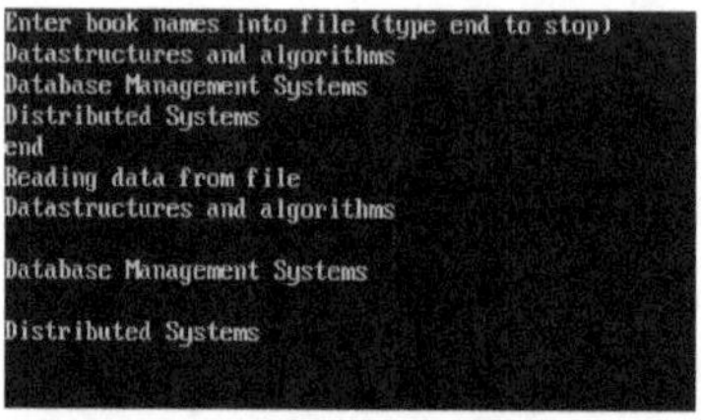

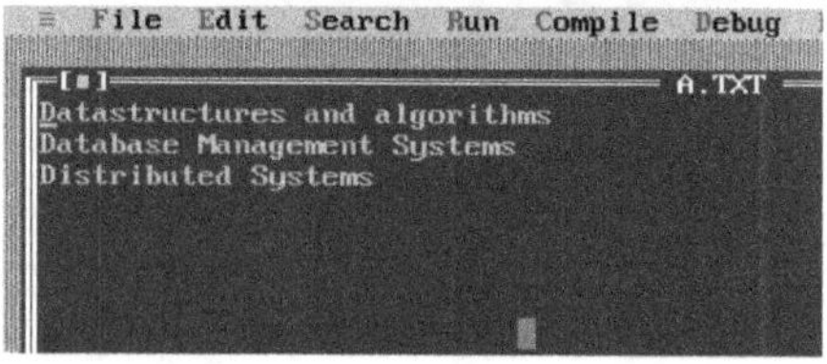

Example: Program to write and read a string using fputs() and fgets()

```
#include<stdio.h>
#include<string.h>
#include<conio.h>
void main( )
{
FILE *fp ;
char college[50];
clrscr();
fp = fopen("z.txt", "w+") ;
if ( fp == NULL )
{
printf( "file error" ) ;
exit(1);
}
printf("enter college name\n");
while ( strlen ( gets( college ) ) > 0 )
```

```
fputs(college, fp) ; // writes college data into the file
rewind(fp);          // it takes fp to the beginning of the file
while( fgets ( college, 50, fp ) != NULL ) // reads the college data from the file
printf( "%s" , college ) ;
fclose(fp) ;     //closes the file
getch();
}
```

Output

```
enter college name
velammal engg college
velammal engg college
```

open z.txt and find the string

```
velammal engg college
```

6.5.9. fgetc()

fgetc(): It reads the character one by one from the input file. It has only one argument the file pointer. It returns character on success EOF on failure

int fgetc(FILE *stream);

"stream" File pointer used to read the character from the input file

Example

```
char c = fgetc(fp);
```

fp reads single character and stores it into a variable c

6.5.10. fputc()

fputc(): It writes the character one by one into the output file. It has two arguments, the character to be written and the file pointer. It returns character on successful written, EOF on failure

int fputc(int ch, FILE *stream);

"ch" holds single character at a time to write

"stream" file pointer points to the output file

Example

```
for (i = 0; string1[i]!='\0'; i++)
fputc(string1[i], fp); //string1[i] has one character at a time and writes it into the file
```

Example: Program to read the character one by one from the file using fgetc() and print it on the screen

```
#include<stdio.h>
#include<conio.h>
void main ()
{
FILE *fp;
char ch;
clrscr();
fp = fopen("vn.txt","r");
if ( fp == NULL )
{
printf( "file error" ) ;
exit(1);
}
do
{
ch = fgetc(fp); // reads single character at a time
if (feof(fp))
break ;
printf("%c", ch);
}while(1);
fclose(fp); //closes the file
getch();
}
```

In vn.txt file, we have the following content

Velammal

Output

Velammal

Example: Program to write characters one by one using fputc() and print it on the screen

```
#include<stdio.h>
#include<conio.h>
void main()
{
int i = 0;
FILE *fp;
char string1[]="C Programming", string2[15];
clrscr();
fp= fopen("sd.txt","w");
if ( fp == NULL )
{
printf( "file error" ) ;
exit(1);
}
for (i = 0; string1[i]!='\0'; i++)
fputc(string1[i], fp); //writes single character at a time into the output file
fclose(fp);
fp = fopen("sd.txt","r");
fgets(string2,15,fp);  //it reads the entire string from the file and stores it into string2
printf("%s", string2);
fclose(fp); //closes the file
getch();
}
```

Output:

C Programming

Open the file sd.txt and find the string

C Programming

Example: Program to append data into the empty file

```
#include <stdio.h>

#include <conio.h>

#include <stdlib.h>

void main()

{

FILE *fp;

char string1[10] = {"\nvelammal"};

clrscr();

fp= fopen("kb.txt", "a");

fputs("\nwelcome to",fp);

fputs(string1,fp);

fclose(fp);

getch();

}
```

Here the kb.txt file is empty and opened in append mode, initially fp will be pointing to the beginning, after append, it starts adding at the end, again if you execute the file, the data is added at the end.

Output:

```
-

welcome to

velammal
```

Execute the file again you will get the following output

```
-

welcome to

velammal

welcome to

velammal
```

File Positioning Functions

6.5.11. fseek()

fseek(): It moves the file pointer position to the respective location of the file. It takes three arguments, the file pointer, the offset or the displacement and current file pointer position. It returns 0 on success otherwise non-zero. In order to make the file pointer to move to the respective location it uses the following parameters along with the displacement.

1. SEEK_SET: To move the file pointer to beginning of the file
2. SEEK_CUR: To move the file pointer to the specified location of the file
3. SEEK_END: To move the file pointer to the end of the file

int fseek(FILE *stream, long offset, int origin);

"stream" file pointer

"offset" also called displacement, denotes how many position to be moved either in the forward direction(positive value) or in the backward direction(negative value) from the pointer position or the origin. The positive or negative value can be attached with L, represents long integer

"origin" also called pointer position, gets added with the displacement or offset. It can take one of the following

1. SEEK_SET or 0
2. SEEK_CUR or 1
3. SEEK_END or 2

Note: If the file is said to be binary, we can move to exact position with the help of offset and origin. In case of text file either offset should set as zero or we have to use ftell() to get the file position.

Example

1. fseek(fp,2L,0)

fp is the file pointer, 2L is the positive displacement or offset value given(L is the long integer) and 0 represents the origin or the pointer position. Here the pointer position is skipped 2bytes forward from the beginning of the file.

2. fseek(fp,-9L,1)

fp is the file pointer, -9L is the negative displacement or offset value given(L is the long integer) and 1 represents the origin or the pointer position. Here the pointer position is skipped 9bytes backward from the current position of the file.

3. *fseek(fp,6L,1)*

fp is the file pointer, 6L is the positive displacement or offset value given(L is the long integer) and 1 represents the origin or the pointer position.

Here the pointer position is skipped 6bytes forward from the current position of the file.

6.5.12. rewind()

It moves the file pointer to the beginning of the file and returns none.

void rewind(FILE *stream);

"stream" file pointer which points to the beginning of the file

It is similar to fseek(fp, 0, SEEK_SET). Where fp is the file pointer, 0 is the displacement or offset and SEEK_SET represents the beginning of the file.

ie., file position = 0(displacement)+beginning of the file(SEEK_SET)

= beginning of the file

= rewind()

Example

rewind(fp); //move the file pointer fp to the beginning of the file

6.5.13. ftell()

ftell(): It returns the file position of the file. If the file is opened in binary mode, it returns the file position as number of bytes from the beginning of the file. If it is opened in text mode, it should take help from fseek() to tell the bytes. It returns number of bytes on success otherwise EOF

long ftell(FILE *stream);

"stream" holds the file position as number of bytes of the file

Example

fseek(fp, 0, SEEK_END);// makes the fp to reach the end

length1 = ftell(fp); /*always ftell() should work along with fseek(), it can tell number of bytes available in the file only with the help of fseek()*/

length1 is the integer variable to hold the number of bytes of the file

Example: Program to find the number of bytes in the file using ftell()

```
#include<stdio.h>

#include<conio.h>

void main ()

{

FILE *fp;

int length1;

clrscr();

fp = fopen("bb.txt", "r");

if ( fp == NULL )

{

printf( "file error" ) ;

exit(1);

}

fseek(fp, 0, SEEK_END);// makes the fp to reach the end

                    // fseek(fp, 0, 2);  also can be used

length1 = ftell(fp); /*always ftell() should work along with fseek(), it can tell number of bytes

             available in the file only with the help of fseek()*/

fclose(fp);

printf("Size of  the file is = %d\n", length1);

getch();

}
```

bb.txt

velammal

Output

Size of the file is = 8

Example: Program to reverse the string using fseek()

```
#include<stdio.h>
#include<conio.h>
#include<errno.h>
void main()
{
int i;
int length1;
char ch, ch1;
FILE *fp1, *fp2;
clrscr();
if (fp1 = fopen("File1.txt", "r"))
{
fp2 = fopen("File2.txt", "w");
//fp is moved to the last character of the file
fseek(fp1, -1L, 2);
length1=ftell(fp1);
length1++;
for(i=length1;i>=0;i--)
{
ch = fgetc(fp1);
fputc(ch, fp2);
fseek(fp1,-2L,1);  //to move to the previous character
}
printf("\nreverse is done\n");
}
else
{
perror("Error ");
}
fclose(fp1);
fclose(fp2);
getch();
}
```

Save some content in file1.txt, say

cprogramming

Output:

reverse is done

Open file2.txt and find the following

gnimmargorpc

Example: Program to Copy Content of One File into Another File

```
#include<stdio.h>
#include<conio.h>
void main()
{
  FILE *fp1, *fp2;
  char ch;
  int i,length1;
  clrscr();
  if ((fp1 = fopen("File3.txt","r")) == NULL)
  {    printf("\nFile cannot be opened");
       exit(1);
  }
  fp2 = fopen("File4.txt", "w");
  fseek(fp1, 0L, SEEK_END); // to move file pointer to the end of file
  length1 = ftell(fp1);
  fseek(fp1, 0L, SEEK_SET); // to move file pointer to the beginning
  for(i=length1;i>=0;i--)//while (length1)
  {    ch = fgetc(fp1);  // copying character by character
       fputc(ch, fp2);
  }
  fcloseall(); //to close all the file
  getch();
}
```

file3.txt

velammal engineering college

file4.txt

velammal engineering college

Example: Program to merge two files and store it into another existing or new file

```
#include<stdio.h>
#include<conio.h>
void main()
{
  FILE *fp1 = fopen("f1.txt", "r");
  FILE *fp2 = fopen("f2.txt", "r");
  FILE *fp3 = fopen("f3.txt", "a");
  char ch;
  clrscr();
  if (fp1 == NULL || fp2 == NULL || fp3 == NULL)
  {
        printf("file error");
        exit(1);
  }
  while ((ch = fgetc(fp1)) != EOF) // content of file f1 is copied to file f3
  fputc(ch, fp3);
  while ((ch = fgetc(fp2)) != EOF) // content of file f1 is copied to file f3
  fputc(ch, fp3);
  printf("file merge is done successfully\n");
  fcloseall();
 getch();
}
```

In f1.txt, we have

CProgramming

In f2.txt, we have

is really interesting

Output

file merge is done successfully

f3.txt is not created initially so if you open f3.txt, you can find the following string

CProgramming is really interesting

You can also open an existing file, say file3.txt, it has velammal engineering college, now execute the above program you will get the following output

file merge is done successfully

open file3.txt

velammal engineering college CProgramming is really interesting

Example: Program to print the numbers from 0 to 9 . Make use of rewind()

```
#include<stdio.h>
#include<conio.h>
char str[20];
void main()
{
FILE *fp;
char ch,c;
clrscr();
fp = fopen("cc.txt", "w+");
for (ch = '0'; ch <= '9'; ch++)
fputc(ch, fp); //fp is at the end of the character
rewind(fp);  // moves fp to the beginning of the file
fgets(str,20,fp);
printf("%s",str);
fclose(fp);
getch();
}
```

Output

0123456789

Open the file cc.txt and find the following

0123456789

Error Handling Functions

6.5.14. feof()

feof(): It checks whether the end of file is reached or not. It returns zero if the end of file is not reached, otherwise non-zero

int feof(FILE *stream);

"stream" file pointer to check the end of file

ferror(): It checks for file error. It returns zero if the file has no error otherwise non-zero

Checks the given stream for errors.

int ferror(FILE *stream);

"stream" file pointer to check for errors

6.5.15. perror()

perror(): It prints the error message to stderr indicating that an error has occurred recently due to system call. It does not return anything.

void perror(const char *str)

"str" contains a custom message that is printed to stderr

Example: Program to display a string, use feof()

```
#include <stdio.h>
#include<conio.h>
#include <stdlib.h>
void main()
{
FILE* fp = fopen("ee.txt", "r");
int c;
clrscr();
if(!fp) {
perror("No such file exists");
exit(1);
}
while ((c = fgetc(fp)) != EOF)
{
putchar(c);
}
if (ferror(fp))
puts("error ");
else if (feof(fp))
puts("\nEOF reached successfully");
fclose(fp);
getch();
}
```

In ee.txt we have the following content

CProgramming

Output:

CProgramming

EOF reached successfully

Operations on Files

6.5.16. Remove()

remove(): It deletes the file. It returns zero on success otherwise non-zero

int remove(const char *fname);

"fname" contains the file to be deleted

Example: Program to delete a file

```
#include <stdio.h>
#include <string.h>
void main ()
{
int dele;
char ch[40];
FILE *fp;
char file11[] = "hh.txt"; //hh.txt is the empty file assigned to file11
clrscr();
fp = fopen(file11, "w");
fprintf(fp, "%s", "CProgramming");
rewind(fp);
fp = fopen(file11,"r");
fscanf(fp,"%s",ch);
printf("%s",ch);
fclose(fp);
dele = remove(file11); //deletes the file file11
if(dele == 0)
printf("File is successfully deleted");
else
printf("could not delete the file");
getch();
}
```

Output

```
Cprogramming
File is successfully deleted
```

6.5.17. rename()

rename(): It renames the existing file. It takes two arguments, a file pointer to point to the old file and another file pointer to point to the new file. It returns zero on success otherwise non-zero

int rename(const char *old_filename, const char *new_filename);

"old_filename" file pointer points to the string contains the path of the old file name

"new_filename" file pointer points to the string contains the path of the new file name

Example: Program to rename a file

```
#include<stdio.h>
#include<conio.h>
void main ()
{
int k;
char old_filename[] = "cc.txt";
char new_filename[] = "gg.txt";
clrscr();
k = rename(old_filename, new_filename);
if(k == 0)
printf("File is successfully renamed");
else
printf("could not do rename");
getch();
}
```

Initially cc.txt has 0123456789 after rename, cc becomes the gg.txt, if you open cc, you cannot find the content, only gg.txt has the content.

File Handling functions

6.5.18. putw() and getw()

putw() : It writes an integer value to a file. It takes two arguments, a number variable to hold the integer value to write and the file pointer. On success, returns the integer value otherwise EOF

int putw(int number, FILE *fp);

"number" contains the integer value to be written

"fp" file pointer points to the file in which the integer value to be written

Example

putw(i, fp); // the variable i holds the integer value to be written to the file through fp

getw() : It reads an integer value from a file. It takes an argument as file pointer through which the integer value can be read. On success, returns the next integer value otherwise EOF

int getw(FILE *fp);

"fp" file pointer though which an integer can be read

Example

getw(fp); //fp is the file pointer to read the integer value from the file

Example: Program to write and read integers one by one using putw() and getw()

```
#include<stdio.h>
#include<conio.h>
void main()
{
FILE *fp;
int n;
clrscr();
fp=fopen("k.dat", "wb+");
printf("\n*****Writing elements into File*****\n");
printf("\nEnter the first element\n");
scanf("%d",&n);
printf("\nenter the next-next element one by one and zero to stop\n");
while(n!=0)
{
putw(n,fp);     //writes an integer to the file
scanf("%d",&n);  }
rewind(fp);
printf("\n*****Reading Elements from File*****\n");
while((n=getw(fp))!=EOF)  //reads an integer from the file
printf("%d\n",n);
fclose(fp);
getch();
}
```

```
*****Writing elements into File*****

Enter the first element
23

enter the next-next element one by one and zero to stop
24
25
0

*****Reading Elements from File*****
23
24
25
_
```

6.6. File Processing Types

1. Sequential access File
2. Random access file

1. Sequential Access File

In Sequential access file elements are arranged in a sequential manner. Reading the element from the file or writing the element into the file should start from the beginning to the end. It does not allow the user to access or modify or delete any record directly

2. Random Access File

It is also called as direct access since we can read or write any record of any location in the file. Records can be arranged randomly in the file. It allows the user to access, modify and delete any record randomly or directly.

6.6.1. Sequential Access File Processing

In Sequential file access, If we want to modify or delete the last record or in-between record, we have to start reading from the beginning of the file. Therefore it consumes more time to process the requested record. Accessing sequential record is faster when compared to random access due to huge number of seek() operations. Every process should be done in a sequential manner.

It is not suitable for storing huge volume of integer elements. For example say an integer 1123 requires 4bytes to be stored in the sequential file since each integer is considered as the character string. Therefore it is well suited for small text applications. It allows records or elements of different length.

Example program: Finding average of numbers stored in sequential access file

```
#include<stdio.h>
#include<conio.h>
void main()
{
int n,t,sum=0,average;
FILE *fp;
clrscr();
printf("\nenter the no of elements\n");
scanf("%d",&n);
t=n;
fp=fopen("p.dat", "wb+");
printf("\nenter the numbers one by one and zero to stop\n");
scanf("%d",&n);
while(n!=0)
{
putw(n,fp);
scanf("%d",&n);
}
rewind(fp);
printf("Read numbers from file one by one and find sum and average");
while((n=getw(fp))!=EOF)
{
sum = sum+n;
}
average=sum/t;
printf("\nsum of %d numbers = %d",t, sum);
printf("\naverage of %d numbers = %d",t, average);
getch();
}
```

```
enter the no of elements
3

enter the numbers one by one and zero to stop
12
13
14
0
Read numbers from file one by one and find sum and average
sum of 3 numbers = 39
average of 3 numbers = 13
```

Example: Program to write and access the employee records sequentially

```
#include<stdio.h>
#include<conio.h>
struct employee_details
{
int eid;
int age;
char ename[20];
char eaddress[20];
char designation[20];
};
void main()
{
struct employee_details e;
FILE *fp;
int n,i;
clrscr();
fp=fopen("emp1.dat","wb+");
printf("How many records?");
scanf("%d",&n);
printf("Enter %d records:\n",n);
for(i=1;i<=n;i++)
{
```

```
printf("\Enter the details of the Record %d:\n",i);
printf("\nenter eid:");
scanf("%d",&e.eid);
printf("enter age:");
scanf("%d",&e.age);
printf("enter employee name:");
scanf("%s",e.ename);
printf("enter employee address:");
scanf("%s",e.eaddress);
printf("enter employee designation:");
scanf("%s",e.designation);
fwrite(&e,sizeof(e),1,fp);
}
fseek(fp,0,0);
for(i=1;i<=n;i++)
{
printf("\nThe details of the Record %d is\n",i);
fread(&e,sizeof(e),1,fp);
printf("\nThe employee id is:%d",e.eid);
printf("\nThe employee age is:%d",e.age);
printf("\nThe employee name is:%s",e.ename);
printf("\nThe employee address is:%s",e.eaddress);
printf("\nThe employee designation is:%s\n",e.designation);
}
fclose(fp);
getch();
}
```

Output

```
How many records?2
Enter 2 records:
Enter the details of the Record 1:
enter eid:12
```

enter age:32

enter employee name:nalayini

enter employee address:puzhal

enter employee designation:lecturer

Enter the details of the Record 2:

enter eid:13

enter age:45

enter employee name:kala

enter employee address:ana nagar

enter employee designation:professor

The details of the Record 1 is

The employee id is:12

The employee age is:32

The employee name is:nalayini

The employee address is:puzhal

The employee designation is:lecturer

The details of the Record 2 is

The employee id is:13

The employee age is:45

The employee name is:kala

The employee address is:anna nagar

The employee designation is:professor

6.6.2. Random Access File Processing

In Random access file individual records can be accessed or modified or deleted in any order without disturbing or overwriting the existing data. It allows only fixed length records.

Record 1	Record 2	Record 3	Record 4	Record 5
10 bytes	10 bytes	10 bytes	10 bytes	10 bytes

For random process, it uses the following functions

1. fseek()
2. ftell()
3. rewind()

Random access file-Example program: Transaction processing using random access files

Program to write the records of the file sequentially and accesses the record randomly

```
#include<stdio.h>
#include<conio.h>
struct book_details
{
int book_id;
char book_name[20];
int price;
char publisher_name[20];
char author_name[20];
};
void main()
{
struct book_details b;
FILE *fp;
int n,i,recno;
char ch[1];
clrscr();
fp=fopen("book.dat","wb+");
printf("How many records?");
scanf("%d",&n);
printf("Enter %d records:\n",n);
for(i=1;i<=n;i++)   //storing the records sequentially
{
printf("\n\nenter bookid:");
scanf("%d",&b.book_id);
printf("enter book name:");
```

```
scanf("%s",b.book_name);
printf("enter book price:");
scanf("%d",&b.price);
printf("enter publisher name:");
scanf("%s",b.publisher_name);
printf("enter author name:");
scanf("%s",b.author_name);
fwrite(&b,sizeof(b),1,fp);
}
while(1)
{
printf("\nEnter the record number:");
scanf("%d",&recno);
if(recno<1||recno>n)
printf("enter valid record number ");
else
{
// placing the file pointer to the respective record in order to access it randomly
fseek(fp,(recno-1)*sizeof(b),0);
fread(&b,sizeof(b),1,fp);
printf("book id:%d\nbook
name:%s\nprice:%d\npublisher:%s\nauthor:%s",b.book_id,b.book_name,b.price,b.publishe
r_name,b.author_name);
}
printf("\nWant to continue...y/n:");
scanf("%s",ch);
if(strcmp(ch,"n")==0)
break;
}
fclose(fp);
getch();
}
```

Output:

```
How many records?

3

Enter 3 records:

book id:12

book name:dbms

price:350

publisher:tata

author:nala

book id:13

book name:ds

price:300

publisher:technical

author:kala

book id:14

book name:oops

price:320

publisher:pearson

author:nila

Enter the record number:2

book id:13

book name:ds

price:300

publisher:technical

author:kala

Want to continue...y/n: n
```

Example: Program to write the records of the file sequentially and updates the record randomly

```
#include<stdio.h>
#include<conio.h>
struct book_details
{
int book_id;
int price;
char book_name[20];
char publisher_name[20];
char author_name[20];
};
void main()
{
struct book_details b;
FILE *fp;
int n,i,recno,p;
char ch[1];
clrscr();
fp=fopen("book.dat","wb+");
printf("How many records?");
scanf("%d",&n);
printf("Enter %d records:\n",n);
for(i=1;i<=n;i++)  //storing the records sequentially
{
printf("\Enter the details of the Record %d:\n",i);
printf("\nenter bookid:");
scanf("%d",&b.book_id);
printf("enter book price:");
scanf("%d",&b.price);
printf("enter book name:");
scanf("%s",b.book_name);
```

```
printf("enter publisher name:");
scanf("%s",b.publisher_name);
printf("enter author name:");
scanf("%s",b.author_name);
fwrite(&b,sizeof(b),1,fp);
}
while(1)
{
printf("\nEnter the record number for modification:");
scanf("%d",&recno);
if(recno<1||recno>n)
printf("enter valid record number");
else
{
printf("enter new price for update:");
scanf("%d",&p);
//to make the file pointer to move to the respective record
fseek(fp,(recno-1)*sizeof(b),0);
//from the current record position, shifts the file pointer 2bytes forward and writes the new
price
fseek(fp,2L,1);
fwrite(&p,sizeof(int), 1, fp);
}
fseek(fp,0,0);
for(i=1;i<=n;i++)
{
printf("\nThe details of the Record %d is\n",i);
fread(&b,sizeof(b),1,fp);
printf("\nThe book id is:%d",b.book_id);
printf("\nThe book price is:%d",b.price);
printf("\nThe book name is:%s",b.book_name);
printf("\nThe publisher name is:%s",b.publisher_name);
printf("\nThe author name is:%s\n",b.author_name);
```

```
}
fclose(fp);
printf("\ntype n to quit/n:");
scanf("%s",ch);
if(strcmp(ch,"n")==0)
break;
}
getch();
}
```

Output

```
How many records?3
Enter 3 records:
Enter the details of the Record 1
enter bookid:24
enter book price:220
enter book name:dsa
enter publisher name:tata
enter author name:nalayini
Enter the details of the Record 2
enter bookid:25
enter book price:300
enter book name:dbms
enter publisher name:pearson
enter author name:kala
Enter the details of the Record 3
enter bookid:26
enter book price:400
enter book name:ds
enter publisher name:technical
enter author name:pari
Enter the record number for modification:2
enter new price for update:560
The details of the Record 1 is
```

The book id is:24

The book price is:220

The book name is:dsa

The publisher name is:tata

The author name is:nalayini

The details of the Record 2 is

The book id is:25

The book price is:560

The book name is:dbms

The publisher name is:pearson

The author name is:kala

The details of the Record 3 is

The book id is:26

The book price is:400

The book name is:ds

The publisher name is:technical

The author name is:pari

type n to quit:n

Difference between Sequential and Random File Access

Sequential file processing	**Random file processing**
Records or elements should be accessed in sequential order 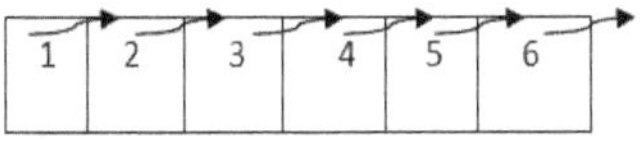	Records or elements can be accessed in any order 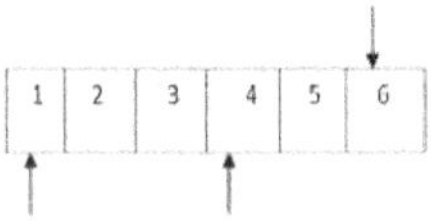
Tape drives incorporate Sequential file access mechanism	In Hard Disks and Optical drives, random access mechanism can also be used
Sequential read is very fast when compared to random read	Number of seek operations takes much time to do random access
In a Sequential file, each record can be of different length	Implemented using fixed length records

Table 6.5: Difference between Sequential File Processing and Random File Processing

6.7. Command Line Arguments

Passing values at the command line to the source program is called the command line arguments. Those passed values are sent as arguments to the main() in the source program. The arguments are argc and argv.

The argc parameter counts the number of arguments or values passed at the command line.

The argv[] parameter is a pointer array pointing to the command line arguments. Command line arguments are mainly used to control the source program from outside.

int main(int argc, char **argv)

"argc" counts the number of arguments at the command line

"argv[]" a pointer array pointing to the command line arguments

Example 1

C:\TURBOC3\SOURCE>cm.exe hi hello welcome

argc counts the command line arguments as 4

argv[0] has cm.exe //cm.exe is the source program's exe file

argv[1] has hi

argv[2] has hello

argv[3] has welcome

Example 2

C:\TURBOC3\SOURCE>p29.exe r.txt

argc counts the value as 2

argv[0] has p29.exe

argv[1] has r.txt

To open the file r.txt in the source program p29.c, we can have the following code:

FILE *fp;

f p= fopen(argv[1], "r"); // argv[1] has r.txt and it is opened in read mode

Example : Program to display the total no of arguments passed and the passed arguments in the command line

```
#include<stdio.h>
#include<conio.h>
void main(int argc, char* argv[])
{
int i;
clrscr();
printf("Total number of arguments: %d",argc);
for(i=0;i< argc;i++)
{
printf("\n %d argument is: %s",i,argv[i]);
getch();
}
}
```

Step 1: Compile the program

Step 2: After executing the program, you will get the exe file and the following will be displayed

Total number of arguments: 1

0 arguments is: C:\TURBOC3\SOURCE\CM.EXE

We did not pass any arguments at the command line, simply we executed the source program cm.c and got the above output. It has taken the cm.exe file as its argv[0]. To pass arguments at the command line do the following steps.

Step 3: Go to file menu

Step 4: Click DOS Shell, u will get a command prompt with C:\TURBOC3\BIN

Step 5: C:\TURBOC3\BIN> CD ..

C:\TURBOC3\CD SOURCE

C:\TURBOC3\SOURCE>cm.exe hi hello welcome

Output Window

Total number of arguments: 4

0 argument is: C:\TURBOC3\SOURCE\CM.EXE

1 argument is: hi

2 argument is: hello

3 argument is: welcome

Note

argc counts the value as 4

argv[0] has C:\TURBOC3\SOURCE\CM.EXE

argv[1] has hi

argv[2] has hello

argv[3] has welcome

Example: Program to display the argument passed in the argv[1]

```
#include <stdio.h>
#include <conio.h>
void main( int argc, char *argv[] )
{
clrscr();
if( argc == 2 )
printf("The argument at argv[1] is %s\n", argv[1]);
else if( argc > 2 )
printf("check the no of arguments\n");
else
printf("The Source file name is:%s.\n",argv[0]);
getch();
}
```

Step 1: Compile the program

Step 2: After executing the program, you will get the exe file and the following output will be displayed

The Source file name is:C:\TURBOC3\SOURCE\p21.EXE

Note: It will take the p21.exe as argv[0],

Step 3: Go to file menu

Step 4: Click DOS Shell, u will get a command prompt with C:\TURBOC3\BIN

Step5: C:\TURBOC3\BIN> CD ..

C:\TURBOC3\CD SOURCE

C:\TURBOC3\SOURCE>p21.exe velammal

Output Window

The argument at argv[1] is velammal

Note:

If you are working in tc, then follow the below given command

C:/tc/bin>TCC filename.c or program name .c

C:/tc/bin>filename or program name   type the respective arguments

Example

C:/tc/bin>TCC p21.c

C:/tc/bin>p21 velammal

Example: Program to pass file as the argument in the command line

```
#include <stdio.h>
#include<conio.h>
void main ( int argc, char *argv[] )
{
char k;
FILE *file;
clrscr();
if ( argc != 2 )
{
printf( "The actual filename is: %s", argv[0] );
}
else
{
file = fopen( argv[1], "r" );
if ( file == 0 )
{
printf( "file open error\n" );
}
else
{
while  ( ( k = fgetc( file ) ) != EOF )
{
printf( "%c", k );
}
fclose( file );
```

```
}
}
getch();
}
```

Create a file say r.txt in any location but not inside bin

The file r.txt has the following content

velammal

Step 1: Compile the program

Step 2: After executing the program, you will get the exe file and the following output will be displayed

The actual filename is: C:\TURBOC3\SOURCE\p29.EXE

Step 3: Go to file menu

Step 4: Click DOS Shell, u will get a command prompt with C:\TURBOC3\BIN

Step 5: C:\TURBOC3\BIN> CD ..

```
C:\TURBOC3\CD SOURCE
C:\TURBOC3\SOURCE>p29.exe  r.txt
velammal
```

Example: Program to pass file and its contents as argument in the command line

```
#include<stdio.h>
#include<conio.h>
void main( int argc, char *argv[] )
{
char c;
FILE *fp;
clrscr();
if ( argc != 2 )
{
printf( "The actual filename is: %s", argv[0] );
}
else
{
fp = fopen( argv[1], "w" );
if ( fp == 0 )
{
```

```
printf( "file open error\n" );
}
else
{
while ((c = getchar()) != EOF)
{
putc(c, fp);
}
fclose(fp);
}
}
getch();
}
```

Create a file say oo.txt in any location but not inside bin

Let the file oo.txt be empty

Step 1: Compile the program

Step 2: After executing the program, you will get the exe file and the following output will be displayed

The actual filename is: C:\TURBOC3\SOURCE\p30.EXE

Step 3: Go to file menu

Step 4: Click DOS Shell, u will get a command prompt with C:\TURBOC3\BIN

Step 5: C:\TURBOC3\BIN> CD ..

```
C:\TURBOC3\CD SOURCE
C:\TURBOC3\SOURCE>p30.exe  oo.txt
hi
welcome
to
velammal
```

press ctrl z and d to end the file

open the file oo.txt, you will get the following content

```
hi
welcome
to
velammal
```

Example: Program to copy the content of one file into another using command line arguments

```
#include<stdio.h>
#include<stdlib.h>
#include<conio.h>
void main(int argc,char *argv[])
{
 FILE *fp1,*fp2;
 char ch;
 clrscr();
 if(argc!=3)
 {
  printf("\n check the no of arguments.\n");
  exit(1);
 }
 fp1=fopen(argv[1],"r");
 if(fp1==NULL)
 {
 printf("file error");
 exit(1);
 }
 fp2=fopen(argv[2],"w");
 if(fp2==NULL)
 {
 printf("file error");
 exit(1);
 }
 while(1)
 {
 ch=fgetc(fp1);
 if(ch==EOF)
 break;
 else
 fputc(ch,fp2);
```

```
}
fcloseall();
getch();
}
```

Create a file g6.txt and it has the following content

Velammal

Create another file g7.txt and make the file empty

Step 1: Compile the program p31.c

Step 2: Execute the program to get the exe file

Step 3: Go to file menu

Step 4: Click DOS Shell, u will get a command prompt with C:\TURBOC3\BIN

Step 5: C:\TURBOC3\BIN> CD ..

C:\TURBOC3\CD SOURCE

C:\TURBOC3\SOURCE>p31.exe g6.txt g7.txt

Open the file g7.txt and find the following copied content from g6.txt

Velammal

Example: Program to create and modify employee details using command line arguments

```
#include<stdio.h>
#include<stdlib.h>
#include<string.h>
#include<alloc.h>
struct emprec
{
int empid;
char *name;
};
typedef struct emprec emp;
void insert(char *a);
void display(char *a);
void update(char *a);
int count=0;
void main(int argc, char *argv[])
{
```

```
int choice;
if(argc!=2)
{
printf("file error");
exit(0);
}
else
{
while (1)
{
printf("Enter the choice\n");
printf("1-Insert a new record into file\n2-Display the records\n");
printf("3-Update the record\n4-Exit\n");
scanf("%d",  &choice);
switch (choice)
{
case 1:
insert(argv[1]);
break;
case 2:
display(argv[1]);
break;
case 3:
update(argv[1]);
break;
case 4:
exit(0);
default:
printf("Enter the correct choice\n");
}
}
}
}
```

```
void insert(char *a)
{
FILE *fp1;
emp *temp1 = (emp *)malloc(sizeof(emp));
temp1->name = (char *)malloc(20 * sizeof(char));
fp1 = fopen(a, "a+");
if (fp1 == NULL)
printf("file error");
else
{
printf("Enter the employee id\n");
scanf("%d", &temp1->empid);
fwrite(&temp1->empid, sizeof(int), 1, fp1);
printf("Enter the employee name\n");
scanf(" %[^\n]s", temp1->name);
fwrite(temp1->name, 20, 1, fp1);
count++;
}
fclose(fp1);
free(temp1);
free(temp1->name);
}
void display(char *a)
{
FILE *fp1;
char ch;
int var = count;
emp *temp = (emp *)malloc(sizeof(emp));
temp->name = (char *)malloc(20*sizeof(char));
fp1 = fopen(a, "r");
if (count == 0)
{
printf("no records to display\n");
exit(1);
```

```
}
if (fp1 == NULL)
printf("file error");
else
{
while(var)    // display the employee records
{
fread(&temp->empid, sizeof(int), 1, fp1);
printf("%d", temp->empid);
fread(temp->name, 20, 1, fp1);
printf(" %s\n", temp->name);
var--;
}
}
fclose(fp1);
free(temp);
free(temp->name);
}
void update(char *a)
{
FILE *fp1;
char ch, name[20],p[20];
int var = count, id, c,recno;
emp *temp = (emp *)malloc(sizeof(emp));
temp->name = (char *)malloc(20*sizeof(char));
fp1 = fopen(a, "r+");
if (fp1 == NULL)
printf("file error");
else
{
printf("\nEnter the record number for modification:");
scanf("%d",&recno);
printf("enter new name for update:");
scanf("%s",p);
```

```
fseek(fp1,(recno-1)*sizeof(temp),0);
fseek(fp1,2L,1);
c=fwrite(&p,20, 1, fp1);
if(c == 1)
printf("record is updated succesfully\n");
else
printf("update unsuccesful enter correct id\n");
fclose(fp1);
free(temp);
free(temp->name);
}
}
```

Step1: Compile the program p66.c

Step2: Execute the program to get the exe file

Step3: Go to file menu

Step4: Click DOS Shell, u will get a command prompt with C:\TURBOC3\BIN

Step5: C:\TURBOC3\BIN> CD ..

```
C:\TURBOC3\CD SOURCE
C:\TURBOC3\SOURCE>p66.exe v9.txt
Enter the choice
1-Insert a new record into file
2-Display the records
3-Update the record
4-Exit
1
Enter the employee id
11
Enter the employee name
nala
Enter the choice
1-Insert a new record into file
2-Display the records
3-Update the record
4-Exit
```

2

11 nala

Enter the choice

1-Insert a new record into file

2-Display the records

3-Update the record

4-Exit

1

Enter the employee id

12

Enter the employee name

kala

Enter the choice

1-Insert a new record into file

2-Display the records

3-Update the record

4-Exit

2

11 nala

12 kala

Enter the choice

1-Insert a new record into file

2-Display the records

3-Update the record

4-Exit

3

Enter the record number for modification: 1

enter new name for update: appa

record is updated succesfully

Enter the choice

1-Insert a new record into file

2-Display the records

3-Update the record

4-Exit

2

11 appa

12 kala

Enter the choice

1-Insert a new record into file

2-Display the records

3-Update the record

4-Exit

4

Exercise

1. Try listing the file's date and time.
2. List the examples of the streams.
3. Use fseek() to reverse the content of the file.
4. Write a program to perform banking application by randomly accessing the content of the file.
5. Write a program to merge two files using command line arguments.

APPENDIX-A

Question Bank

Part A and Part B Questions with Answers

Unit I

Part-A

1. Write the technologies used in various Generations of Computers.
    - First Generation – Vacuum tubes
    - Second Generation – Transistors
    - Third Generation – Integrated Circuits (IC)
    - Fourth Generation – Microprocessors (Large Scale Integration and VLSI)
    - Fifth Generation – Artificial Intelligence
2. Write the Classification of Computers.

    Based on size and types, it can be classified into four types

    - Microcomputers
    - Minicomputers
    - Mainframe Computers
    - Super Computer
3. Define Laptop

It resembles a note book computer. They are portable and have all features of a desktop computer. The advantage is that it is small in size and be carried anywhere. It has a battery backup and functionality of desktop.

4. Define Tablet Computer.

It has the features of notebook computer. It can accept input from a stylus or a pen instead of keyboard or mouse. It is a portable computer and new kind of PCs.

5. What is dumb terminal and intelligent terminal?

A dumb terminal cannot store data or do processing of its own. It has the input and output device only. An intelligent terminal has the input and output device, can do processing, but cannot store data of its own.

6. Define Computer

Computer is an electronic device that accepts data as input, processes the input data by performing mathematical and logical operations on it and gives the desired output.

7. What are the parts of the computer system?
    - Hardware
    - Software
    - Data
    - Users
8. Define Hardware

The hardware consists of physical devices of the computer. The devices are required for input, output, storage and processing of data. Keyboard, monitor, hard disk drive, floppy disk drive, printer, processor and mother board are some of the hardware devices.

9. Define Software

It is a set of instructions that tells the computer about the tasks to be performed and how these tasks are to be performed. A set of programs and documents are collectively called software.

10. Define Program

Computer programs are set of instructions, written in a language understood by the computer, to perform a specific task.

11. What are the basic operations of a computer?
    - Input
    - Process
    - Storing
    - Controlling and Output
12. Define Data and Information

Data – Raw fact for information Processing

Information –The Processed data is called information.

13. Define cache memory

Cache memory is a very high speed memory placed in between RAM and CPU. It increases the speed of processing. It is a storage buffer that stores the data temporarily and makes them available to CPU at a fast rate.

14. Define RAM

RAM is volatile. It stores data when the computer is on. The information stored in RAM gets erased when the computer is turned off. RAM provides temporary storage for data and instructions.

15. Define ROM

ROM is non–volatile and read only memory. The storage in ROM is permanent in nature. It is used for storing standard processing programs that permanently reside in the computer.

16. List out the applications of the computer.

- Education
- Entertainment
- Sports
- Advertising
- Medicine
- Science and Engineering
- Government
- Home

17. Define Algorithm.

Algorithm is an ordered sequence of finite, well defined, unambiguous instructions for completing a task. It is a step by step procedure for solving a task or a problem.

18. Define Flowchart.

A flowchart is a diagrammatic representation of the logic for solving the task. It is drawn using boxes of different shapes with lines connecting them to show the flow of control. The purpose of drawing a flowchart is to make logic of the program clearer in a visual form.

19. Define Pseudo code

Pseudo code consists of short, readable and formally styled English language used for explaining the algorithm. It is a short–hand way of describing the program. It does not include details like variable declarations, subroutines, etc.

20. What is the Purpose of drawing the flowchart?

- Define and analyze the processes
- Build a step by step picture of the process for analysis, discussions and Communications.

21. How algorithm can be represented in different forms?

- Normal English
- Flowchart
- Pseudo code
- Decision table

22. Write pseudocode to find the area and circumference of the circle.

Read radius

Compute area by multiplying pi and the square of radius

Compute circumference by multiplying 2, pi and radius

Print the area and circumference

23. Convert decimal to binary – $(34.24)_{10}$

Ans : $(100010.00111)_2$

24. Convert binary to octal – $(11000.0010)_2$

Ans : $(30.1075)_8$

25. Convert hexadecimal to decimal – $(96.470A)_{16}$

Ans : $(150.64)_{10}$

Part-B

1. Briefly Explain the Generation of Computers

(i) First Generation

- Vacuum tubes
- Instructions were written in Machine language
- Computation time–milliseconds
- Large in size
- (e.g.) UNIVAC, ENIAC, EDVAC

(ii) Second Generation

- Transistors
- Instructions were written in Assembly language
- Computation time–microseconds
- Small in size
- (e.g.) PDP–8, IBM 1401, CDC 1604

(iii) Third Generation

- Integrated Circuits
- Operating System was used. High level languages were used.
- Computation time–nanoseconds
- Small in size
- (e.g.) IBM 370, PDP 11

(iv) Fourth Generation

- Microprocessors (LSI and VLSI)
- Operating System like MS-DOS and MS Windows were developed.
- Supports GUI
- Small in size.
- (e.g.) Intel 4004 Chip.

(v) Fifth Generation

- Artificial Intelligence (SLSI chips)
- Parallel processing is used
- Intel dual core microprocessor uses parallel processing

2. Explain the classification of computers in detail.

The computers are classified into four categories based on their size and type.

- Microcomputers
- Minicomputers
- Main frame computers
- Super computers

(i)Microcomputers

- Small, low cost and single user digital computer.
- It consists of CPU, input unit, output unit, storage unit and the software.
- (e.g.) IBM PC based on Pentium microprocessor and Apple Macintosh.

(ii) Minicomputers

- Digital Computers used in multi user systems
- Have high processing speed and high storage capacity.
- It can support 4-200 users simultaneously
- Applications - Industries, research centres
- (e.g.) PDP 11, IBM (8000 series)

(iii) Mainframe Computers

- Multi user, multi programming and high performance computers
- High Speed and High storage capacity
- Large and Powerful Systems used in centralizes databases.
- Dumb terminal, intelligent terminal.
- Applications-Banks, Companies.

- (e.g.) CDC 6600, IBM ES000 series.

(iv) Super computers

- Fastest and most expensive machines.
- Have High Processing Speed
- Speed–FLOP (Floating point Operations per second)
- Used for highly calculation intensive tasks such as weather forecasting, climate research, molecular research, biological research, nuclear research and aircraft design.
- (e.g.) IBM Roadrunner, IBM Blue gene and Intel ASCI red.

3. Explain the different components of a computer system with block diagram
   - Input/Output Unit
   - Central Processing Unit
   - Memory Unit

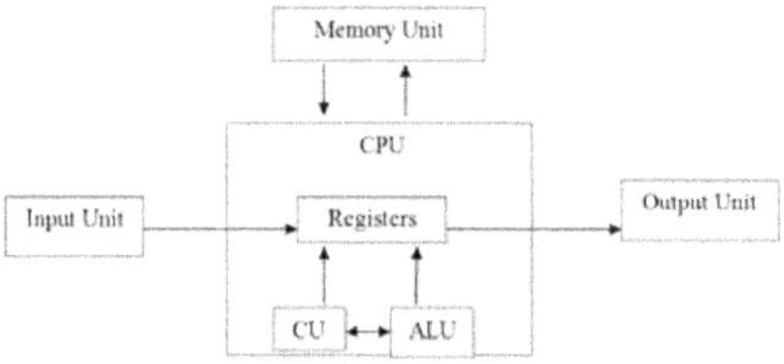

Input Unit

The Input unit accepts data from the user. It converts the data that it accepts from the user into a form that is understandable by the computer. Input is provided to the system using input devices like keyboard, trackball, and mouse.

Output Unit

It provides the processed data. The Output unit provides the output in a form that is understandable by the user. The output devices are monitor, printer.

Central Processing Unit

CPU controls, coordinates and supervises the operations of the computer. It is responsible for processing of the input data. CPU consists of ALU and Control unit.

ALU

It performs all the arithmetic and logic operations on the input data.

Control Unit

It controls the overall operations of the computer.

Memory Unit

It stores the data, instructions, intermediate results and output temporarily during the processing of data. This memory is called main memory.

4. Explain the Central Processing Unit in detail.

CPU is the brain of the computer. It consists of ALU and control unit. It has a set of registers which are temporary storage areas for holding data and instructions. CPU uses the registers to store data, instructions during processing.

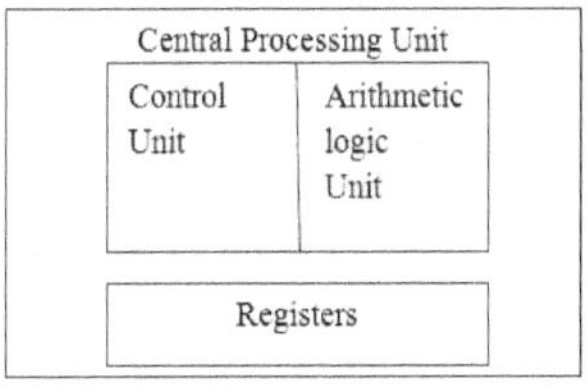

Arithmetic and Logic Unit:

- ALU consists of two units–arithmetic unit and logic unit
- Arithmetic unit–performs arithmetic operations on the data.
- Logic unit–performs logic operations.

Registers:

- High speed storage areas within the CPU but have least storage capacity. These are directly accessed by CPU during instruction execution.
- The data and instructions that require processing must be brought in the registers of CPU before they can be processed.

  (i)Accumulator – stores the result of arithmetic and logic operations.

  (ii)Instruction Register – Current instruction most recently fetched.

  (iii)Program Counter – Address of next instruction to be processed.

  (iv)Memory Address Register (MAR)–Address of next location in the memory to be accessed.

  (v)Memory Buffer Register (MBR)–Temporarily stores data from memory or the data to be sent to memory.

  (vi)Data Register–stores the operands and any other data.

Control Unit:

- It organizing the processing of data and instructions. It acts as s supervisor, control and coordinates the activity of other units of the computer.

5. Explain the memory unit in a computer.

The memory unit consists of cache memory and primary memory. Main memory of the computer is used to store the data and instructions during execution of the instructions. RAM and ROM are primary memory.

(i)Cache memory diagram with explanation

(ii)Primary memory

(iii)Secondary memory

Cache Memory

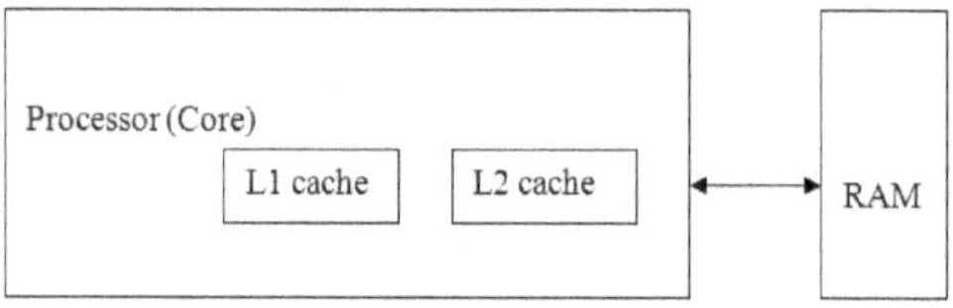

6. What is Number System? Explain Number System with example.
   - Definition of Number System
   - Decimal Number System – Base 10
   - Binary Number System – Base 2
   - Octal Number System – Base 8
   - Hexadecimal Number System – Base 16
   - Conversion of all types of number system with example.
7. Define Algorithm and Explain with an example.

Definition:

Algorithm is an ordered sequence of finite, well defined, unambiguous instructions for completing a task. It is a step by step procedure for solving a task or a problem.

Example

8. Draw and explain the various symbols of flowchart with an example.
   - Definition of flowchart
   - Draw a flow chart symbols with explanation
   - Example : Addition of two numbers flowchart
9. Define Pseudo code and explain with an example
   - Definition of Pseudo code
   - How to prepare s Pseudo code steps?
   - Example : Product of any two numbers

Unit II

Part-A

1. What is meant by global variable?

The variable that is used in more than one function throughout the program are called global variables and declared outside of all the function.

(e.g.)

```
#include<stdio.h>

int a = 5;

main()

{

  int b=6, c;

  c = a+b;

  printf("The value of c is %d",c);

}
```

2. Define logical and data errors

Logical errors: These are the errors, in which the conditional and control statements cannot end their match after some sequential execution.

Data errors: These are the errors, in which input data given, is not in syntax as specified in the input Statement

3. What is meant by tokens?

The tokens are usually referred as individual text and punctuation in the passage of text. The C language program can contain the individual units called the C tokens.

4. What are keywords?

Keywords are reserved words that have standard and pre-defined meaning in C. These keywords can be used only for their intended purpose. (e.g.) break, int, else, void

5. What are the types of input statements available in c?

- Formatted I/O statements – printf(), scanf()
- Unformatted I/O statements – getchar(), getc(), gets(), putchar(), putc() and puts().

6. Define getchar () function.

The getchar () function reads a single character from a standard input device. This function do not requires any arguments.

7. What is meant by local variable?

The variables which are defined inside a function block or inside a compound statement of a function sub-program are called local variables

(e.g.)

```
#include<stdio.h>
main()
{
    int a =5, b=6, c;
    c = a+b;
    printf("The value of c is %d",c);
}
```

8. Define constant.

The items whose values cannot be changed during the execution of program are called constants.

```
Const char a='A';
```

9. Define statements.

Statements can be defined as set of declarations or sequence of action. Statement causes the program to perform some action.

10. List the types of operators

- Arithmetic operators
- Relational operators
- Logical operators
- Increment and Decrement operators
- Bitwise operators
- Assignment operators
- Miscellaneous operators.

11. Difference between Initialization and assignment

S.NO	Initialization	Assignment
1	First time assignment at the time of definition is called initialization. (e.g.) int a = 10; is a initialization of a.	Value of the data object after initialization can be changed by means of assignment. (e.g.) int a=10; a=20; The value of a is changed to 20 by the assignment statement.
2	Initialization can be done only once	Assignment can be done any number of times
3	Qualified constant can be initialized with a value. (e.g.) const int a=10; is valid.	Qualified constant cannot be assigned a value. It is erroneous to write a=10; if 'a' is a qualified constant.

12. List out the miscellaneous Operators.

- Function call operator (())
- Array subscript operator ([])
- Member select operator
  - Direct member access operator (.Dot operator or period)
  - Indirect member access operator (-> arrow operator)
- Indirection operator (*)
- Conditional operator
- Comma operator
- Size of operator
- Address of operator (&)

13. Define Jump statements and list out the jump statements.

A jump statement transfers control from one point to another without checking any condition.

- goto statement
- break statement
- continue statement
- return statement

14. Difference between while statement and do while statement

S.NO	while statement	do while statement
1.	This is top tested loop	This is bottom tested loop
2.	The condition is first tested, if condition is true then the block is executed until the condition becomes false.	It executes the body once, after it checks the condition, if it is true the body is executed until the condition becomes false.
3.	Loop will not be executed if the condition is false	Loop is executed at least once even though the condition is false.

15. What is meant by break statement?

The break statement is used to terminate the loop. When the keyword break is used inside any loop, the control automatically get transferred to the first statement after the loop.

16. What is meant by continue statement?

Continue statement is used to transfer the control back to the beginning of the loop, before executing the rest of the statements inside the loop.

17. Define goto statement.

The goto statement transfers the control unconditionally from one place to another place in the program.

Syntax:

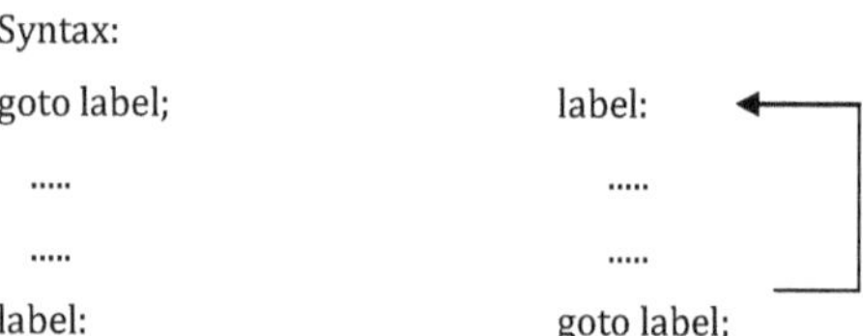

```
goto label;                label:   <-----+
  .....                      .....        |
  .....                      .....        |
label:                     goto label; ---+
```

18. What are the three main ingredients of counter controlled looping?

- Initialization of the loop counter
- A condition determining whether the loop body should be executed or not.
- An expression that manipulates the value of the loop counters so that the condition in step2 eventually becomes false and the loop terminates.

19. Compare counter controlled and sentinel controlled loop

Counter controlled loop	Sentinel Controlled loop
The number of times the loop will execute is known in advance. It starts with initial value of loop counter and terminates when the final value of the loop counter is reached. It is also known as definite repetition loop.	The number of times the loop will execute is not known in advance. The execution of loop depends upon a special value called sentinel value. If this value is true, the loop body gets executed else not. It is also known as indefinite repetition loop.

20. What is an Operator and Operand?

An operator is a symbol that specifies an operation to be performed on operands.

Example: *,+,-,/ are called arithmetic operators.

The data items that operators act upon are called operands.

Example: a+b; In this statement a and b are called operands.

21. What is Ternary operator or Conditional operators?

Ternary operator is a conditional operator with symbols? and:

Syntax: variable=exp1 ? exp2:exp3

If the exp1 is true variable takes value of exp2. If the exp2 is false, variable takes the value of exp3.

22. What is the difference between '='and '=='operator?

Where =is an assignment operator and == is a relational operator.

Example:

while (i=5) is an infinite loop because it is a nonzero value and while(i==5) is true only when i=5.

23. What is typecasting?

Type casting is the process of converting the value of an expression to a particular data type.

Example:

int x,y;

c=(float)x/y; where a and y are defined as integers. Then the result of x/y is converted into float.

24. What is the difference between if and while statement?

if	while
(i)It is a conditional statement	(i)It is a loop control statement
(ii)If the condition is true, it executes some statements.	(ii)Executes the statements within the while block if the condition is true.
(iii)If the condition is false then it stops the execution the statements.	(iii)If the condition is false the control is transferred to the next statement of the loop.

25. Define storage class specifier and its types

The storage class of an identifier can be specified with the help of a storage class specifier. The storage class specifiers are:

- auto
- register
- static
- extern
- typedef

26. What are the different pre-processor directives?

- Macro Inclusion
- Conditional Inclusion
- File Inclusion
- Line directive
- Pragma directive
- Error directive
- Null directive

27. List the conditional compilation directives

- #if
- #ifdef
- #ifndef
- #else
- #elif
- #endif

28. What are the 3 types of lifetime?

- Static or global
- Automatic or local
- Allocated

29. List the types of macro

- Object-like macros – macro without arguments
- function-like macros – macro with arguments

30. What is a pre-processor directive?

The pre-processor is a translator that works and processes the source code before it is given to the compiler. It operates under the control of commands known as pre-processor directives.

31. Define enumeration constant with syntax and example.

Enumeration is a user-defined data type with the keyword "enum". The only constraint of enum is that it fits in only with the integers i.e., it is a collection of integer values and it takes only one value out of the collection. The size of the enumeration will be the size of the integer as shown in the second example program. This makes enum the right choice for the use of flags.

Syntax:

```
enum identifier
{
        Enumeration_list,
};
```

Example:

enum week { sunday, monday, tuesday, wednesday, thursday, friday, saturday };

32. Define compiling and linking.

Compilation:

The compiler does the compilation process. The compiler takes the file containing the source code and translates the code to the machine code. The compiler then places that machine code into an output file called an object file and has the file extension .obj. The process of translating the source code into an object file is called C*ompiling.*

Linking:

After the compiler has created all the object files, another program is called to bundle them into an executable program file. That program is called *Linker* and the process of bundling them into the executable file is called *Linking.*

Part-B

1. Explain the different types of Operators in C with an example

   Define Operator

   Types

   - Arithmetic operators with example
   - Relational operators with example
   - Logical operators with example
   - Increment and Decrement operators with example
   - Bitwise operators with example
   - Assignment operators with example
   - Miscellaneous operators with example

2. Explain the formatted and Unformatted I/O statements in C with example

   Formatted Input Statements:

   - scanf() function

   Formatted Output Statements:

   - printf() function

Unformatted Input Statements:

(i)getchar() function

(ii)gets() function

(iii) getch() and getche() function

(iv) cgets() function

Unformatted Output Statements:

(i)putchar() function

(ii) puts() function

(iii) putch() function

(iv) cputs() function

3. Explain the branching statements with example.

Branching statements are used to transfer program control from one point to another.

- Conditional branching – Selection Statements
- Unconditional branching – Jump Statements

Selection Statements

(i)if statement – Syntax, Flow chart, Example program

(ii)if–else statement – Syntax, Flow chart, Example program

- Nested if statement – Syntax, Example program
- Nested if – else statement – Syntax, Flow chart, Example program

(iii) Switch statement – Syntax, Example program

Jump Statements

(i)goto statement – Syntax, Example program

(ii) break statement – Syntax, Example program

(iii) continue statement – Syntax, Example program (iv) return statement – Syntax.

4. Explain the iteration or looping statements with example.

Iteration is the process of repeating same set of instructions again and again until the specified condition holds true.

(i)for statement – Syntax, Flow chart, Example program

(ii) while statement – Syntax, Flow chart, Example program

(iii) do – while statement – Syntax, Flow chart, Example program.

5. Explain in detail about 'C' declarations and variables.

General rules of 'C' language:

- program execution begins at main()
- keywords are written in lower-case
- statements are terminated with a semi-colon
- text strings are enclosed in double quotes
- C is case sensitive, use lower-case and try not to capitalize variable names
- \n means position the cursor on the beginning of the next line
- printf() can be used to display text to the screen
- The curly braces{} define the beginning and end of a program block.

Initialising Data Variables at Declaration Time

In C, variables may be initialized with a value when they are declared. Consider the following declaration, which declares an integer variable count which is initialized to10. int count=10;

Simple Assignment of Values to Variables

The= operator is used to assign values to data variables. Consider the following statement, which assigns the value 32 an integer variable count, and the letter A to the character variable letter

count=32;

letter= 'A'

Variable Formatters

%d decimal integer

%c character

%s string or character array

%f float

%e double

6. Explain the structure of C program

Basic Structure of C Programs

C programs are essentially constructed in the following manner, as a number of well defined sections.

/* HEADERSECTION */

/* Contains name, author, revisionnumber*/

```
/* INCLUDE SECTION */
/* contains #include statements*/
/* CONSTANTSANDTYPESSECTION */
/* contains types and #defines */
/* GLOBAL VARIABLESSECTION */
/* any global variables declared here */
/* FUNCTIONSSECTION */
/* user defined functions*/
/* main()SECTION */
int main()
{
}
```

A Simple Program

The following program is written in the C programming language.

```
#include <stdio.h>
main()
{
printf("Programming in C is easy.\n");
}
```

Header Files

Header files contain definitions of functions and variables which can be incorporated into any C program by using the pre-processor #include statement.

#include<stdio.h>should be at the beginning of the source file, because the definition for printf() is found in the file stdio.h All header files have the extension .h and generally reside in the /include subdirectory.

```
#include <stdio.h>
#include "mydecls.h"
```

7. Explain in detail about the constants, expressions and statements in 'C'.
    1. Constants:(with examples)
        1.Numeric constants
            a. Integer Constants
            b. Real Constants

2.Character constants

a. Single character Constants

b. String Constants

2. Expressions: An expression represents a single data item, such as number or a character. Logical conditions that are true or false are represented by expressions.

   Example: a =p – q /3 +r* 2 -1

3. Statements

   - Assignment Statements – Definition and examples
   - Null Statements – Definition and examples
   - Block of statements – Definition and examples
   - Expression statements – Definition and examples
   - Declaration statements – Definition and examples

8. Discuss about the various data types in 'C'. (MAY2009)

The four basic data types are

a. INTEGER

b. FLOATINGPOINT

c. DOUBLE

d. CHARACTER

9. Discuss the storage classes with an example

   - auto – Syntax, example
   - register – Syntax, example
   - static – Syntax, example
   - extern – Syntax, example
   - typedef – Syntax, example

10. Discuss about pre-processor in C

   - Preprocessor directives
   - Macros
   - Simple macro substitution
   - Macros as arguments
   - Nesting of macros
   - Undefining a macro
   - File inclusion

Unit III

Part A

1. Define an Array

An array is a collection of elements of the same data type. The data type of an element is called element type. It is a data structure that is used for the storage of homogenous data.

2. What are the types of arrays?

- One dimensional array
- Two dimensional array
- Multi dimensional array

3. What is one dimensional array?

One dimensional array consists of a fixed number of elements of the same data type organized as a simple linear sequence. The elements of a one-dimensional array can be accessed by using a single subscript, they are known as single-sub-scripted variables.

(e.g.) int a [10];

4. What are two dimensional arrays?

A two dimensional array has its elements arranged in a rectangular grid of rows and columns. The elements of a two-dimensional array can be accessed by using a row subscript and a column subscript. A two dimensional array is known as a matrix.

(e.g.) int a [5][10];

5. Give the syntax of the declaration of two dimensional arrays.

<storage_class_specifier><type_qualifier><type_modifier>typeidentifier [<row_specifier>]

[column_specifier]<=initialization_list<...>>;

6. What is array of pointers?

An array of pointers is a collection of addresses. The addresses in an array of pointers could be the addresses of isolated variables or the addresses of array elements or any other addresses.

7. What is pointer to an array?

To create a pointer that points to a complete array instead of pointing to the individual elements of an array or isolated variables. Such a pointer is known as a pointer to an array.

Syntax:

int (*p1)[5];

8. What are the merits and demerits of Arrays?

Merits:

Direct Indexing – The time required to access any element in an array of any dimension is almost the same irrespective of its location in the array.

Demerits:

- The memory to an array is allocated at the compile time.
- Arrays are static in nature. The size of an array cannot be expanded or cannot be squeezed at the run time.
- The size of an array has to be kept big enough to accommodate the worst cases. Therefore, memory usage in case of arrays is inefficient.

9. What is meant by linear search?

A list can be searched sequentially wherein the search for the data item starts from the beginning and continues till the end of the list.

10. What is meant by sorting?

It is an operation in which all elements of a list are arranged in a predetermined order. The elements can be arranged in a sequence from smallest to largest such that every element is less than or equal to its next neighbour in the list. Such an arrangement is called ascending order.

11. Define Strings.

A string literal is a sequence of zero or more characters enclosed within double quotes. (e.g.) "Viji"

12. What is meant by length of the string?

The length of the string is defined as the number of characters present in it. The terminating null character is not counted while determining the length of the string.

(e.g.) strlen("abc");

The length of the string is 3

13. Give the syntax for string variable or a character array.

<s_class_specifier><type_qualifier><type_modifier>charidentifier [<size_specifier>]

<=initialization_list OR string literal>;

14. Give the syntax of array of strings.

<sclass_specifier><type_qualifier><type_modifier>charidentifier [row_specifier]

[column_specifier]<=initialization_list>;

15. What is array of character pointers?

An array of strings can be stored by using an array of character pointers.

16. List the steps in binary search in an ordered list

Step 1: the middle element is tested for the required entry if found then its position is reported else

Step 2: if val < middle, search the left half of the list else search the right half of the list

Step 3: repeat step 1 and 2 until the entry is found

17. List the matrix operations

- Matrix addition
- Matrix subtraction
- Matrix multiplication
- Matrix transpose

18. List the sorting operations

- Selection sort
- Bubble sort
- Insertion sort
- Merge sort
- Quick sort
- Shell sort
- Radix sort

19. How to concatenate 2 strings?

Strcat() is used to concatenate 2 strings

Example : strcat(dest,src);

The source string is appended with the destination string

20. What is the use of'\0'character?

When declaring character arrays(strings),'\0'(NULL)character is automatically added

At end. The '\0' character acts as an end of character array.

21. Defines scanf()and print() functions.

The scanf(): This function allows to store character from a character Array and writes to another array. Similar to scanf(), but instead of reading from standard input, it reads from an array.

The printf():This function writes the values of any data type to an array of characters.

22. List the characteristics of Arrays.

All elements of an array share the same name, and they are distinguished form one another with help of an element number. Any particular element of an array can be modified separately without disturbing other elements.

23. What is an empty string?

A string literal constant of 0 length is an empty string. It still takes one byte in the memory to store the null character.

24. What are multi dimensional arrays?

Multi-dimensioned arrays have two or more index values which specify the element in the array. multi[i][j]...[n];

25. Distinguish linear search and binary search

s.no	Linear search	Binary search
1	It searches Sequentially	It uses divide and conquer technique
2	starts searching from the first element in the list and proceeds towards the last element until the element is found	starts searching from the middle element in the list and proceeds to one end of the list based on the search value.
3	It is very slow	It is comparatively fast
4	Ex.magnetic tapes	Ex. Binary search tree

Part-B

1. Explain the string Library Functions with example.
   - Strlen() – Definition, Syntax and example.
   - Strcpy() – Definition, Syntax and example.
   - Strcat() – Definition, Syntax and example.
   - Strcmp() – Definition, Syntax and example.
   - Strcmpi() – Definition, Syntax and example.
   - Strrev() – Definition, Syntax and example.
   - Strlwr() – Definition, Syntax and example.
   - Strupr() – Definition, Syntax and example.
   - Strset() – Definition, Syntax and example.
   - Strchr() – Definition, Syntax and example.
   - Strrchr() – Definition, Syntax and example.
   - Strstr() – Definition, Syntax and example.
   - Strncpy() – Definition, Syntax and example.
   - Strncat() – Definition, Syntax and example.
   - Strncmp() – Definition, Syntax and example.

- Strncmpi() – Definition, Syntax and example.
- Strnset() – Definition, Syntax and example.

2. Explain the selection sort.
   - Definition of Selection sort
   - Example
   - Program
3. Explain the bubble sort.
   - Definition of bubble sort
   - Example
   - Program
4. Explain the Insertion sort.
   - Definition of Insertion sort
   - Example
   - Program
5. Explain the merge and Quick sort.
   - Definition of merge and Quick sort
   - Example of merge and Quick sort
   - Program of merge and Quick sort
6. Explain linear and binary search with program
   - Definition of linear and binary search
   - Example of linear and binary search
   - Program of linear and binary search
7. Write a program to perform matrix addition and matrix subtraction
   - Program for matrix addition and subtraction
   - Sample input and output
8. Write a program to perform matrix multiplication
   - Program for matrix multiplication
   - Sample input and output
9. Write a program to perform matrix determinant and scaling.
   - Program for matrix multiplication
   - Sample input and output
10. Write a program to compute the mean, median and mode using array.
    - Program for matrix multiplication
    - Sample input and output

Unit IV

Part-A

1. What is 'C' functions? Why they are used?

A function is a self-contained block(or)a sub-program of one or more statements that performs a special task when called. To perform a task repetitively then it is not necessary to re-write the particular block of the program again and again. The function defined can be used for any number of times to perform the task.

2. What are the two types of functions?

Predefined functions or Library functions – Built in functions.

User defined functions – The function defined by the users according to their requirements.

3. Differentiate library functions and User-defined functions.

Library Functions	User-defined Functions
a) Library functions are pre-defined set of functions that are defined in C libraries.	a) The User-defined functions are the functions defined by the user according to his/her requirement.
b) User can only use the function but cannot change(or)modify this function.	b) User can use this type of function. User can also modify this function.

4. What are the steps in writing a function in a program.
   a. Function Declaration(Prototype declaration): Every user-defined functions has to be declared before the main().
   b. Function Callings: The user-defined functions can be called inside any functions like main(), user-defined function, etc.
   c. Function Definition: The function definition block is used to define the user-defined functions with statements.

5. What is a use of 'return' Keyword?

The 'return' Keyword is used only when a function returns a value.

6. Give the syntax for using user-defined functions in a program.

Syntax for using user-defined functions in a program

```
Syntax:
    Function declaration;                         function definition;
     main()                                              main()
     {                                            {
     ======                                       ======
function calling;          (or)                   functioncalling;
     ======                                       ======
}                                                 }
function definition;
```

7. Classify the functions based on arguments and return values.

Depending on the arguments and return values, functions are classified into four types.

a. Function without arguments and return values.
b. Function with arguments but without return values.
c. Function without arguments but with return values.
d. Function with arguments and return values.

8. Distinguish between Call by value and Call by reference.

Call by value	Call by reference.
a) In call by value, the value of actual arguments are passed to the formal arguments and the operation is done on formal arguments.	a) In call by reference, the address of actual argument values is passed to formal argument values.
b) Formal arguments values are photocopies of actual arguments values.	b) Formal arguments values are pointers to the actual argument values.
c) Changes made in formal arguments valued do not affect the actual arguments values.	c) Since Address is passed, the changes made in both the arguments values are permanent.

9. What is function definition?

It is the process of specifying and establishing the user defined function by specifying all of its elements and characteristics.

Syntax:

```
return_type  function name (parameters list);
(e.g.) int add (int x, int y, int z);
```

10. What is function declaration?

The function can be declared before they defined and invoked.

Syntax:

```
datatype function_name (parameters list)
parameters declaration;
{
        local variables declaration;
        ..........
        body of the function;
        ..........
        return(expression);
}
```

11. What is function call?

The function can be called by simply specifying the name of the function, return value and parameters if presence.

Syntax:

```
function name ();
function_name (parameter);
return value = function_name (parameter);
```

12. What are actual and formal parameters?

Actual parameters – These are the parameters transferred from the calling program (main program) to the called program (function).

Formal parameters – These are the parameters transferred into calling function from the called program.

(e.g.)

```
main()                              fun1 (x,y)
{                                   {
 .....                               .....
 .....                               .....
 fun1(a,b);                          .....
 .....                               .....
 .....                               .....
}                                   }
```

a, b – Actual parameters.

x, y – Formal parameters.

13. What is Recursion?

It is the process of calling the same function itself again and again until some condition is satisfied. This process is used for repetitive computation in which each action is satisfied.

Syntax:

```
function1()
{
        function1();
}
```

14. What are the two methods to pass arrays to functions?

- Passing individual elements of an array one by one
- Passing an entire array at a time.

15. List the pattern of recursive calls.

(i) Linear recursion

(ii) Binary recursion

(iii) n–ary recursion.

16. What is a Pointer? How a variable is declared to the pointer?(MAY2009)

Pointer is a variable which holds the address of another variable.

Pointer Declaration:

datatype*variable-name;

Example:

int*x, c=5;

x=&a;

17. What are the uses of Pointers?

- Pointers are used to return more than one value to the function
- Pointers are more efficient in handling the data in arrays
- Pointers reduce the length and complexity of the program
- They increase the execution speed
- The pointers save data storage space in memory

18. What are*and & operators means?

'*' operator means 'value at the address'

'&' operator means 'address of'

19. List out the advantages of using pointers.

- Pointers are more compact and efficient code
- Pointers can be used to achieve clarity and simplicity.
- Pointers are used to pass information between function and its reference point.
- Pointers provide a way to return multiple data items from a function using its function arguments.
- Pointers provide an alternate way to access an array element.
- Pointer enables us to access the memory directly.

20. What is Null pointer?

A pointer is said to be a null pointer when its right value is 0. A null pointer can never point to a valid data.

```
(e.g.) int *a;
       int *b;
       b=a=0;
```

21. What is pointer to pointer variable?

Pointer is a variable that contains the address of another variable. Similarly another pointer variable can store the address of this pointer variable. This is a pointer to pointer variable.

22. How the array elements to be accessed using pointers?

- Standard array notation
- Pointer arithmetic

23. What is the difference between an array and pointer?

Array	Pointer
1.Array allocates space automatically. 2.It cannot be resized. 3.It cannot be reassigned. 4.Sizeof(array name)gives the number of bytes occupied by the array.	1.Pointer is explicitly assigned to point to an allocated space. 2.It can be resized using realloc (). 3.Pointers can be reassigned. 4.Sizeof(pointer name)returns the number of bytes used to store the pointer variable.

24. What is the purpose of the function main()? (MAY2009)

The function main() invokes other functions within it. It is the first function to be called when the program starts execution. Some salient points about main()are as follows:

1. It is the starting function.
2. It returns an int value to the environment that called the program.
3. Recursive call is allowed for main() also.
4. It is a user-defined function.
5. Program execution ends when the closing brace of the function main() is reached.
6. It has two arguments

   (a) argument count and(b)argument vector(represents strings passed.)
7. Any user-defined name can also be used as parameters for main()instead of argc and argv

25. What is dangling pointer?

In C, a pointer may be used to hold the address of dynamically allocated memory. After this memory is freed with the free() function, the pointer itself will still contain the address of the released block. This is referred to as a dangling pointer. Using the pointer in this state is a serious programming error. Pointer should be assigned NULL after freeing memory to avoid this bug.

Part-B

1. Discuss about the elements of user defined functions and its use in C
    - Function Definition – Definition, Syntax, Example.
    - Function Declaration – Definition, Syntax, Example.
    - Function call – Definition, Syntax, Example.
2. Discuss the function prototypes in C

    Function with no arguments and no return values – Definition, Syntax, Example program.

    Function with arguments and no return values – Definition, Syntax, Example program.

    Function with arguments and with return value - Definition, Syntax, Example program.

    Function with no arguments and with return value - Definition, Syntax, Example program.
3. Explain the parameter passing methods using functions.
    - Call by value
    - Call by reference.
4. Define Recursion. Explain with an example
    - Definition
    - Syntax
    - Factorial Program using function
5. Explain the parameters to the function using pointers
    - Call by value
    - Call by reference
6. Discuss about pointers and its use in C
    - Introduction
    - Pointer declaration
    - Address operator
    - Pointer expressions and pointer arithmetic
    - Pointers and function
    - Pointers to arrays
    - Pointers to structures
    - Pointers on pointers

Unit V

Part-A

1. Define Structure

A structure is a collection of variables under a single name and provides a convenient way of grouping several pieces of related information together. It can be used for the storage of heterogeneous data.

2. Give the syntax for structure

```
[storage_class_specifier][type_qualifier]struct [ structure_name]
{
  type member_name1 [,member_name11,...];
  type member_name2 [,member_name22,...];
  .....
}[variable_name];
```

3. What are the two operations on structures?

- Aggregatc operations
- Segregate operations

4. List out the aggregate operations that can be applied on an object of a structure type.

- Accessing members of an object of a structure type.
- Assigning a structure object to a structure variable
- Address of a structure object
- Size of a structure.

5. Give a syntax for pointer to a structure.

[storage_class_specifier][type_qualifier]structnamed_structure_type*identifier_name [=lvalue[...]];

6. How will you access structure members via pointer to a structure?

(i) By using the dereference or indirection operator and the direct member access operator.

(*pointer_to_structure_type).structure_member_name

(ii) By using the indirect member access operator (- > arrow operator).

Pointer_to_structure_object - > Structure_member_name.

7. Define Union

A union is a collection of one or more variables of different types. All the members of an object share the same memory.

8. Give the syntax for union object.

[storage_class_specifier][type_qualifier]union named_union_type identifier_name [=initialization_list[...]];

9. Compare arrays and structures.

Arrays	Structures
An array is a collection of data items of same data type.	A structure is a collection of data items of different data types.
Arrays can only be declared. There is no keyword for arrays.	Structures can be declared and defined. The keyword for structures is struct.
An array name represents the address of the starting element.	A structure name is known as tag. It is a shorthand notation of the declaration.
An array cannot have bit fields.	A structure may contain bit fields.

10. Compare structures and unions.

Structure	Union
Every member has its own memory.	All members use the same memory.
The keyword used is struct.	The keyword used is union. Different interpretations for the same memory location are possible.
All members occupy separate memory location, hence different interpretations of the same memory location are not possible.	
Consumes more space compared to union.	Conservation of memory is possible.

11. Is it better to use a macro or a function?

Macros are more efficient(and faster)than function, because their corresponding code is inserted directly at the point where the macro is called. There is no overhead involved in using a macro like there is in placing a call to a function. However, macros are generally small and cannot handle large, complex coding constructs. Incases where large, complex constructs are to handled, functions are more suited, additionally; macros are expanded inline, which means that the code is replicated for each occurrence of a macro.

12. What is the use of 'typedef"?

It is used to create a new data using the existing type.

Syntax: typedef data type name;

Example: typedef int hours:hours hrs;/*Now,hours can be used as new data type */

13. Define a structure for an employee

```
Struct employee
{
char name[20];
int age;
double salary;
char designation[20];
}emp;
```

14. Define Self-Referential Structure.

A self referential structure is a dynamic structure that contains a pointer member that points to another structure that is of same structure type (pointing to them self).For example,

Syntax:

```
struct name
{
member 1;
member 2;
......
member n;
struct name *pointer;
};
```

15. What are the ways to implement a list.
    - Array implementation
    - Linked list implementation
    - Cursor based implementation
16. List the types of linked list

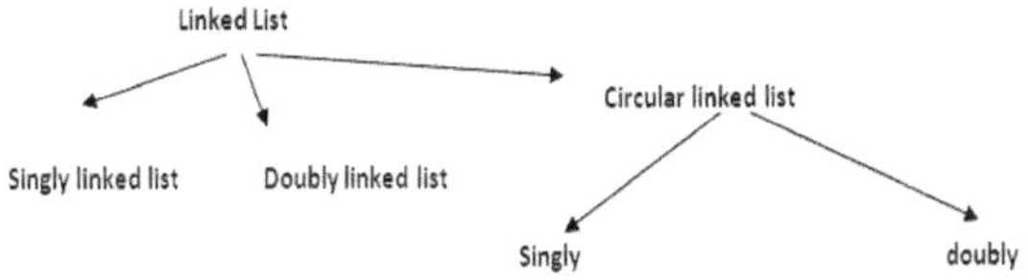

17. Define ADT

ADT stands for Abstract Data Type. ADT is a mathematical specification whose behavior is given by a set of operations and set of values. It gives you only the set of operations to be performed and not how it can be implemented. It is called "abstract" since it gives an implementation independent view.

18. Differentiate static and dynamic memory allocation

static memory allocation	**dynamic memory allocation**
Memory is allocated at compile time.	Memory is allocated at run time.
Memory can't be increased while executing program.	Memory can be increased while executing program.
Used in array.	Used in linked list.

19. List the dynamic memory allocation functions with syntax.

Function	Description/Use	Syntax
malloc()	Allocates requested size of bytes and returns a pointer first byte of allocated space	ptr=(cast-type*)malloc (byte_size);
calloc()	Allocates space for an array elements, initializes to zero and then returns a pointer to memory	ptr=(cast-type*)calloc (number, byte_size);
free()	deallocate the previously allocated space	realloc (pointer_name, new_size);
realloc()	Change the size of previously allocated space	free (pointer_name);

20. Differentiate array and linked list

Array	Linked List
Array is a contiguous static memory allocation where the size of the array should be fixed.	Linked list has dynamic memory size and involves dynamic memory allocation
Inserting a new element in an array of elements is expensive.	Ease of insertion and deletion
The elements can be accessed randomly. Binary search can be done.	Random access is not possible. Elements should be accessed sequentially from the first node. Binary search can't be performed.

Part-B

1. Explain about structure and Union declaration in C with suitable example
    - Definition
    - Giving values to members
    - Initializing structure
    - Functions and structures
    - Passing entire function to functions
    - Arrays of structure
    - Structure within a structure
    - Union
2. Define Union. Explain Union in detail.(JAN2009)

Union is a collection of variables similar to structure. The union requires bytes that are equal to number of bytes required for the largest number.

Example:

```
union student
{
char name[20];
int rollno,m1,m2,m3,tot;
float avg;
}s1;
```

Union of structure

Union can be nested with another union.

Example program: Program to use structure within union. Display the contents of structure elements.

3. With suitable example explain how pointer variable is used to access the members of a structure variable.

   i. By using the dereference or indirection operator and the direct member access operator.

      (*pointer_to_structure_type).structure_member_name

   ii. By using the indirect member access operator (- > arrow operator).

      Pointer_to_structure_object - > Structure_member_name.

Example

4. Give an example of nested structure. Explain how the structure members are accessed in a nested structure with a suitable example.

Nested structure – structure within structure

Example

```
Struct address
{
int doorno;
char streetname[15];
char city[15];
char state[15];
};
struct employee
{
char name[20];
int age;
double salary;
 char designation[20];
struct address addr;
}emp;
```

To access members of the nested structure

Ex:

Doorno.addr.emp;

5. Write a C program that gets *and* displays *the* report *of* n students with their personal an*d* academic details using structures.

   Define the structure for the student

   Get the details for each student

   Print the details

6. Write the ADT to perform all the operations in a singly linked list.

   Definition

   Operations – Insertion, Deletion, Search, Count, Display

   ADT and Example.

Unit VI

Part A

1. What is the necessity for files?

It is difficult to manage large volume of data by main memory (volatile), after the programs are executed, the data will be lost because they are stored in the temporary variables and arrays. Therefore it is necessary to store our data permanently in some place. Files are the solution for the permanent retention of data.

In C language, files are stored inside the disk or secondary storage devices, so that the data can be stored permanently and retrieved when required

2. Define File

A file is a collection or group of related records, placed on the disk or secondary storage devices.

A record is the collection or group of related fields, Use structure or class to represent the record

A Field is the group of characters which contains the actual data

Eg. employee(name, id, age, designation, address)

Here the employee record has 5 fields, and each field can have the meaningful values.The name field has the value nala, id field has 11, age field has 32, designation field has lecturer, and address field has puzhal

3. List the types of files

   1. Text files
   2. Binary files

4. Define Text File

It consists of text related information such as special symbols, alphabets and digits. It stores the the ASCII value of the characters into the file and uses only 7 bits for character and last bit(8th bit) has 0. Text files are easily readable. Each text file should be properly saved with extensions such as, .txt, .c, etc

5. Define Binary File

It is the combination of all type of data such as text, image, audio, video, etc. It stores all complex type data and uses entire byte(8 bits) to store the information. Binary files are not in a readable format. It can saved with .mp3, .doc, etc depending on the type of data.

6. List the areas where text and binary mode files are different.
   1. Handling of newlines
   2. Representation of end of file
   3. Storage of numbers
7. Write the difference between binary and text file.

Text File	Binary File
It consists of text related information such as special symbols, alphabets and digits	It contains custom data(text, audio, video, images, etc)
Uses only 7 bits for character and last bit(8th bit) has 0	Uses entire byte(8 bits) to store the information
Easily readable	Unreadable for humans
Time taken to access data is more	Takes less time to access the data
Handling of newline (end of line) character occupies an extra space in memory since it is converted into carriage return while writing into the disk and converted back into newline while reading. Therefore text files occupies more space compared to binary files	It requires less space compared to text file and there are no conversions taken place
It uses a special character to denote the EOF(end of file), that special character is stored with the ASCII 26 into the file, as soon as it is encountered in the file, immediately it returns EOF to the program	It does not require any special character to denote the end of file
Each character occupies 1 byte (but only 7 bits) in text file. For example, the integer value 5040 will occupy 2 bytes in the memory but 5 bytes in the text files	Here the integer value 5040 occupies the same 2 bytes in both memory and the binary file

8. Define Streams

It is also a file or any physical device such as monitor or printer or keyboard. It provides communication between the programs and the files. Reading characters from the file and writing characters into the file are also said to be sequence of streams.

9. List the functions to read and write data into the binary file

fread(): reads the no of objects stored from a file.

int fread(void *buffer, int size, int count, FILE *stream);

fwrite(): writes specified no of objects to a file.

int fwrite(const void *buffer, int size, int count, FILE *stream);

10. List the file positioning functions

ftell():returns the current file position indicator.

long ftell(FILE *stream);

fseek():moves the file position indicator to a specific location in a file.

int fseek(FILE *stream, long offset, int origin);

rewind():moves the file position indicator to the beginning of the file.

void rewind(FILE *stream)

11. How to declare a file?

To declare a file, use FILE structure as the base ,which is the predefined structure available in stdio.h and then declare a file variable as pointer to it.

FILE *fp; // fp is the file pointer that points to a FILE structure.

12. Define File Pointer

File Pointer: It is a pointer to a FILE structure and contains the following file information

1. file name
2. its current position
3. status about read and write process
4. error and EOF status.

13. List the basic file operations

1. Opening a file
2. reading from or writing into the file
3. Closing the file

14. Write the difference between write and append mode

Write mode	Append mode
If an existing file is opened in the write mode, its contents are overwritten.	If an existing file is opened in the append mode, pointer is moved to end of the file and starts adding or appending data at the end. It does not overwrite the already existing data
FILE *fp; fp=fopen("g.txt", "w");	FILE *fp; fp=fopen("g.txt", "a");

15. Give an example for fputs and fgets

fgets(book,80,fp); //book is the string reads and stores the set of characters, 80 the length of the string, fp is the file pointer

fputs(book,fp); //writes book data into the file

book is a string has the data to be written, fp is the file pointer

16. Write the functionality of fseek() function.

fseek(): It moves the file pointer position to the respective location of the file. It takes three arguments, the file pointer, the offset or the displacement and current file pointer position. It returns 0 on success otherwise non-zero. In order to make the file pointer to move to the respective location it uses the following parameters along with the displacement.

1. SEEK_SET: To move the file pointer to beginning of the file
2. SEEK_CUR: To move the file pointer to the specified location of the file
3. SEEK_END: To move the file pointer to the end of the file

17. What is ftell()?

ftell(): It returns the file position of the file. If the file is opened in binary mode, it returns the file position as number of bytes from the beginning of the file. If it is opened in text mode, it should take help from fseek() to tell the bytes. It returns number of bytes on success otherwise EOF

fseek(fp, 0, SEEK_END);// makes the fp to reach the end
length1 = ftell(fp); /*always ftell() should work along with fseek(), it can tell number of bytes available in the file only with the help of fseek()*/
length1 is the integer variable to hold the number of bytes of the file

18. Which function is used read and write an integer from a file?

putw() : It writes an integer value to a file. It takes two arguments, a number variable to hold the integer value to write and the file pointer. On success, returns the integer value otherwise EOF

getw() : It reads an integer value from a file. It takes an argument as file pointer through which the integer value can be read. On success, returns the next integer value otherwise EOF

19. Define Sequential file

In Sequential access file elements are arranged in a sequential manner. Reading the element from the file or writing the element into the file should start from the beginning to the end. It does not allow the user to access or modify or delete any record directly

20. Define Random access file:

It is also called as direct access since we can read or write any record of any location in the file. Records can be arranged randomly in the file. It allows the user to access, modify and delete any record randomly or directly.

21. Write the difference between sequential and random access file

Sequential file processing	Random file processing
Records or elements should be accessed in sequential order 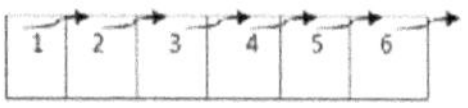	Records or elements can be accessed in any order 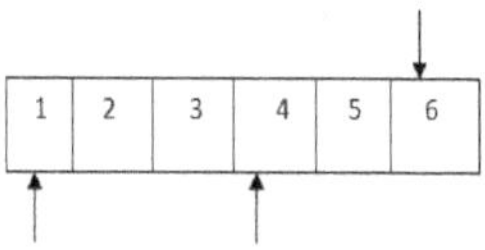
Tape drives incorporate Sequential file access mechanism	In Hard Disks and Optical drives, random access mechanism can also be used
Sequential read is very fast when compared to random read	Number of seek operations takes much time to do random access
In a Sequential file, each record can be of different length	Implemented using fixed length records

22. What are all the functions used by random access file?
    1. fseek()
    2. ftell()
    3. rewind()
23. Define Command line argument. Write the purpose too

Passing values at the command line to the source program is called the command line arguments. Those passed values are sent as arguments to the main() in the source program. The arguments are argc and argv. The argc parameter counts the number of arguments or values passed at the command line and argv[] parameter is a pointer array pointing to the command line arguments. Command line arguments are mainly used to control the source program from outside.

24. Give an example for command line arguments

int main(int argc, char **argv)

"argc" counts the number of arguments at the command line

"argv[]" a pointer array pointing to the command line arguments

Example 1:

C:\TURBOC3\SOURCE>cm.exe hi hello welcome

argc counts the command line arguments as 4

argv[0] has cm.exe //cm.exe is the source program's exe file

argv[1] has hi

argv[2] has hello

argv[3] has welcome

Example 2:

C:\TURBOC3\SOURCE>p29.exe r.txt

argc counts the value as 2

argv[0] has p29.exe

argv[1] has r.txt

To open the file r.txt in the source program p29.c, we can have the following code :

FILE *fp;

f p= fopen(argv[1], "r"); // argv[1] has r.txt and it is opened in read mode

25. List any two applications of file
    1. Creating Calculator Application
    2. Bank Management Application(transaction processing)

Part-B

1. Explain File Handling functions in 'C'.

List all the file functions with proper syntax, its role and give an example each:

fopen(),fclose(), fgetc(), fputc(), fgets(), fputs(), fscanf(), fprintf(), fread(),fwrite(), fseek(), rewind(), ftell(), feof(), remove(),ferror(), rename(), putw(), getw()

2. Describe in detail about File Access Modes for both binary and text files

   List all the modes for both text and binary files –r,rb,w,wb,a,ab,r+,rb+,w+,wb+,a+,ab+

   Write the characteristics of each mode

3. Write a program to reverse the string stored in the file
   - Declare the FILE Structure and a file pointer
   - Open the file in the respective mode
   - Use respective file handling functions to reverse the string
   - Finally close the file through file pointer
4. Write a program to Copy Content of One File into Another File
   - Declare the FILE Structure and two file pointers
   - Open both the files in the respective modes(read | write)
   - Use respective file handling functions to copy the string
   - Finally close both files through fcloseall() or close the files individually
5. Write a program to merge two files and store it into another existing or new file
   - Declare the FILE Structure and three file pointers
   - Open two files in the read mode and third one in the write mode
   - Use respective file handling functions to merge the content of those two files and store it into the third file
   - Finally close all the files.
6. Explain fseek() and ftell() with suitable example programs
   - Write the definition of fseek() and its sub parameters and ftell()
   - Write the Syntax and an example snippet for both
   - Declare the FILE Structure and a file pointer
   - Open the file in the respective mode
   - Use both the functions to find the size of the file
   - Print the size of the file
   - Finally close the file.

7. Write a program to find average of numbers stored in sequential access file
    - Declare the FILE Structure and a file pointer
    - Open the file in the respective mode
    - Use respective file handling functions to read the number sequentially from the file
    - Do average on the numbers
    - Finally close the file through file pointer
8. Write a program to write and access the student records sequentially
    - Declare the FILE Structure and a file pointer
    - Define the structure for student and declare a structure variable
    - Open the file in the respective mode
    - Use respective file handling functions to read and write the student records sequentially in the file
    - Finally close the file through file pointer
9. Define Random access file and list out the fuctions used in random access file. Write a program to do the following book transactions in the library.
    A. accessing the book details of a given book
    B. updating the price details of a given book
        - Defile Random access file
        - Give syntax and characteristics of the functions fseek(), ftell() and rewind()
        - Declare the FILE Structure and a file pointer
        - Define the structure for book and declare a book variable
        - Open the file in the respective mode
        - Use respective file handling functions to access and update the details of a given book randomly in the file
        - Finally close the file through file pointer
10. Explain Command line arguments in detail with a suitable example program.
    - Define command line arguments
    - give the syntax and an example snippet
    - Write a program using files and pass the file in the command line as argument
    - Compile the source program
    - Execute the source program to get the exe file
    - Go to file menu and click DOS Shell, you will get a command prompt with C:\TURBOC3\BIN
    - change the bin to source C:\TURBOC3\BIN> CD ..

- C:\TURBOC3\CD SOURCE
- C:\TURBOC3\SOURCE>source_filename.exe g6.txt
- Write the purpose of command line argument.

Question Paper Code: 50648

B.E/B.Tech DEGREE EXAMINATION, NOV/DEC 2017

First Semester

Mechanical Engineering

GE6151 – Computer Programming

(Common to ALL Branches)

(Regulation 2013)

Time: Three hours **Maximum: 100 Marks**

Answer ALL questions

Part A – (10 x 2 = 20 marks)

1. Convert the given octal number 12570_8 into decimal number.

   Ans:$(5496)_{10}$ [Refer pg no:20,21]

2. What is Flowchart? **Refer pg no: 27**
3. What is the difference between while loop and do while loop? **Refer pg no: 71**
4. What is the use of sizeof() operator? **Refer pg no: 57**
5. What are the features of array? **Refer pg no: 89**
6. Differentiate between linear search and binary search.

   Refer Annexure 1 Question Bank Unit 3 Q.No: 25

7. Distinguish between call by value and call by reference.

   Refer Annexure 1 Question Bank Unit 4 Q.No: 8

8. What are the advantages of using pointers in a program?

   Refer Annexure 1 Question Bank Unit 4 Q.No: 19

9. Define in C++. Define 'Structure' of C language. Give an example.

   Refer pg no: 181,182

10. What storage classes are available in C language? **Refer pg no: 51**

Part B – (5 x 16 = 80 marks)

11. (a) (i) Explain in detail about the characteristics of Computer. (6)

    Refer pg no: 1

    (ii) Describe in detail about the classification of computers with their features and limitations. **Refer pg no: 10** (10)

    (or)

    (b) (i) Give Pseudo code algorithm and the flowchart to print the Fibonacci series of n terms. (8)

Algorithm

Step 1: Start

Step 2: Declare variables n, first, second, next, c

Step 3: Initialize first=0,second=1

Step 4: Read the value of n

Step 5: Repeat the Steps until c<n

5.1: if c<=1

5.1.1: next=c

5.2: else

5.2.1: next = first + second

5.2.2: first = second

5.2.3: second = next

Step 6: display next

Step 7: Stop

Flowchart

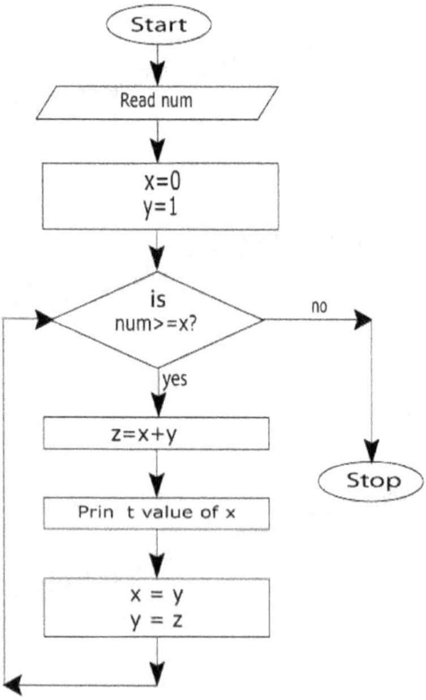

(ii) Draw an algorithm and draw the flowchart to find the largest among three numbers.

Refer pg no: 25,30 (8)

12. (a) Explain the different types of operators available in C with example. (16)

Refer pg no: 53

(or)

(b) (i) With an example program explain the various decision making statements available in C. **Refer pg no: 61** (8)

(ii) Explain switch case statement and 'for' loop statement with suitable example.

Refer pg no: 65,69 (8)

13. (a) (i) What is an array? Write a C program to arrange the given 10 numbers in ascending order using one dimensional array. **Refer pg no: 89** (8)

(ii) Write a C program to multiply two 3x3 matrices. **Refer pg no: 101** (8)

(or)

(b) (i) Write a C program to count the number of vowels, Consonants, Digits and Spaces in a given string. Discuss the algorithm for the same. (16)

```
#include <stdio.h>
int main()
{
  char line[150];
  int i, vowels, consonants, digits, spaces;
  vowels =  consonants = digits = spaces = 0;
  printf("Enter a line of string: ");
  scanf("%[^\n]", line);
  for(i=0; line[i]!='\0'; ++i)
  {
    if(line[i]=='a' || line[i]=='e' || line[i]=='i' ||
      line[i]=='o' || line[i]=='u' || line[i]=='A' ||
      line[i]=='E' || line[i]=='I' || line[i]=='O' ||
      line[i]=='U')
    {
      ++vowels;
    }
    else if((line[i]>='a'&& line[i]<='z') || (line[i]>='A'&& line[i]<='Z'))
    {
      ++consonants;
    }
```

```
        else if(line[i]>='0' && line[i]<='9')
        {
          ++digits;
        }
        else if (line[i]==' ')
        {
          ++spaces;
        }
      }
      printf("Vowels: %d",vowels);
      printf("\nConsonants: %d",consonants);
      printf("\nDigits: %d",digits);
      printf("\nWhite spaces: %d", spaces);
      return 0;
}
```

ALGORITHM:

Step 1: Start

Step 2: Input a String

Step 3: Initialize vowels, consonants, digits and spaces to 0.

Step 4: Repeat Steps 4.1 to 4.6 till string[i]!='\0'

Step 4.1: if line[i] == 'a'||'A' or line[i]=='e'||'E' or line[i]=='I'||'i' or line[i]='o'||'O' or line[i]='u'||'U' then increment the vowels count by 1.

Step 4.2: else if line[i] is between 'a' & 'z' or 'A' &'Z' then increment consonants count by 1.

Step 4.3: else if line[i] is between 0 and 9 then increment digits count by 1.

Step 4.4: else if line[i] is a blank spaces then increment spaces count by 1.

Step 5: Display the count of vowels, consonants, digits and spaces.

Step 6: End

14. (a) Explain about the different parameter passing methods in functions with examples.

Refer pg no:168 (16)

(or)

(b) (i) Write a C program to swap the content of two variables using pointers (8)

Refer pg no: 170

(ii) Write a C program to read integers into an array and reversing them using pointers. **Refer pg no: 177** (8)

15. (a) Write a C program and algorithm to create mark sheet for students using structure. **Refer pg no:187** (16)

(or)

(b) Write algorithm and a C program using unions, to prepare the employee pay roll of a company (16)

Algorithm:

Step 1: Start

Step 2: Define union with a member variable netpay and structure with member variables employee name, number, basic pay, allowance and deduction

Step 3: Declare structure and union variable as an array to work for 'n' number of employees

Step 4: Store the details of employee into the structure

Step 5: Store the net payment of employee into the union

Step 6: Display the employee details using both structure and union

Step 7: Stop

```
#include<stdio.h>
#include<conio.h>
struct emp
{
int empno ;
char name[10] ;
int bpay, allow, ded;
}e[2] ;
union emp1
{
int npay;
}u[2];
void main()
{
```

```
int i, n;
clrscr() ;
printf("Enter the number of employees : ") ;
scanf("%d", &n) ;
for(i = 0 ; i < n ; i++)
{
printf("\nEnter employee number :");
scanf("%d", &e[i].empno) ;
printf("\nEnter the name : ") ;
scanf("%s", e[i].name) ;
printf("\nEnter the basic pay, allowances & deductions : ") ;
scanf("%d%d%d", &e[i].bpay, &e[i].allow, &e[i].ded) ;
printf("\nemployee number is:%d\nemployee name is:%s\nbasic pay is:%d\nallowance
is:%d\ndeduction is:%d\n",e[i].empno,e[i].name,e[i].bpay,e[i].allow,e[i].ded);
u[i].npay = e[i].bpay + e[i].allow - e[i].ded ;
printf("\nNetpay is:%d",u[i].npay);
}
getch() ;
}
```

OUTPUT:

```
Enter the number of employees : 2
Enter employee number :1
Enter the name : nala
Enter the basic pay, allowances & deductions : 20000 3000 1000
employee number is:1
employee name is:nala
basic pay is:20000
allowance is:3000
deduction is:1000
Netpay is:22000
```

Enter employee number :2

Enter the name : kala

Enter the basic pay, allowances & deductions : 30000 3000 1000

employee number is:2

employee name is:kala

basic pay is:30000

allowance is:3000

deduction is:1000

Netpay is:32000

Question Paper Code: 27655

B.E/B.Tech Degree Examination, Dec 2015/Jan 2016

First Semester

Civil Engineering

GE6151 – Computer Programming

(Common to ALL Branches)

(Regulation 2013)

Time: Three hours **Maximum: 100 Marks**

Answer All Questions

Part A-(10*2=20 marks)

1. Convert $(1011101)_2$ to octal.

   Ans:$(135)_8$ [Refer pg no:21]

2. Differentiate algorithm and pseudocode.

S.NO	ALGORTIHM	PSEUDOCODE
1	Algorithm is an ordered sequence of finite, well defined, unambiguous instructions for completing a task.	Pseudo code consists of short, readable and formally–styled English language for explaining an algorithm.
2	Converting an algorithm into a program code is not easy	Converting a pseudo code to a program code is easy

3. What is meant by linking process? **Refer pg no: 76**

4. What are the input and output functions in C? **Refer pg no: 57**

5. Write a C program to store Fibonacci series in an array.

```
#include<stdio.h>
#include<conio.h>
void main()
{
  int i,n,a[100];
  clrscr();
  printf("How many terms to be display : ");
  scanf("%d",&n);
  a[0]=0;a[1]=1;
  for(i=2;i<n;i++)
    a[i]=a[i-1]+a[i-2];
 printf("First %d Terms of fibonacci series \n",n);
```

```
  for(i=0;i<n;i++)
    printf("%5d",a[i]);
  getch();
}
```

6. List the string functions available in C. **Refer pg no: 147**

7. State the significance of pointers.
   - Pointers provide direct access to memory and address of the variables can be extracted.
   - Pointers provide a way to return more than one value to the functions
   - Reduces the storage space, execution time and complexity of the program
   - Provides an alternate way to access array elements
   - Pointers can be used to pass information back and forth between the calling function and called function.
   - Pointers allow us to perform dynamic memory allocation and deallocation.
   - Pointers helps us to build complex data structures like linked list, stack, queues, trees, graphs etc.

8. Write a program to print the first 50 prime numbers recursively.

```
#include<stdio.h>
void main()
{
int count=0;
int num=1;
int i;
printf("prime nums \n");
while(count<50)
{
num++;
for (i=2;i<=num-1;i)
{
if(num%i==0)break;
i++;
}
if(i>=num-1)
{
```

```c
printf("%d ",num);
count++;
}}}
```

9. Define a structure called ID_Card to hold the details of a student.

```c
struct ID_Card
{
   int id_no;
   char name[50];
   char dept[20];
   long int batch;
};
```

10. List some C preprocessor directives. **Refer pg no: 72**

Part B-(5*16=80 marks)

11. a (i) Elaborate the various generations of computers and their characteristics and represent them in a tabular format. **Refer pg no: 6** (8)

(ii) Write in detail about the basic organization of a computer. **Refer pg no:12** (8)

(OR)

b Write an algorithm and flowchart to simulate the railway ticket booking process. (16)

Algorithm:

Step 1: Start

Step 2: Read train_no, train_name, from, to and class type

Step 3: Check for ticket availability

Step 3.1 if tickets are available then book ticket(go to step4) with the following data

No_of_passengers, from, to, age, train_no, train_name and class type

Step 3.2 else Quit the process

Step 4: Book ticket with the following check

Step 4.1 if age is greater than or equal to 60, allocate lower berth and payment is 1/3

Step 4.2 if age is lesser than 60 then regular payment with the requested berth

Step 5: Read payment amount and make the payment

Step 6: Stop

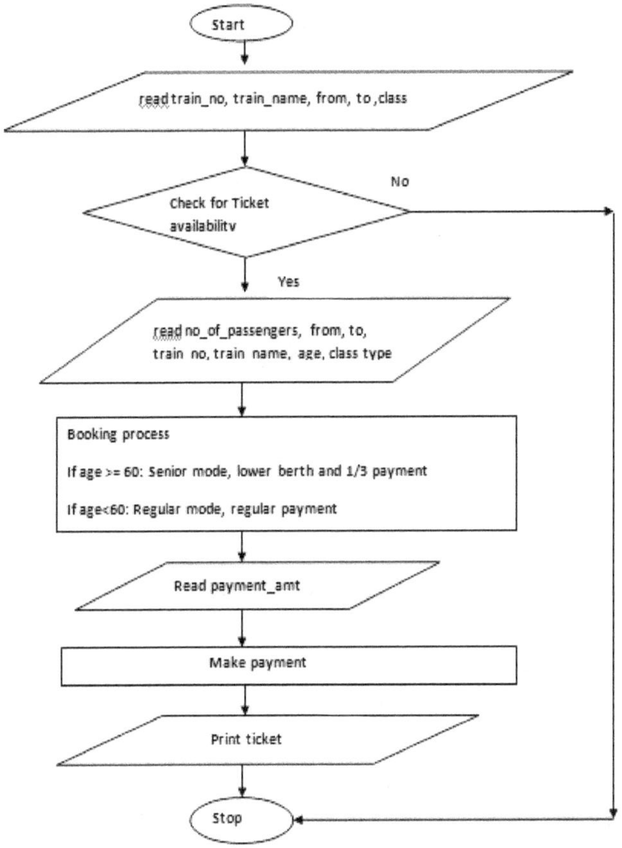

12. a (i) Describe the structure of a C program using "Calculator Program" example. (8)

Refer pg no:37

Calculator Program:

```
 #include<stdio.h>  /*header files*/
#include<conio.h>
#include<stdlib.h>
void add(int a,int b)  /*user defined functions definition*/
{
printf("Addition of %d and %d is %d \n",a,b,a+b);
}
void sub(int a,int b)
```

```
{
printf("Subtraction of %d and %d is %d \n",a,b,a-b);
}
void mult(int a,int b)
{
printf("Multiplication of %d and %d is %d \n",a,b,a*b);
}
void div1(int a,int b)
{
printf("Division of %d and %d is %d \n",a,b,a/b);
}
void main() /*main function*/
{
int a,b,c;
int n=0;
clrscr();
printf("************* Calculator program ***************\n");
printf("\n Enter two numbers");
scanf("%d%d",&a,&b);
do
{
printf("______________________");
printf("\n1.addition\n");
printf("2.subtraction\n");
printf("3.multiplication \n");
printf("4.division\n");
printf("5.exit \n");
printf("______________________");
printf("\nenter your choice \n");
scanf("%d",&c);
switch(c)
{
case 1: add(a,b);
break;
```

```
case 2:sub(a,b);
break;
case 3: mult(a,b);
break;
case 4:div1(a,b);
break;
case 5:exit(0);
default:printf("wrong chioce \n");
}
printf("you want to continue press 1");
scanf("%d",&n);
}while(n==1);
getch();
}
```

(ii) Write short note on branching statement in C. **Refer pg no: 61** (8)

(OR)

b (i) Write in detail about the various looping statements with suitable examples.(16)

Refer pg no: 68

13. a (i)Write a C program to multiply two 3 * 3 matrix. **Refer pg no: 101** (10)

(ii) Write a C program to find the determinant of the resultant matrix. **Refer pg no: 107** (6)

(OR)

b Write the following programs:

(i) to sort a given set of strings alphabetically. **Refer pg no: 122** (6)

(ii) to print whether each word is a palindrome or not. (6)

```
#include <stdio.h>
#include <string.h>
int main()
{
  char a[100], b[100];
  printf("Enter a string to check if it is a palindrome\n");
  gets(a);
  strcpy(b,a);
  strrev(b);
  if (strcmp(a,b) == 0)
```

```
    printf("Entered string is a palindrome.\n");
  else
    printf("Entered string is not a palindrome.\n");
  return 0;
}
```

(iii) to count the length of each string. **Refer pg no: 116** (4)

14. a (i)What is the difference between call by value and call by reference? What are the problems associated with each? Explain with suitable examples (8)

Refer pg no: 168 and Annexure 1 Question bank unit 4 Q.No:8 for table

(ii) What are the advantages of using recursion? Demonstrate with examples. (8)

Refer pg no: 150,154

(OR)

b. Write in detail about pointer arithmetic. Support your answer with appropriate examples. **Refer pg no: 162** (16)

15. 15. a (i) What is the need for structure data type? Does structure bring additional overhead to a program? Justify **Refer pg no: 181** (10)

(ii) Write short note on structure declaration. **Refer pg no: 182** (6)

(OR)

b. What are the storage classes available in C? Demonstrate the working of each storage class. **Refer pg no: 45** (16)

Question Paper Code: 57408

B.E/ B.Tech Degree Examination, May/June 2016

First Semester

Civil Engineering

GE6151 – Computer Programming

(Common to ALL Branches)

(Regulation 2013)

Time: Three hours **Maximum: 100 Marks**

Answer All Questions

Part A-(10*2=20 marks)

1. Classify the computers based on performance, size, cost and capacity **Refer pg no: 10**
2. Convert the binary number 10110111.1101 into decimal number

   Ans:$(183.8125)_{10}$ [Refer pg no:20]
3. What are variables? Give examples. **Refer pg no: 42**
4. Define implicit type conversion

Implicit Type Conversion Also known as 'automatic type conversion'.

- Done by the compiler on its own, without any external trigger from the user.
- Generally takes place when in an expression more than one data type is present. In such condition type conversion (type promotion) takes place to avoid lose of data.
- All the data types of the variables are upgraded to the data type of the variable with largest data type.

5. What is an array? **Refer pg no: 89**
6. Define String. Give examples. **Refer pg no: 112**
7. Specify the advantages of functions. **Refer pg no:141**
8. How is pointer arithmetic done? **Refer pg no:162**
9. What do you mean by structures? **Refer pg no:181**
10. State the importance of Union **Refer pg no:194**

Part B-(5*16=80 marks)

11. a (i) Describe the basic computer organization with neat diagram **Refer pg no:12** (10)

    (ii) Draw the flow chart to solve the quadratic equation (6)

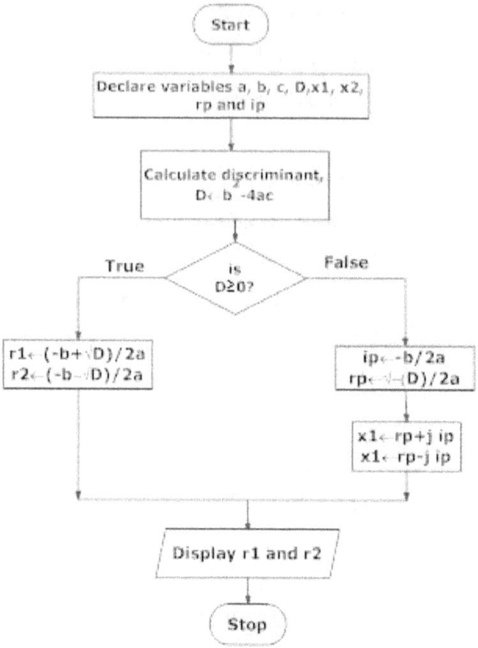

(OR)

b (i) Explain the various generations of computers. **Refer pg no:6** (8)

(ii) What is pseudo code? Explain its guidelines and benefits **Refer pg no: 25** (8)

12. a (i)Explain the different types of operators available in C **Refer pg no: 53** (10)

(ii) Discuss the basic data types in C **Refer pg no: 43** (6)

(OR)

b (i) Describe the various input and output statements in C with suitable examples. (10)

Refer pg no:57

(ii) Write a C program for the following series: (6)

1 + 2 + 3 + 4 + ... + n

```
#include<stdio.h>
int main(){
int n,i;
int sum=0;
printf("Enter the n i.e. max values of series: ");
scanf("%d",&n);
sum = (n * (n + 1)) / 2;
```

```
printf("Sum of the series: ");
for(i =1;i <= n;i++){
if (i!=n)
    printf("%d + ",i);
else
   printf("%d = %d ",i,sum);
}
    return 0;
}
```

13. a (i) Write a C program to count the number of vowels in your name (6)

```
#include<stdio.h>
#include<conio.h>
void main()
{
int i, v=0;
char s1[20];
clrscr();
printf("\n Enter the Text: ");
gets(s1);
for(i=0;s1[i]!='\0';i++)
{
switch(s1[i])
{
case 'A':
case 'E':
case 'I':
case 'O':
case 'U':
case 'a':
case 'e':
case 'i':
case 'o':
case 'u':
v++;
```

```c
break;
default:
break;
}
}
printf("\n The number of vowels is: %d",v);
getch();
}
```

(ii) Write a C program to multiply two matrices **Refer pg no: 101** (10)

(OR)

b (i) Write a C program to check whether the given string is palindrome or not. (6)

Refer Question paper code:27655, Q.No. 13.b.(ii)

(ii) Write a C program to arrange the given 10 numbers in descending order.

Refer pg no: 125 (10)

14. a (i) Write a C program to find the smallest and largest number from the given 10 numbers using functions. (10)

```c
#include <stdio.h>
int max(int num1, int num2);
int min(int num1, int num2);
int main()
{
  int num1, num2, maximum, minimum;
  printf("Enter any two numbers: ");
  scanf("%d%d", &num1, &num2);
  maximum = max(num1, num2);
  minimum = min(num1, num2);
  printf("\nMaximum = %d\n", maximum);
  printf("Minimum = %d", minimum);
  return 0;
}
int max(int num1, int num2)
{
  return (num1 > num2 ) ? num1 : num2;
}
```

```
int min(int num1, int num2)
{
   return (num1 > num2 ) ? num2 : num1;
}
```

(ii) Explain the pass by reference with an example **Refer pg no:170** (6)

(OR)

b (i) Write a C program to find the factorial of a given number using recursion

Refer pg no:151 (8)

(ii) Write a C program to count the number of words in a string using pointers (8)

```
#include<stdio.h>
void main() {
  int now, pos = high;
  char *str;
  now = 0;
  clrscr();
  printf("Enter any string : ");
  gets(str);
  while (*str != '\0') {
    if (*str == ' ') {
         pos = high;
    }
else if (pos == high) {
      pos = low;
      ++now;
    }
    str++;
  }
  printf("\nNumber of words  %d", now);
  getch();
}
```

15. a Define a structure called student would contain name, register number and marks of five subjects and percentage. Write a program to read the details of name, register number and marks of five subjects for 25 students, calculate the percentage and display the name,

register number, marks of 5 subjects, percentage of all the students and also the name of the student who got highest percentage among the 25 students. (16)

```
#include<stdio.h>
#include<conio.h>
struct student
{
char student_name[20];
int reg_no;
int marks[5];
int percentage;
};
void main()
{
struct student s[25];
int i,j,k=0,total=0,t=0;
clrscr();
printf("Enter student details:\n");
for(i=0;i<25;i++)
{
printf("Enter student name: ");
scanf("%s",s[i].student_name);
printf("Enter register number");
scanf("%d",&s[i].reg_no);
printf("\nEnter 5 subject marks: ");
for(j=0;j<5;j++)
scanf("%d",&s[i].marks[j]);
printf("\n");
}
printf("students details:\n\n");
for(i=0;i<25;i++)
{
printf("\nThe student name is:%s",s[i].student_name);
printf("\nThe student register no is:%d",s[i].reg_no);
printf("\nThe student marks are:");
```

```
for(j=0;j<5;j++)
{
printf("\n%d",s[i].marks[j]);
total=total+s[i].marks[j];
}
k=total/5;
s[i].percentage=k;
total=0;
printf("\nThe student percentage is:%d",s[i].percentage);
}
t=s[0].percentage;
for(i=0;i<=1;i++)
{
if( t > (s[i+1].percentage))
t=s[i].percentage;
else
t=s[i+1].percentage;
}
printf("\nThe highest percentage is:%d",t);
for(i=0;i<25;i++)
{
if(s[i].percentage==t)
printf("\nThe student who got highest percentage is:%s",s[i].student_name);
}
getch();
}
```

(OR)

b (i) Explain the various storage classes in C. **Refer pg no: 45** (8)

(ii) Describe about the pre-processors with suitable examples. **Refer pg no:72** (8)

Question Paper Code:77156

B.E/B.Tech DEGREE EXAMINATION, APRIL/MAY 2015

First Semester

Civil Engineering

GE6151 – Computer Programming

(Common to ALL Branches)

(Regulation 2013)

Time: Three hours **Maximum: 100 Marks**

Answer ALL questions

Part A–(10 x 2 = 20 marks)

1. What is super computer? Give an example. **Refer pg no: 12**
2. Define pseudo code. **Refer pg no: 25**
3. What is the importance of keywords in C?

   Keyword is a predefined reserved word that has a particular meaning in the programming language. There are 32 keywords in C. A program cannot be written without the keywords. They are used to implement specific features in the language and cannot be as user defined identifiers.
4. List the various input and output statements in C.**Refer pg no: 57**
5. What is an array? Give an example.**Refer pg no: 89**
6. How is a character string declared?**Refer pg no: 121**
7. Compare actual parameters and formal parameters.**Refer pg no: 168**
8. What is the output of the following program?

```
main()
{
int a=8, b=4, c, *p1=&a, *p2=&b;
c=*p1**p2-*p1/*p2+9;
printf("%d",c);
}
```

   Ans: Program gives error on compiling
9. What do you mean by structures? **Refer pg no: 181**
10. Give the use of pre-processor.
    - To make writing source code easier (more portable)
    - To make the source code more understandable

Part B–(5 x 16 = 80 marks)

11. (a) (i) Describe various generations of Computers. **Refer pg no: 6** (10)

(ii) Convert the decimal number 681.75 into binary, octal and hexadecimal equivalent. (6)

Binary = $(1010101001.1100000)_2$

Octal = $(1251.600)_8$

Hexadecimal = $(2A9.C0)_{16}$

(or)

(b) (i) Explain the basic organization of a computer with neat diagram.

Refer pg no: 12 (10)

(ii) Draw a flowchart to check whether the given number is zero, positive or negative. (6)

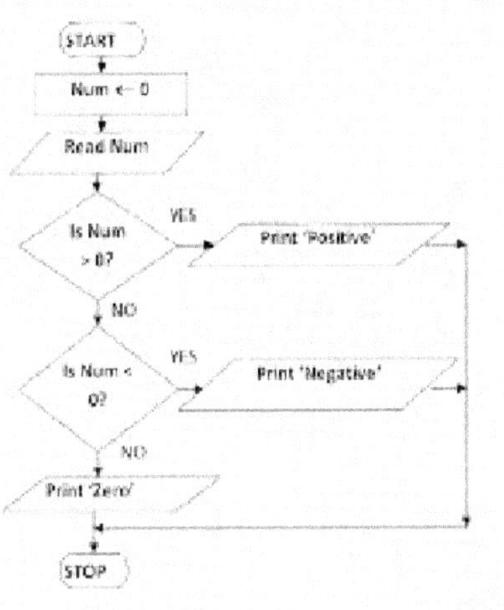

12. (a) (i) Explain the different types of operators available in C. **Refer pg no: 53** (8)

(ii) What are constants? Explain the various types of constants in C.

Refer pg no: 40 (8)

(or)

(b)(i) Describe the various looping statements used in C with suitable examples.

Refer pg no: 68 (8)

(ii) Write the C program to solve the quadratic equation. **Refer pg no:83** (8)

13. (a) (i) Write a C program to add two matrices. **Refer pg no: 99** (10)

(ii) Write a C program to search a given number in an array of elements.

Refer pg no: 132 (6)

(or)

(b) (i) Write a C program to arrange the given 10 numbers in ascending order.

Refer pg no: 125 (10)

(ii) Explain the various string handling functions. **Refer pg no: 147** (6)

14. (a) (i) Write a C program to find the factorial of a given number using function (8)

Refer pg no: 151

(ii) Write a C program to exchange the values of two variables using pass by reference

Refer pg no: 170 (8)

(or)

(b) (i) Write a C program to find the sum of the digits using recursive function. (8)

```
#include <stdio.h>
int sum (int a);
int main()
{
int num, result;
printf("Enter the number: ");
scanf("%d", &num);
result = sum(num);
printf("Sum of digits in %d is %d\n", num, result);
return 0;
}
int sum (int num)
{
if (num != 0)
{
return (num % 10 + sum (num / 10));
}
else
{
return 0;
}
}
```

(ii) Write a C program using pointers to read in an array of integers and print its elements in reverse order. **Refer pg no: 177** (8)

15. (a) Define a structure called book with book name, author name and price. Write a C program to read the details of book name, author name and price of 200 books in a library and display the total cost of the books and the book details whose price is above Rs.500. (16)

```
#include<stdio.h>
#include<conio.h>
struct book_details
{
char book_name[20] ;
char author[20];
int price;
}b[200];
void accept(struct book_details b1[], int n)
{
int i, k=500, total_price=0;
for(i=1;i<=n;i++)
{
printf("\nenter book name author name and price");
scanf("%s", b1[i].book_name);
scanf("%s",b1[i].author);
scanf("%d", &b1[i].price);
total_price=total_price+b[i].price;
}
printf("\nThe total price of all the book is: %d",total_price);
printf("\nBooh Details\n");
for(i=1;i<=n;i++)
{
printf("\nThe details of book %d is: ", i);
printf("\nThe book name: %s", b1[i].book_name);
printf("\nThe author name: %s",b1[i].author);
printf("\nBook price is: %d", b1[i].price);
}
printf("\nThe details of book whose price is greater than 500");
for(i =0 ; i <= n ; i++)
```

```
{
if(b[i].price>k)
{
printf("\n%s", b1[i].book_name);
printf("\n%s",b1[i].author);
printf("\n%d", b1[i].price);
}
 }
}
void main()
{
clrscr();
accept(b,200);
getch();
}
```

(or)

(b) (i) Explain the various storage classes in C. **Refer pg no: 45** (10)

(ii) What is union? Discuss with an example. **Refer pg no: 193** (6)

Question Paper Code : 97078

B.E/B.Tech DEGREE EXAMINATION, NOV/DEC 2014

First Semester

Civil Engineering

GE6151 – Computer Programming

(Common to ALL Branches)

(Regulation 2013)

Time: Three hours **Maximum: 100 Marks**

Answer ALL questions.

Part A–(10 x 2 = 20 marks)

1. Define flow chart. Why is flowchart required? **Refer pg no:27**
2. What is an algorithm? **Refer pg no:24**
3. What is a variable? Illustrate with an example. **Refer pg no:42**
4. Give an example for Ternary variable. **Refer pg no:55**
5. Declare a float array of size 5 and assign 5 values to it.

   float array[5];

   array[5]={2.1,4.5,3.4,6.8,9.3};
6. Give an example for initialization of string array. **Refer pg no:112**
7. What is a function? **Refer pg no:138**
8. What is an address operator and indirection operator? **Refer pg no:56**
9. Define static storage class. **Refer pg no:49**
10. What is the use of #define pre-processor? **Refer pg no:73**

Part B–(5 x 16 = 80 marks)

11. (a) (i) Explain in detail with neat diagram about the Digital Computer organization and each of its unit **Refer pg no:12** (10)

    (ii) What is pseudo code? write a pseudo code for swapping two numbers without using temporary storage. **Refer pg no: 25** (6)

    READ values A and B

    COMPUTE

    A← A + B

    B ← A - B

    A ← A - B

    DISPLAY A and B

(or)

(b) (i) Perform the following: (12)

(1) $(100101)_2 - (11111001)_2$ **Ans: $(-11010100)_2 = (-212)_{10}$**

(2) $(1011101)_2 \times (1011)_2$ **Ans: $(1111111111)_2 = (1023)_{10}$**

(3) $(2A947)_H = (\ ?\ )_2$ **Ans: $(101010100101000111)_2$**

(4) $(4872) = (\ ?\ )_8$ **Ans: $(11410)_8$**

(ii) Discuss the need for logical analysis with an example in brief.

Refer pg no:22 (4)

12. (a) What are the various operators available in C? Discuss each one of them with suitable iilustrations. **Refer pg no:53** (16)

(or)

(b) Explain in detail about various looping structures available in C with illustrative programs. **Refer pg no:68** (16)

13. (a) (i) Write a C program for sorting an array of numbers **Refer pg no:125** (8)

(ii) Explain the various string operations. Write a C program to find out the length of the string without using built-in function **Refer pg no:118,147** (8)

(or)

(b) (i) Write a C program to multiply two matrices **Refer pg no:101** (8)

(ii) Write a C program to search an element in a given array **Refer pg no:132** (8)

14. (a) What is function in C? Discuss about call by value and call by reference with illustrations. **Refer pg no:138,168** (16)

(or)

(b) What is recursion? Explain a recursive function with suitable example. Write a iterative and recursive function to find the power of a number. **Refer pg no:150** (16)

```
#include <stdio.h>
long power (int, int);
int main()
{
int pow, num;
long result;
printf("Enter a number: ");
scanf("%d", &num);
printf("Enter it's power: ");
scanf("%d", &pow);
```

```
result = power(num, pow);
printf("%d^%d is %ld", num, pow, result);
return 0;
}
long power (int num, int pow)
{
if (pow)
{
return (num * power(num, pow - 1));
}
return 1;
}
```

15. (a)(i) What is structure? Create a structure with data members of various types and declare two structure variables. Write a program to read data into these and print the same. **Refer pg no: 181,184** (10)

(ii) Justify the need for structured data type. **Refer pg no:181** (6)

(or)

(b) Write short notes on : (4 x 4 = 16)

(i)Unions **Refer pg no:193**

(ii) Register storage class **Refer pg no:50**

(iii) #include statement **Refer pg no:72**

(iv) #ifndef...#endif **Refer pg no: 74**

Question Paper Code: 57019

B.E/B.Tech DEGREE EXAMINATION, MAY/JUNE 2014

First Semester

Civil Engineering

GE6151 – Computer Programming

(Common to ALL Branches)

(Regulation 2013)

Time: Three hours **Maximum: 100 Marks**

Answer ALL questions.

Part A–(10 x 2 = 20 marks)

1. Convert the binary number 110 100 111 101 to octal.

   Ans:$(6475)_8$ [Refer pg no:21]

2. Draw a flowchart to find biggest of two numbers

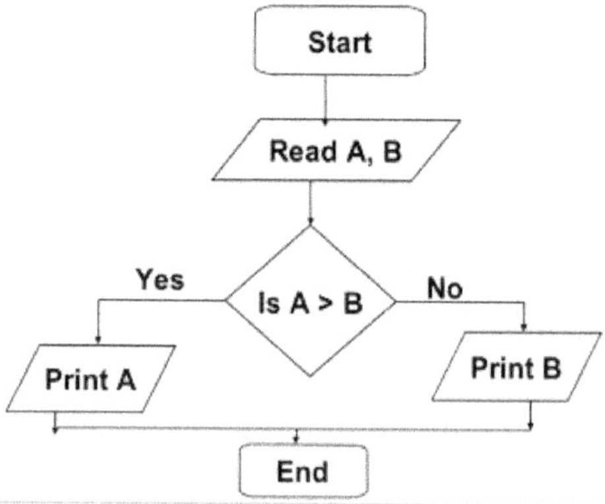

3. List different data types available in C. **Refer pg no:43**
4. Write a C program to find the factorial of a given number using iteration. **Refer pg no:81**
5. Write example code to declare two dimensional array **Refer pg no:93**
6. List any four string handling functions. **Refer pg no:113**
7. Define recursion. **Refer pg no:150**
8. What is the difference between pass by value and pass by reference?

   Refer Annexure 1 Question Bank Unit 4 Q.No: 8

9. What is the purpose of Unions in C? **Refer pg no:194**
10. What is the use of pre-processor directives? **Refer Q.Code:77156 Q.No:10**

Part B–(5 x 16 = 80 marks)

11. (a) (i) Discuss about Generation of Digital Computer. **Refer pg no:6** (10)

(ii) Draw a flowchart to find factorial of a number. (6)

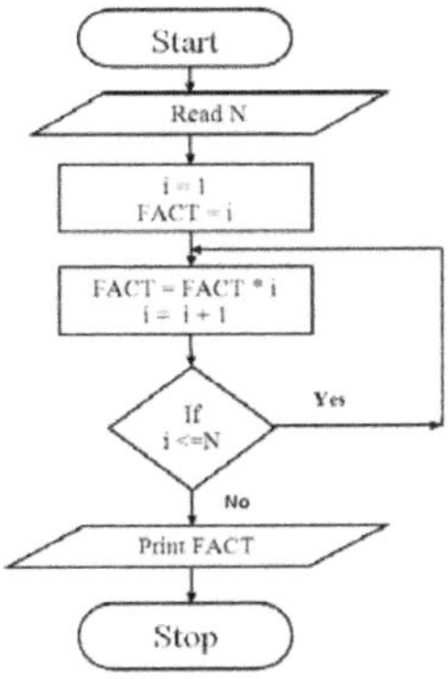

(or)

(b) (i) Explain the basic organization of a computer. **Refer pg no:12** (10)

(ii) Draw a flowchart to find sum of first 100 natural numbers. (6)

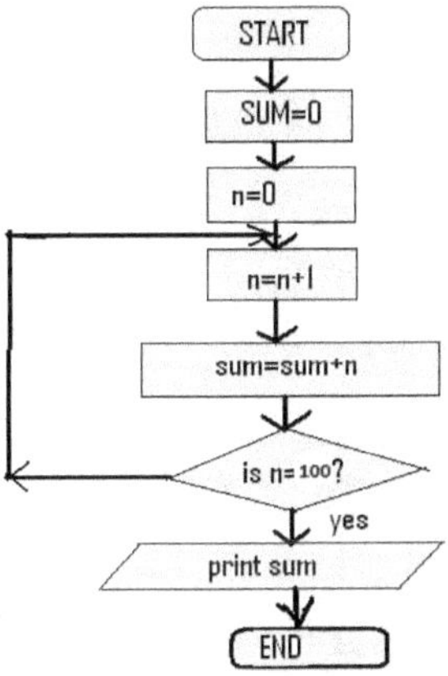

12. (a) (i) Write a program to check whether a given number is prime or not.

Refer pg no:85 (8)

(ii) Write a C program to find sum of digits of an integer. **Refer pg no:86** (8)

(or)

(b)(i) Write a C program to find roots of a quadratic equation. **Refer pg no:83** (8)

(ii) Differentiate entry and exit checked conditional constructs with an example

Refer pg no: 70,71 (8)

13. (a) (i) Explain the concept of pass by reference with suitable example.

Refer pg no:170 (8)

(ii) Write a C program to find factorial of a number using recursion.

Refer pg no:151 (8)

(or)

(b) (i) Write a C program to swap the content of two variables using pointers

Refer pg no:170 (8)

(ii) Explain the use of pointers in arrays with suitable example.

Refer pg no:165 (8)

14. (a) Write a C program to arrange the numbers in ascending order.

Refer pg no:125 (16)

(or)

(b) Write a C program to subtract two matrices and display the resultant matrix (16)

```
#include<stdio.h>
#include<conio.h>
void main()
{
int a[3][3],b[3][3],c[3][3],i,j,m,n;
printf("Enter the rows and columns of two matrices\n");
scanf("%d %d",&m,&n);
printf("Enter the elements of A matrix");
for(i=0;i<m;i++)
{
for(j=0;j<n;j++)
scanf("%d",&a[i][j]);
}
printf("Enter the elements of B matrix");
for(i=0;i<m;i++)
{
for(j=0;j<n;j++)
scanf("%d",&b[i][j]);
}
printf("The elements of A matrix");
for(i=0;i<m;i++)
```

```
{
printf("\n");
for(j=0;j<n;j++)
printf ("\t%d",a[i][j]);
}
printf("\nThe elements of B matrix");
for(i=0;i<m;i++)
{
printf("\n");
for(j=0;j<n;j++)
printf ("\t%d",b[i][j]);
}
printf("\nThe subtraction of two matrices");
for(i=0;i<m;i++)
{
printf("\n");
for(j=0;j<n;j++)
{
c[i][j]=a[i][j]-b[i][j];
printf ("\t%d",c[i][j]);
}
}
getch();
}
```

OUTPUT:

```
Enter the rows and columns of two matrices
3 3
Enter the elements of A matrix 4 5 6 1 2 3 7 8 9
Enter the elements of B matrix 1 2 3 1 1 1 7 8 9
The elements of A matrix
        4   5   6
        1   2   3
        7   8   9
```

The elements of B matrix

1	2	3
1	1	1
7	8	9

The subtraction of two matrices

3	3	3
0	1	2
0	0	0

15. (a) Explain the concept of storage classes with suitable example **Refer pg no:45** (16)

(or)

(b) Write a C program to store the employee information using structure and search a particular employee using Employee Number. (16)

```
#include<stdio.h>
#include<conio.h>
struct emp
{
int empno ;
char name[10] ;
char desig[10];
char address[30];
}e[2] ;
void main()
{
int i, n ,k;
clrscr() ;
printf("Enter the number of employees : ") ;
scanf("%d", &n) ;
for(i = 0 ; i < n ; i++)
{
printf("\nEnter employee number :");
scanf("%d", &e[i].empno) ;
printf("\nEnter the name : ") ;
scanf("%s", e[i].name) ;
printf("\nEnter the designation:");
```

```
scanf("%s", e[i].desig) ;
printf("\nEnter the address:");
scanf("%s",e[i].address);
}
printf("\nEnter the employee no\n") ;
scanf("%d",&k);
for(i =0 ; i < n ; i++)
{
if(e[i].empno==k)
{
printf("\nEmployee number is:%d",e[i].empno);
printf("\nEmployee name is:%s",e[i].name);
printf("\nEmployee designation is:%s",e[i].desig);
printf("\nEmployee address is:%s",e[i].address);
break;
}
}
getch() ;
}
```

OUTPUT:

```
Enter the number of employees :2
Enter employee number :1
Enter the name:nala
Enter the designation:AP
Enter the address:puzhal
Enter employee number :2
Enter the name:kala
Enter the designation:AP
Enter the address:AnnaNagar
Enter the employee no 1
Employee number is:1
Employee name is:nala
Employee designation is:AP
Employee address is:puzhal
```